Media and Middle Class Moms

Written by nationally recognized anthropologists Conrad P. Kottak and Lara Descartes, this ethnography of largely white, middle class families in a town in the Midwest explores the role that the media play in influencing how those families cope with everyday work/family issues. The book insightfully reports that families struggle with, and make, work/family decisions based largely on the images and ideas they receive from media sources, though they strongly deny being so influenced. An ideal book for teaching undergraduate family, media, and methods courses.

Lara Descartes is an Associate Professor of Family Studies at Brescia University College. She earned her doctorate in Anthropology from the University of Michigan. Her research interests include work and family, popular culture, and how identity factors (race, class, gender, geographic locale, etc.) impact family life.

Conrad P. Kottak is the Julian H. Steward Collegiate Professor (and former Chair) of Anthropology at the University of Michigan. He has done ethnographic fieldwork on work/family issues in Brazil, Madagascar, and the United States. His research interests also encompass global change, national and international culture, and mass media.

Media and Middle Class Moms
Images and Realities of Work and Family

Lara Descartes and Conrad P. Kottak

NEW YORK AND LONDON

First published 2009
by Routledge
270 Madison Ave, New York, NY 10016

Simultaneously published in the UK
by Routledge
2 Park Square, Milton Park, Abingdon, Oxon OX14 4RN

Routledge is an imprint of the Taylor & Francis Group, an informa business

© 2009 Taylor & Francis

Typeset in Minion by
RefineCatch Limited, Bungay, Suffolk

All rights reserved. No part of this book may be reprinted or reproduced or utilized in any form or by any electronic, mechanical, or other means, now known or hereafter invented, including photocopying and recording, or in any information storage or retrieval system, without permission in writing from the publishers.

Trademark Notice: Product or corporate names may be trademarks or registered trademarks, and are used only for identification and explanation without intent to infringe.

Library of Congress Cataloging in Publication Data
Descartes, Lara
   Media and middle class moms: images and realities of work and family / Lara Descartes and Conrad P. Kottak.
     p. cm.
   Includes bibliographical references and index.
   1. Working mothers—Michigan—Dexter.   2. Middle class women—Michigan—Dexter.
   3. Middle class families—Michigan—Dexter.   4. Mass media and the family—Michigan—Dexter.   5. Work and family—Michigan—Dexter.   6. Dexter (Mich.)—Social conditions.
   7. Dexter (Mich.)—Economic conditions.—I. Kottak, Conrad Phillip.—II. Title.
   HQ759.48.D48 2008
   306.874′308622—dc22

                                             2008032481

ISBN10: 0–415–99308–3 (hbk)
ISBN10: 0–415–99309–1 (pbk)
ISBN10: 0–203–89273–9 (ebk)

ISBN13: 978–0–415–99308–1 (hbk)
ISBN13: 978–0–415–99309–8 (pbk)
ISBN13: 978–0–203–89273–2 (ebk)

To all the moms in our own lives

CONTENTS

List of Figures		ix
Acknowledgments		x
Chapter 1	Media-ting Work and Family	1
Chapter 2	Studying a Midwestern Town	20
Chapter 3	Media Representations: Constancy and Change	39
Chapter 4	Parents' Media Usage, Consumption, and Reflections about Media	58
Chapter 5	Work–Family Choices	78
Chapter 6	Middle Class Moms: You Feel Guilty if You Work, You Feel Guilty if You Stay Home	107
Chapter 7	Isolation, Boundaries, and Connection: Six Case Studies	128
Chapter 8	Comparison, Connection, and Common Ground	146
Appendix A	Demographic Data	159
Appendix B	Individual Interview Guide	162
Appendix C	Interview Data Entry Form	165
Appendix D	Focus Group Script and Interview Guide	169

viii · Contents

Appendix E	Research Participants' Demographic Information	172
References		177
Index		189

FIGURES

2.1	Main Street	22
2.2	Feed Store	23
2.3	Cider Mill	23
2.4	Subdivision	24
2.5	Subdivision	24

ACKNOWLEDGMENTS

We would like to acknowledge the Alfred P. Sloan Foundation for their generous support of this project. We also wish to thank Thomas Fricke, the Director of the Center for the Ethnography of Everyday Life (CEEL) at the University of Michigan, an Alfred P. Sloan Foundation Center for the Study of Working Families, for his ongoing encouragement through the years of our research and writing. As well, we thank our fellow researchers at CEEL and throughout the Sloan community for regularly sharing with us and each other their findings and insights. We also thank Kathleen Christensen, Director of the Program on the Workplace, Work Force, and Working Families at the Alfred P. Sloan Foundation. Without her support none of this would have been possible.

We are particularly grateful to Anita Garey for her constructive criticism of the complete draft of the manuscript and Elizabeth Rudd for providing us with valuable feedback on Chapter 1. Conrad Kottak wishes to thanks the graduate and undergraduate students in his two fall 2007 seminars for their comments on the manuscript. We are grateful to all our reviewers, especially Jodi O'Brien, for their helpful comments and constructive suggestions.

For their assistance at various stages we thank: Autumn Kelly, who helped transcribe interviews and assist with focus groups; Mollie Callahan, who enabled our completion of the ethnographic observation portion of this project; Melissa Fleiss; and Alison Levitch. Lara Descartes thanks the skilled child care providers whose help gave her the time to complete this manuscript. We are grateful as well to Isabel (Betty) Kottak, who facilitated our initial contacts in Dexter. Judy

Baughn and Jana Bruce deserve our thanks, too, for their organization and managerial support. At Routledge and Taylor & Francis we thank Steve Rutter for his confidence in our work and his suggestions for making this a better manuscript.

And finally, we wish to express our gratitude to the many people in Dexter who made our research experience there a lively, intriguing, and memorable one.

1

MEDIA-TING WORK AND FAMILY

The shows we watched, like *Father Knows Best*, absolutely have no relevance today. The times have just changed so much. It's old news.

—Gus,[1] full time working father of two, married to a stay-at-home mother

Those fathers back then, *Ozzie and Harriet*, I think they get a bad rap. I think they were a good family ... And those dads were not the doofuses that we see now. They were real dads. If their kids needed money, I'm sure they wouldn't go to their moms.

—Brianna, stay-at-home mother of two, married to a full time working father

We do tend to watch shows, the old shows like *Leave it to Beaver*, just so that our son and daughter kind of see "Well, gee, maybe that's how moms were." ... It's good for them to see a mix of work/family situations on TV because they're going to see that when they're out there. They already realize that. Their friends have an entirely different makeup than my friends did when I was a kid. They've got friends who have one parent, two parents, four parents, because they spend some time with mom and dad here and some time with the other mom and dad over there, they've got a dad with a girlfriend, a mom with a boyfriend, they've got friends where there are two moms that are together,

2 • Media and Middle Class Moms

and we've had discussions about that as well, or situations where a grandparent lives there.

> —Morgan, full time working mother of two, married to a full time working father

Father Knows Best, Ozzie and Harriet, Leave it to Beaver: the television programs cited by these parents are American cultural referents that still evoke potent images of middle class family life. Their titles have become shorthand for very specific configurations of family, gender, class, and work—breadwinner fathers, stay-at-home mothers, and obedient, industrious children. Media are a significant and pervasive part of the American cultural landscape. Our central argument in this book is that the mass media, and the representations they offer (whether based in fiction, myth, or "real life"), powerfully shape the ways in which people organize themselves and their expectations, albeit in a manner that is more complex than simple analysis might indicate.

This book is based on an anthropological study that examined how American parents received, interpreted, processed, used, avoided, and resisted media messages about work and family, in the context of their actual work/family choices. Since *Father Knows Best* and *Ozzie and Harriet* first aired in the 1950s, American patterns of family, work, and gender have changed dramatically, as Gus observed in the first quotation. The basis of the American economy has shifted from manufacturing to services and information. Most jobs now are non-union, and many are temporary and/or part time. Such positions often pay poorly and lack fringe benefits. Simultaneously, living costs have risen, along with expectations about what defines a middle class lifestyle. Such shifts have lessened the ability of middle class families to maintain their living standard with just one income. Today's middle class parents must find ways to earn enough to satisfy their needs (and desires), and to care for their children, while reconciling any conflicts that result. Contemporary families meet these challenges in different ways. Some have two working parents; some have one employed and one stay-at-home parent; still others are single-parent families, with that parent usually working outside the home.

Anyone exposed to television, radio, magazines, newspapers, books, or movies encounters an abundance of imagery and information about work and family. Media messages are cultural products that communicate norms and standards. Media reveal and express changes taking place in society. On almost any topic, for the media consumer, some sources will supply reinforcement and validation, some will not, and some will provide contradictory messages. For example, some media offer negative opinions about working mothers. One ready instance is the radio advice provided by Dr. Laura Schlessinger, who advocates strongly that children not attend day care. Other media, such as the magazine with this title, are more pro-*Working Mother*.

Our research for this book focused on parents of young children in Dexter, a small but rapidly growing middle class community in southeastern Michigan. Although the title of our book highlights mothers, because of their central and often-contested roles in families, fathers were an important part of our research as well. We explored parents' media consumption in the context of their work/family patterns and their feelings and rationales about the career and child care choices they had made. This book is distinguished from others on work and family precisely by our focus on media—if and how parents drew on (or avoided) media as they made and evaluated decisions about how to best earn a living and care for their families. It is, we believe, critically important to incorporate media studies into analyses of social life, so as to gain a fuller understanding of the sources from which people get "scripts" for understanding and evaluating who they are, and what they might or should be and do. We paid particular attention to parents' exposure to and interpretation of work/family imagery and messages. What were those messages? What did parents think of them and do with them? How did they evaluate media messages about work and family in the context of their own work/family decisions? What social functions did the media serve?

Our study revealed that Dexter parents processed considerable work and family content, and were well aware of the kinds of messages being transmitted and received. They proved to be attentive and critical consumers of media who could discuss, often eloquently, portrayals of men's and women's roles in families and the workplace. They expressed concern when content seemed to do a disservice to real parents and children. Our informants tended to select media messages that validated and reinforced their own opinions, aspirations, and life choices.

Media served several *social functions* for these parents, of which three will receive particular attention throughout this book. The first is social comparison, of themselves and their families with others, including media representations. The second is the possibility of connection, to a wider world beyond the local community, which some Dexterites valued, while others vigorously resisted. The third is common ground—the social cement and shared knowledge created through exposure to the same media.

Although the role of the media is of interest regardless of class status, our study concentrated on families in the *middle class*—which we defined broadly as indicating that one or both of the parents in the family had a college degree, a professional job, and usually that the family owned or was buying their own home. The middle class represents something powerful in American society: it is an ideal, symbolizing comfort, success, normality (Kendall 2005). The middle class also represents something powerful to American media: consumers with discretionary income, and thus a very important audience. Our focus on the middle class reflected our affiliation with the Center for the Ethnography of Everyday Life (CEEL), a research center at the University of Michigan funded by the Alfred P. Sloan Foundation. CEEL's mandate was to study middle class families, particularly their work/family situations, using ethnographic techniques. Conrad Kottak, a cultural anthropologist with research interests in popular culture, joined CEEL at its inception in 1999 and wrote the proposal for the study on which this book is based. Lara Descartes, at the time a graduate student in anthropology, was invited to work on the project, and this extended into a postdoctoral research position.

We arrived at our interest in the intersections of family, work, and media by different paths. Kottak has studied family structure and work patterns in Brazil and Madagascar. His interest in media and popular culture is longstanding. He is the author of *Prime-Time Society: An Anthropological Analysis of Television and Culture* (1990), an investigation of media use and cultural change in the United States and Brazil. Kottak has been *Researching American Culture* (the title of a 1982 book he edited) since 1976. His early work on the United States focused on American mass culture and popular culture (Kottak 1982). His main concern then was in identifying unifying themes, values, and behavior in American national culture—institutions and experiences that transcend particular regions and social divisions. More recently, Kottak has examined American society in terms of its increasing diversity. With Kathryn A. Kozaitis, he is the author of *On Being Different: Diversity and Multiculturalism in the North American Mainstream* (2008).

Descartes' interest in the connection of media to family ideology developed during her dissertation research on family life in Southern California. Working with a racially diverse population, she recorded how, unprompted, people of very different backgrounds used similar popular media illustratively when talking about their own families, demonstrating media's utility in providing points of common reference—the common ground mentioned previously (see also Walzer 1998). For example, many research participants referred to shows such as *The Waltons* and *The Andy Griffith Show* when discussing elder care within the home and child care by grandparents. The most commonly mentioned program was *Leave it to Beaver*, always used to refer to idealized visions of family life, such as those we talk about later in this volume.

WHAT ETHNOGRAPHY ADDS TO STUDIES OF WORK, FAMILY, AND MEDIA

The understanding of human behavior, experience, and meaning is fundamental to cultural anthropology, which is concerned with what people think, say, and do, and why. Such interests lend themselves to experiential research in the form of ethnography, one of anthropology's hallmarks. Ethnography—firsthand field work among people as they lead their everyday lives—seeks to understand how people interpret and explain what they do, and what their life circumstances mean to them. To this end, ethnographic interviews include open-ended questions that encourage people to discuss their experiences at length and in detail. The ethnographer also spends time in the community being studied. By sharing surroundings and activities with the local people, the ethnographer learns what those things feel like and what they mean to the people experiencing them. Ethnography assumes collaboration between the researcher and the research participant, with the ethnographer in a learning role (Agar 1985). Recognizing this, anthropologists call research participants "informants"—people who inform the researcher about their culture. Ethnographic investigation takes everyday experiences, such as media consumption, and analyzes them contextually. That context may include cultural, historical, social, material, and/or economic factors. A study of how middle class families use media, for example, must consider the larger-scale factors of the changes in work, family, and gender roles and expectations framing their lives.

Ethnographic approaches are being used increasingly in both media research and family studies. Many scholars, including anthropologists Faye Ginsburg (1994) and Lila Abu-Lughod (1997) and communications researchers Alison Alexander (1993) and Patrick Murphy (1999), have commented on the need for in-depth, qualitative, experiential—ethnographic—research on television and other media. This reflects a growing research interest in how audience members perceive and use media in their daily lives. In media studies, survey research and experiments have been much more common than in-depth qualitative studies. As Murphy notes, these usual media research strategies do little to illuminate questions about audiences: How do people use media? In what contexts? What do media mean to them? Abu-Lughod and

6 • Media and Middle Class Moms

Ginsburg agree that anthropologists are particularly suited to study media, because of their "less ethnocentric stance, their attention to the contexts of media texts, and their recognition of 'the complex ways in which people are engaged in processes of making and interpreting media works in relation to their cultural, social and historical circumstances' " (Abu-Lughod 1997:111, citing Ginsburg 1994:13).

Some media scholars have taken steps toward filling in the ethnographic gap. One of us (Kottak 1990) used ethnographic methods in a multi-sited study of Brazilian media and culture change. Other rich ethnographic media audience research includes Marie Gillespie's (1995) work with Asian British youth, Ellen Seiter's (1999) studies of American parents and teachers of young children, and Stewart Hoover, Lynn Clark, and Diane Alters' investigation into how American families use media as part of creating their identities as families (2004). There are still too few such studies—ours adds to this small but growing body of research in its use of context-sensitive qualitative data and firsthand experience to explore media's place and meaning in the everyday lives of families.

Our research and analysis also was informed by and, we hope, will contribute to, the field of work/family studies. Much of what is interesting about belonging to a family is what that feels like and means to its members; what their everyday experiences in their families are, and how they perceive them (see Descartes 2007). In the field of work and family studies there is a relative paucity of ethnographic studies to shed light on how real families cope with the daily challenges of balancing work and home life. The value of ethnography in illuminating such issues is highlighted by the stellar example of Arlie Hochschild's *The Second Shift* (1989). In it, Hochschild drew upon interviews and the time she spent in families' homes to reveal eloquently the tensions caused by women's unequal share of household labor. Ethnographic interviews also have provided insight into women's efforts at blending work and motherhood (Garey 1999, Hays 1996), men's concerns as they combine work, marriage, and fatherhood (Townsend 2002), and couples' attempts to coordinate their work lives with their children's needs (Hansen 2005, Darrah, Freeman, and English-Lueck 2007). In addition, a collection of ethnographic essays by Elizabeth Rudd and Lara Descartes (2008) explores the diversity of middle class families as they balance a range of work and family issues.

Our book, with its focus on everyday media use and its connection to parents' work and family lives, unites and adds to the bodies of ethnographic research on audiences' media usage and work/family studies. Drawing on interviews, focus groups, participant observation, and media content analysis, we provide an in-depth look at our informants' lives. We explore the media they consume, what they do with them, how media function socially, and how media use reflects and shapes parents' perspectives on and decisions about work and family.

IN, ABOUT, AND OF: MEDIA DISCOURSES

Issues of work and family always have been part of American media content, which is expected for such key cultural domains. Sometimes work/family messages are implicit, as in the configurations of male paid labor and female home and child care depicted in *Leave it to Beaver* or, more recently, the situation comedy *Everybody Loves Raymond*. Sometimes such messages are very explicitly foregrounded, as in news coverage of working mothers or day care. Media attention to mothers and working women increased significantly during the 1970s and 1980s, as American women were entering the work force en masse (Douglas and Michaels 2004). While reflecting increased female employment, this media focus simultaneously provided a site for the phenomenon to be examined, and concerns over the changes expressed. Susan Douglas and Meredith Michaels contend that much of the ensuing coverage has focused on negatives, such as child endangerment, and has promoted ever-escalating standards for mothers to meet.

Media treatments of work/family issues are important, especially because of the quantity of media messages most Americans encounter each day. One recent observational study found that in one day Americans spent, on average: over one hour reading newspapers, magazines, and books; more than two hours listening to the radio; over five hours watching television; and nearly two and a half hours on their home computer (Papper, Holmes, and Popovich 2004). The media also enter our lives through postal mail, cell phones, compact discs, and MP3 players. Media technologies constantly change, offering new avenues of connection, new ways to supply us with entertainment, information, and, of course, advertising. Television and the Internet are becoming ever more intertwined: recent developments include CNN-YouTube presidential debates, network programs available online, and programming and ads placed in other virtual environments such as secondlife.com (Itzkoff 2007). Wireless technology now allows us to access media more easily than ever before. By the time this book is a few years old, entirely new media devices likely will be bringing information and entertainment to people wherever and whenever they want.

Despite, and because of, America's fascination with TV, movies, the

Internet, and more, it is common to demonize the media as forces whirling family members away from meaningful interactions with each other and creating isolated worlds of retreat. The popular imagination associates media with an assumed deteriorating quality of family life, another sign of troubled modern times. There is evidence, however, that media can play a positive role in family cohesion and social interaction. Choices people make about using or avoiding media can work either to connect or to isolate people. Robert Kubey and Mihály Csikszentmihályi (1990) found, for example, that although families talked less while watching TV together (as opposed to engaging in other activities), the experience provided family members with time spent together and common reference points. Stewart Hoover (2001) likewise noted the social functions of media, which allow people to bond through shared knowledge, tastes, or opinions. One can think of co-workers discussing politics or last night's football game, or teenagers voicing their opinions about contestants on *American Idol*. Someone who consumed no media would be entirely left out of such interactions. Our own study reveals how media can play a vital role in connecting people to, and providing shared knowledge about, a world beyond their local community.

There also is a popular belief that media exposure promotes antisocial behavior, including violence and unacceptable sexuality (Seiter 1999). Tragedies such as the Columbine and Virginia Tech killings routinely raise questions about the role of the media (most commonly TV, violent movies, video games, and the Internet) in forming personalities that commit such acts. What people do and why is more complex, however, than a simple one-to-one modeling of behavior based on television (Bandura 1977) or other media. Media consumers always bring their own prior experiences, preconceptions, structural positions (race, class, gender, sexual orientation, etc.), and cultural identities with them when they select and experience media. People filter media messages to fit their pre-existing knowledge and beliefs (Kitzinger 1995). As well, people use media deliberately and selectively, often choosing media content specifically because it supports their beliefs. For example, our own results demonstrate how women select media messages and sources on child-rearing that already appeal to them (cf. Hays 1996).

Hoover (2001) created a tripartite typology (discourses *in, about,* and *of* the media) to describe how media enter people's lives. The intended meaning of a program, book, podcast, and so on is a discourse *in* the media—a message the media want to convey to consumers (e.g., Dr. Laura stating that children should have a stay-at-home parent). Discussing a program with friends or family ("What did you think of Dr. Laura's first caller yesterday?") is an example of discourse *about* the media. A comment such as "I spend too much time on the Internet" or "TV is trash" is a discourse *of* the media, one that reflects the speaker's perceptions of appropriate attitudes toward media.

This typology may help illuminate how people receive and experience various messages, including those about work and family. For example, some programs, as noted, illustrate discourses *in* the media that do or do not support employed mothers. Media consumers selectively choose content that fits—and can reinforce—their own beliefs, while avoiding contrary voices. As well, people may resist the intended meaning (also called the hegemonic meaning, the "right" meaning) of the "text"—the discourse *in* the media—by creating alternative meanings that support their own views and life choices (Fiske 1989). Any cultural product—an event, an artifact, an ideology, or a media-borne message—can be considered a text. This term applies to something that can be creatively "read," interpreted, and assigned meaning by *anyone* (a "reader") who receives it. The particular meanings that each of us finds in a given text or discourse *in* the media, although likely constrained by the original meaning, can be very different from what its producers imagined.

Interpreting a text in a non-canonical way is very common. In our study, for instance, a fan of Dr. Laura Schlessinger felt sure that Schlessinger would approve of her decision to have her children in day care, because they were there only part time. Schlessinger's message on this, however, is very clear: no day care. The mother, without realizing it consciously, had resisted the hegemonic message, and had drawn an alternative meaning from the text, one that suited her own life choices. Her interpretation was still bound by the text's intent—to promote the idea that day care is bad for children—but within that she found room to personalize the message.

Whatever individuals may make of discourses *in* the media, they also engage in discourses *about* the media. Such discussions with family, friends, and co-workers can help people process and develop ideas, learn about differing views, form opinions, and even make decisions. People who choose to tune out Dr. Laura's messages about the "selfishness" of working mothers, for example, still may learn about her opinions from other people and other media that discuss her program, books, and views. Discussions *about* the media can illustrate, and create, common ground—social cement—among people who know about and find shared meaning in those media.

Exemplifying discourses *of* the media, several of our informants told us that media are solely for entertainment and shouldn't be taken seriously. Frequently this statement was expressed in tandem with the opinion that only the inexperienced, such as children, or the marginalized, such as the elderly, consume much media or give media credence. This discourse *of* the media shapes discourses *about* the media, and may influence discussion of discourses *in* the media. People who believe that TV is trash, or at least that it is socially desirable to say so, may underreport their own media consumption, and may scoff at any implication that media content is meaningful to them, as some of our informants did. Almost always, however, further conversation revealed greater media consumption than originally indicated, along with awareness of various work and family messages put forth by media. Despite initial denial, such discourses *of* the media did not prevent our informants from talking *about* the media or knowing what was *in* them. During our study we had to ponder the paradox of why our informants, like so many other Americans, tended to downplay the impact of the media, when media effects are so obvious to researchers. It also was paradoxical when our informants denied any influence on themselves, while demonizing the media for perceived (usually harmful) effects on others.

CHANGING WORK/FAMILY PATTERNS

Perhaps the media are blamed so often and for so much because of their unceasing proliferation and diversification since the mid-twentieth century. Consider how far we have come from the rabbit ears, channel knobs, and black and white sets that allowed Americans of the 1950s to learn how *Father Knows Best*. Media penetrate every aspect of our lives, as we know from our daily experiences at home, in schools, in malls, and riding in trains, planes, buses, and automobiles. Fueling our increasingly mass-mediated lives since the 1950s has been a sweeping economic transformation, whose social correlates include dramatic alterations in family life and gender norms. Work and family roles have undergone a revolution, in tandem with changes in the nature of work itself. Service jobs have supplanted the earlier production-centered workplace (Reskin and Padavic 1994). Labor union membership has declined drastically (Cornfield and Fletcher 2001), along with union impact (Strobel 1993). Part time and temporary positions have become more common (Lester 1996, Houseman 2001, Kalleberg, Reynolds, and Marsden 2003). Such jobs are less likely than traditional full time positions to offer security, good pay, and fringe benefits (Kalleberg, Reskin, and Hudson 2000). Given falling real wages since the 1970s, it has become more difficult for a family to maintain a middle class lifestyle with just one income (Strobel 1993, Dube 2006):

> In 1997, a child in a two-parent family with only the father employed had a per capita income level about two-thirds as high as that of a child in a dual-earner, two-parent family. Interestingly, two decades earlier, in 1977, such a child would have had an average per capita income about 82 percent that of a child in a dual-earner, two-parent family. (Casper and Bianchi 2002:254)

According to U.S. Census data, from 1967 to 2000 only the top (richest) fifth, or quintile, of American households increased their share of national income—by 13.5 percent. All other quintiles fell, the lowest one falling most dramatically, by 17.6 percent. This divergence continues: the richest fifth of American households, with a mean annual income of $159,583 in 2005, was 15 times wealthier than the poorest fifth, with a mean annual income of $10,655 (DeNavas-Walt, Proctor, and Lee 2006). Encompassing most of the middle class—including our informants in Dexter—the other three quintiles lie somewhere in between. In this context, the movement of large numbers of middle class women into the work force has helped maintain their families' economic equilibrium (Margolis 1984). Women's labor force participation increased by 42 percent between 1970 and 1980 and by 27 percent from 1980 to 1990 (Strobel 1993:61). Only 32 percent of wives worked outside the home in 1960, but by 2004 61 percent did so (Kottak 2008:469).

Historically, minority and working class women have had little choice but to engage in paid labor (Landry 2000), but for white and middle class women the move into the work force has been more recent (Reskin and Padavic 1994). In 1970 51 percent of American families consisted of a married couple with the man as sole breadwinner. By 1998 this figure had fallen to 16 percent (Casper and Bianchi 2002). In 1960 just 19 percent of married women with children under age six were in the work force, compared with 59 percent in 1990 and 2004 (Kottak 2008:469). Jerry Jacobs and Kathleen Gerson (2004) note that parents in dual-earner and single-parent households always have faced a time bind in fulfilling work and family responsibilities. A major change since 1970 has been a marked growth in the number of people living in such households. In 1970 only 36 percent of American family households were dual earner, compared with 60 percent in 2000 (Jacobs and Gerson 2004).

As it was changing gender roles, the new economy also led to changes in educational norms. In 1953 C. Wright Mills could observe that a

12 • Media and Middle Class Moms

high school education usually was sufficient to support a middle class lifestyle; college educations were associated with "higher" level positions. Fifty years later, a high school degree no longer grants access to most middle class jobs. A college degree increasingly is necessary for professional and financial success, especially in engineering, computer, and business fields (Weston 2006). A college graduate's mean annual income now is more than twice that of someone with only a high school degree, compared with just 18 percent more in the 1970s (Francese 1995, Weston 2006).

With the baccalaureate almost mandatory for a middle class lifestyle, there is an increased emphasis on gaining access to the best colleges. By opting to live in school districts known for their quality (see Warren and Tyagi 2003), such as the one in our study, or by paying for private schools, middle class parents strategize to obtain the best possible educations for their children. Based partly on the belief that extracurricular pursuits impress college admissions boards, parents involve their kids in a host of activities, which are costly in terms of parental time and money (Lareau 2003, Descartes, Kottak, and Kelly 2007). Today's parents pay proportionately more of their wages to raise their children, with child care and (pre-college) education costs having risen from 1 percent of household spending in 1960 to 11 percent in 2005 (Kottak and Kozaitis 2008:288).

As the U.S. economy has transformed, interrelated changes in lifestyle goals, gender norms, and reproductive technologies have interacted to produce smaller families. As more and more middle class women entered the work force, medical advances offered them greater control over their fertility. At the same time, the rising cost of raising children so as to ensure their class positions became an important point to consider in planning family size. With higher standards for their children's education and material comfort, contemporary Americans have fewer children on average than did their mid-twentieth century counterparts. In 2002 women's fertility was 45 percent lower than in 1960: a rate of 65 compared to 118 births per thousand women (Hamilton and Ventura 2006).

Forms of marriage and the family changed as well. In 1960, nuclear families—married couples with children—made up 44 percent of all American households. By 2000 that number had dropped below 25 percent (Sado and Bayer 2001). With women increasingly able to make it "on their own," the economic importance of marriage declined. Only 52 percent of American women and 56 percent of American men were married in 2000, versus 60 and 65 percent, respectively, in 1970 (Fields and Casper 2001). By 2007 the figure for women had dipped below 50 percent, so that more than half of all American women are not currently married, for the first time in the nation's history (Roberts 2007). A dramatic shift in marital stability occurred between 1970 and 2000, especially between 1970 and 1990, as divorce rates rose in tandem with women's new employment opportunities. By 2000 the divorced population of the United States had more than quadrupled, while the overall population increased by only 40 percent, compared with 1970. The percentage of children living in mother-only households in 2000 was three times the 1970 rate, and the percentage of children in father-only households was five times greater (Fields and Casper 2001).

The social meaning of marriage itself is changing, with both attitudes and behavior less likely to indicate that marriage is necessary for a couple to live together or to have children (Axinn and Thornton 2000). As Morgan, a working mother, noted in the third quotation at the beginning of this chapter, today's family configurations feature diversity and permeable boundaries. People cohabit, marry, separate, divorce, cohabit anew, and/or remarry, with each action creating new relationships. As Judith Stacey (1990, 1996) has noted, labeling these new family forms "postmodern," the emergence of so many choices can breed insecurity. These possibilities—and their representations in the media—provide varied sites for cultural negotiation about what "family" means. Marriage and family become arenas of cultural comparison and conflict, illustrated by movements from James Dobson's conservative Focus on the Family association to the gay and lesbian rights organization Love Makes a Family.

WORK PATTERNS: OUTSIDE AND INSIDE

Most American women now expect to join the paid labor force, just as men do. One survey of more than 4,000 teens found that "The majority (over 80 percent) of teen girls and boys expect to work full time as adults, and almost all girls (97 percent) and boys (99 percent) expect to provide financially for themselves or for themselves and their families" (Marlino and Wilson 2003:8). Most young women plan to stay home with small children but return to the work force once their children enter school. Although just 6.5 percent of surveyed female 11th-graders planned to work if they had children between ages one and three, almost 80 percent expected to do so with children between three and twelve years old (Tittle 1981).

In local discussions, as well as in the media, issues associated with redefining work, family, and gender often get essentialized to working mothers. Despite America's socioeconomic transformation, our cultural ideals still associate women with caring for the home and nurturing children, and men with earning a living (e.g., Hochschild 1989, McMahon 1995, Potuchek 1997, Williams 2000). As Lisa Silberstein (1992) has observed, the rapidity of the move away from the 1950s model of stay-at-home mother and breadwinning father means that many of today's adults were socialized with those ideals, even if they themselves have changed that pattern dramatically (cf. Hochschild 1997). Future generations probably will have more flexible ideas about gender roles based on the media content they consume and their own experiences in society.

However, given the lingering salience of the 1950s model, even today when couples have two incomes, both members may expect the husband's career to be primary (Silberstein 1992, Potuchek 1997). Many women, both self- and socially identified as children's primary caretakers, turn to part time work after the birth of their children. Indeed, more women than ever see this as a desirable option, allowing them to attend to their children and homes while also contributing to family income. In 2007, sixty percent of employed mothers saw part time work as ideal, a jump of 12 percent in ten years (Pew Research Center 2007b).

Without doubt, however, paid employment is socially privileged, because it establishes and maintains a family's material circumstances (Becker and Moen 1999). Power relations at home still reflect the career imbalance by gender. For women who work only part time, family power dynamics—as measured by female input into financial matters and male participation in housework—are similar to those of full time stay-at-home mothers (Shelton 1990, Stier and Lewin-Epstein 2000). More egalitarian roles emerge when women work full time.

Debates about mothers' work *outside* the home takes place on a national scale—for example, and perhaps most notably, in and through the media. There is much less public discussion of fathers' work *inside* the home. It is well documented that married women who work outside, even full time, still do most housework and child care. Hochschild (1989) eloquently described the predicament of women engaged in this "second shift," which husbands do not take up if their wives lay it down. Micaela di Leonardo (1987) noted that the wide scope of female work in maintaining a family extends beyond laundry, cooking, and cleaning to such tasks as card writing and holiday preparation.

In 1995 women did nearly twice as much housework as men did—a dramatic change, however, from 1965, when women did over six times as much (Casper and Bianchi 2002). Hochschild (1989) found that men and women frequently compared their own household responsibilities with what they knew or suspected about the division of labor in other families. Men felt they did more than their fair share when they perceived they did more housework than other men did. Women, on the other hand, felt fortunate when their husbands seemed to do more housework than other men did. According to Nancy Grote, Kristen Naylor, and Margaret Clark (2002), women tend to compare their own housework with that of other wives, rather than assessing their husband's actual contribution. As a result, women may perceive an unbalanced workload within their own home as fair. Men are most uncomfortable doing housework when they don't know other men also are doing it (Silberstein 1992). Material for comparison comes from the media as well as from personal experience, but because public discussion of *male work inside* is so limited compared with the attention paid to *female work outside*, Americans know little about the actual range of male domestic activities. It is true, however, that there has been a sea change in the awareness of the importance of sharing household work. Sixty-two percent of Americans today see sharing household chores as important for a successful marriage, versus just 47 percent in 1990 (Crary 2007). There is little difference in this statistic by gender (Pew Research Center 2007a).

PERFORMING MOTHERHOOD

Part of what makes balancing domestic and extradomestic duties so difficult is an ethos, reinforced by the media, that places work and family in opposed spheres (Nippert-Eng 1996). This separation is based in an ideology that associates the inside world of home and family with femininity and the outside world of work with masculinity. Given this dichotomy, wives—but not husbands—have to justify why external employment does not make them a bad parent (Coltrane 2000).

Jane Ribbens concluded that a mother is more than a role; she is a symbol, "the heart of 'the family', and in herself its most potent representation. Hence concerns that, if mothers 'go out to work', 'family life' is threatened" (1994:71). Local TV channels and 24/7 cable news magnify this risk perception when they dwell on cases in which children are endangered or lost through the absence or inattention of parents—especially working mothers. Anita Garey (1999) observed how working women frame their actions so as to demonstrate, to themselves and others, that they are good mothers:

In a cultural context in which mothers who are not employed are referred to as "full-time mothers," mothers who are employed understandably feel the need to assert their status as mothers in a number of contexts, particularly contexts that directly involve their children. They also want to be perceived this way by others. Their attempts to make their actions, as expressions of their identities as mothers, known to others is what I call "maternal visibility" . . . Maternal visibility is one response to the potential criticism that . . . employment prevents [a mother] . . . from properly caring for her child. (1999:29–30)

In the United States, "intensive mothering" is the ideal, and "correct" mothering is a moral duty (Hays 1996, cf. Newman 1993). According to Sharon Hays, "giving of oneself and one's resources freely is the appropriate code of maternal behavior, and any concern for maximizing personal profit is condemned" (1996:125). This view creates what Hochschild (1997) calls a time-debt, an amount of parental time owed to children if any is "taken away" by working.

Although most mothers work outside the home, many women are vocal about wanting to be home to care for their children. If 61 percent of married women are in the work force, 39 percent are not. These choices are made in a context in which withdrawal from paid labor can undermine a woman's financial security, her long-term employability, and her power within the marriage. In American culture, as social conservatives are fond of saying, it doesn't take a village to raise a child; "It takes a family to raise a child." Child care normatively is privatized and individualized (cf. Chira 1998). The child is considered to be a product of the self, and the primary parental self is the mother, reflecting traditional gendered work–family roles. Women bear not only the moral burden of mothering, they also have a possessive interest in it, for they are judged by the product of their labor—their children.

Furthermore, the American ethos that privatizes the nuclear family corresponds to a certain exclusivity attached to one's children and their love. Two frequently heard sentiments in our research were "I don't want someone else raising my children," and "I don't want my child calling the babysitter 'Mommy'." Even the other, non-primary, parent can fall under this mandate. For example, Susan Chira (1998), herself a working mother, recalled feeling bereft when her husband assumed some child-related tasks, such as transportation to a doctor's appointment. Such errands made her feel closer to her children and were difficult to give up.

THE MEDIA AND SOCIAL COMPARISON

The ongoing proliferation of media makes them more important than ever. They are an insistent part of our social landscape, and that alone makes them of interest to social scientists and commentators. Media are cultural products that help reveal aspects of us to ourselves—our concerns, our stereotypes, our fears, our dramas, our humor (of course, who the "us" and "our" are is open to debate). Although media do not dictate people's actions or behavior, they can, through their content and portrayals, contribute to and reinforce attitudes and beliefs (Gerbner and Gross 1976, Shrum, Wyer, and O'Guinn 1998). For media consumers, discourses *in* the media offer constant and varied points of social comparison: how others live, what they do, what mistakes they make, how they are or are not like one's self. The media offer material with which to think through one's own circumstances by contemplating alternatives, including some that are unavailable in the local setting. Discourses *about* the media offer this as well; think of family members sharing Dr. Laura's opinions even with those who don't listen to her program.

Leon Festinger's (1954) seminal work on social comparison described how individuals look to the experiences of others to gain information and to evaluate themselves (Buunk and Gibbons 2007). This can include upward social comparison: people choose role models to emulate. Feeling kinship with a successful someone can make people believe that they too can achieve, and offers ideas about how to do so. Yet subsequent work on social comparison suggested that people may react defensively to upward social comparisons they cannot attain, by emphasizing their differences from more successful people (Mussweiler et al. 2000). Downward social comparison (Hakmiller 1966) occurs when people who feel threatened in some way compare themselves to others whom they see as worse off. Downward social comparison can decrease one's sense of threat and increase a sense of well-being (Gibbons and Gerard 1997). Most people who watch Jerry Springer's TV program or *The People's Court*, even if facing no threat, can engage easily in downward social comparison.

The parents in our study inhabited a fairly homogeneous local community within a complex socioeconomic world. They had to earn a living, care for children, maintain a home, and try do these things in ways that were meaningful and satisfying. Their choices in such matters were not unconstrained. They lived in a structured world shaped by workplace norms, school days, and gendered life trajectories. Within those constraints, however, there still were important decisions to be made about division of labor, at least for those in couples: one income or two, outside child care or not, who does the household chores. Information contributing to how people made their decisions was available from a variety of sources: cultural ideals, childhood experiences, and comparisons with friends, family, and, via the media, a world of fictional and non-fictional others. Hoover, Clark, and Alters wrote: "we look at media engagement as part of a process of reflexivity in dealing with modern life, as media brings us the world in some ways or, more precisely, a particular set of statements about the world that invite some kind of negotiation" (2004: 175). Our research examined how parents in Dexter engaged with the media and how they processed, interpreted, and negotiated media statements about work and family. This book is concerned with those processes, their social functions, and their cultural meanings. To reiterate our central argument: the media, and the representations they offer, play a key role in shaping how people organize their arrangements, behavior, and expectations involving work, family, and social interaction more generally.

COMING UP NEXT

This chapter has provided a rationale for our study and for our argument that media matter in understanding contemporary social life, including the key domains of family and work. In addition, this chapter has reviewed the economic and social shifts that have shaped American work, family life, and gender roles in recent decades. Chapter 2 describes Dexter, Michigan—our fieldwork site—along with the methods we used and who our participants were. To provide background for discussing our research participants' media exposure and use, Chapter 3 considers in detail past and contemporary media representations of work and family. Chapter 4 lays out what we learned in Dexter about media consumption through our interviews, focus groups, and ethnographic observations. Chapter 5 discusses Dexter parents' actual work and family patterns, choices, dilemmas, and solutions. Chapter 6 focuses on the media messages on work and family that participants in our study received and what they made of them. Chapter 7 uses case studies and vignettes from our informants' lives to illustrate key findings and conclusions. Chapter 8 provides a synthesizing analysis of the work and family lives of Dexter parents and the role the media play for those middle class Americans.

ORIENTING QUESTIONS

Here are some of the key questions to be addressed and answered in subsequent chapters:

- How do the media contribute to expectations about lifestyle, including matters involving work, family, and gender?
- How do contemporary media representations of work, family, and gender accord with social reality? To what extent are such representations mired in 1950s images?
- How do people use media creatively, deliberately, and selectively to fit, support, and reinforce their pre-existing knowledge and beliefs?
- How do individuals and social groups use media differently?
- Why must researchers take seriously the effects of the media even when their informants discount them?
- How do people draw on media representations and "real life" examples in making social comparisons?
- What role does the use of media play in isolating—and connecting —people?
- Given that culture, in the anthropological sense, refers to shared knowledge and expectations, what role do the media play in creating such common ground?

NOTE

1 All personal names used in this book are aliases, in order to protect research participants' confidentiality.

2

STUDYING A MIDWESTERN TOWN

On Dexter, Michigan: its changing character:

I haven't seen a real sense of community here . . . I'm not saying that there's not, you know, two people in the [grocery store] aisle talking about soccer practice and are you going to PTA meetings, that does happen, but I see more people that are from out of state or from out of town that have new families that have just moved from Ann Arbor and into this community. It's a beautiful place, but I think it's just starting out, and it's doing a lot of growing.

> —Lisbeth, full time working mother of three, married to a full time working father

I grew up here, and we all wanted to get out of here. It's just a farmer, hick town. We wanted to go to Ann Arbor. Well, now everybody wants to come here, and it's . . . we used to walk down the street and know pretty much everybody, seriously . . . It's different now, and it's not that it's not just as nice, but it's not the small little town that it used to be . . . I can walk down Main Street and not see people I know, which, it never was like that, even ten years ago or so.

> —Dora, part time working mother of two, married to a full time working father

On Dexter's standard of living:

My husband, he does good, but we still struggle. And a lot of kids in Dexter, they don't. The families live in, well, nice houses. And my son will say, "Why can't we have all this money?" I'm like, "We just don't, Gavin, we just don't have it."

—Tyra, part time working mother of two, married to a full time working father

Oh, everybody's got a beautiful house.

—Annaliese, part time working mother of two, married to a full time working father

On Dexter's people:

It's been real hard for me to feel plugged in in Dexter because of the full time job and the commute and the soccer and the Girl Scouts and the music lessons. So, you know, what Dexter? You live your life in the holes that your schedule creates for you.

—Bonny, full time working mother of two, divorced

There are just some more neighbors around that are, if they're not alike in age as my children, they are at least like mine in that they have the same values, orientation towards work, and that type of stuff. And so, we're all pretty much singing out of the same hymnbook, which is not to say—we may not see each other until we go to lunch once a month. Which is not to say we don't see each other in the neighborhood. But we're not running over for coffee or anything like that, you know, on a daily basis or anything.

—Brianna, stay-at-home mother of two, married to a full time working father

Dexter, Michigan consists of a small, picturesque village surrounded by a semi-rural township. Founded early in the nineteenth century, its original economy centered on local mills and the surrounding farmland. Dexter retains a small town feel. In the village, Main Street (Figure 2.1) is lined with brightly painted buildings that house an array of service-oriented businesses. Bakeries, gift shops, and restaurants stand alongside a bank, grocery store, gasoline station, and hardware store. Recent additions to the landscape include flower beds and brick-lined sidewalks. Shoppers can relax and enjoy the views from wooden and ironwork benches in front of the buildings. Dexter's serene, mani-cured residential streets are lined with large clapboard homes whose open front porches offer an inviting picture of small town family life. Outside the village proper lies the township, where most homes are newer. They are located primarily in clustered developments bearing a

Figure 2.1 Main Street.

variety of pastoral names, such as Fox Ridge. These subdivisions are filled mostly with large, bi-level homes surrounded by expansive lawns. The houses uniformly are neatly kept and landscaped. Driving from the village center out to the subdivisions, one encounters reminders of Dexter's agricultural heritage, including a feed store, cider mill, and remaining farmland. Figures 2.2 through 2.5 provide views of the businesses on the outskirts of the village and a few of the many housing developments.

TOWN AND TOWNSHIP

Dexter is experiencing brisk growth. Although the town itself has relatively few employment opportunities, especially at the professional level, it is a 20- to 30-minute drive from the Ann Arbor region's universities, hospitals, and corporations. Urban centers including Detroit, Dearborn, Flint, Jackson, and Lansing are within driving distance for those willing to take on longer commutes.

In some ways a bedroom community, Dexter has become a place where parents move their families and then travel out to their jobs, with drives of up to an hour and a half each way. According to data from the 2000 Census, half the township residents who commute to work drive

Figure 2.2 Feed Store.

Figure 2.3 Cider Mill.

one-way for a half hour or more; 18 percent have an even longer drive—45 minutes or more (U.S. Census 2000a). Among our informants, men usually had the longest commutes, in part because they were likely to hold professional jobs commensurate with their training level,

Figure 2.4 Subdivision.

Figure 2.5 Subdivision.

which usually were unavailable in Dexter. Women who worked for pay tended to seek jobs closer to home, in order to be more available for their children's needs (see Descartes, Kottak, and Kelly [2007] for a discussion of how transportation issues affect men and women in Dexter).

Dexter grew rapidly between 1990 and 2000 (Table 1 in Appendix A). The village population increased by 56 percent, from 1,497 to 2,338 residents, and the township grew by 19 percent, from 4,407 to 5,248. Despite its many new residents, Dexter's racial/ethnic profile remained unchanged—98 percent white (Washtenaw County, where Dexter is located, is just over three quarters white, roughly the same as the United States as a whole [U.S. Census 2006]). Most Dexter households are family households, where family is defined as "a householder and one or more other persons living in the same household who are related to the householder by birth, marriage, or adoption" (U.S. Census n.d.). In the village, 63 percent of the households were families in 2000; in the township that figure was 80 percent. For comparison, in the United States overall, 68 percent of all households were families (U.S. Census 2000d). Married couple families represented 47 percent of all households in Dexter village and 72 percent in Dexter township (compared with about 52 percent in the United States as a whole). The proportion of married couple families is higher in the township because the new housing developments there consist of large, expensive, single family homes, which are beyond the financial reach of most single parent families.

In Dexter township, 88 percent of children under age six lived with two parents in 2000 (Appendix A, Table 2). In the village this figure was 67 percent. Nationally, the percentage is 72 percent (U.S. Census 2000f). In Dexter's dual parent families, if only one parent worked, it was almost always the father. As is true nationwide, mothers were much more likely to stay home with younger children (under age six) than with older children (ages 6–17). In Dexter township, for example, 34 percent of married couple families with young children (under six) were "father only in labor force." This figure fell to 13 percent for families with children six and over.

Most married couple families in Dexter had dual incomes. The definition of "dual income" is clarified, however, in Appendix A, Table 3, where it can be seen that men were much more likely than women to work full time. About 76 percent of the men who work were employed full time, versus about 50 percent of the women. Compared with figures at the national level, the figure for full time female employment in Dexter is low. In the United States overall, 71 percent of employed

26 • Media and Middle Class Moms

women work full time (U.S. Census 2000h). Despite this, Dexter's median household income was high compared with the U.S. national average of $41,994 (1999 dollars) (U.S. Census 2000i). The village median household income was $50,510. The township, as expected, was much higher, at $75,085 (1999 dollars) (U.S. Census 2000j).

Our overall impression of Dexter was one of a quiet, pleasant place to live, characterized by homogeneity in race, ethnicity, family configuration, class, and even religion: an Internet search pulled up ten houses of worship in Dexter, all them Christian (yellowpages.com n.d.). This homogeneity was part of Dexter's appeal to many of our informants, who also spoke of it as a safe place to raise their families. Parents, particularly those living in the township's subdivisions, told us they appreciated living in a place where their neighbors were like them and shared their values. They talked about how happy they were to have such families' children as peers for their own (we address this issue of homogeneity and ideologies of appropriate middle class child rearing in Descartes and Kottak [2008]).

OUR METHODS

We used various methods, including ethnography, to investigate Dexterites' use of media and the role of media in shaping behavior, attitudes, and expectations. Traditional ethnography can be difficult to operationalize in researching media, especially in countries like the United States (cf. Moores 1993). This reflects inherent difficulties in gaining access to family time, which most Americans consider to be private, as well as the sporadic nature of media consumption (see Descartes 2007). Recognizing such difficulties at the outset, we used a mixed methods research design to obtain multiple perspectives on media, work, and family. Each method added a different type of data that contributed to our analyses. With parents we conducted individual interviews, ran focus groups, and did ethnographic observation.

Individual Interviews

To explore parents' perspectives on their work and family lives and their use of media, we began with individual interviews. The first step was to develop an interview guide that addressed our research focus in ways and with categories that were relevant to our research population. We developed the interview guide by conducting pilot interviews with 30 parents of young children, recruited through personal contacts and by posting advertisements in the Dexter area. The pilot interviews included broad, open-ended questions on our topics of interest: how parents had made their choices in dividing up the labor of paid employment and caring for children; their media consumption; and how they felt about the portrayals of work and family in those media. We used the responses to develop the interview guide included in Appendix B. It includes open-ended questions about parents' work and family configurations, encompassing daily paid labor and child care routines. More structured items ask about the form, frequency, and content of media consumption, including television, movies, radio, Internet, magazines, and other print material.

We obtained the interview sample for our study by working through a primary school in Dexter. Following the mandate of Michigan's Center for the Ethnography of Everyday Life, we wanted to work with a middle class community. Dexter fit the bill and was located conveniently close to our university. We chose this elementary school because it was the first suitable one we contacted that agreed to help with our study. We limited this sample to parents of first and second graders, for consistency in the types of child care issues parents faced. The principal selected five of the 10 first grade classes, and five of the 10 second grade classes, according to her sense of which teachers would be most willing to help. We sent home letters to the parents of 250 students, explaining our research and requesting their participation in an individual interview. Half the letters asked for an interview with a mother and half with a father. Thirty-six parents, of whom only eight were men, agreed to be interviewed. Descartes conducted all the interviews, which ran about 1.5 hours and were audio-taped. Data from the structured portions of the interviews were organized in tabular fashion for easy comparison. Our data entry forms had space for each family member's daily schedule and types of media intake (Appendix C). We transcribed material from our open-ended responses verbatim, as we also did with our focus groups.

Focus Groups

Focus groups allow multiple participants to interact, exchanging thoughts and building on each other's comments. Such a group setting produces a range of conversational dynamics, including teasing and banter, which reveal different aspects of the topic under discussion (Kitzinger 1995). This method is "appropriate when the interviewer has a series of open-ended questions and wishes to encourage research participants to explore the issues of importance to them, in their own vocabulary, generating their own questions and pursuing their own priorities" (Kitzinger 1995:4). When described in this way, focus group data bear similarities to ethnography, which also explores locally significant beliefs, categories, and meanings.

Our individual interview guide provided a template for the focus group guide (Appendix D). The main difference between the two was that the more structured part of our interview guide, in which we asked for data on parents' work schedules and media consumption, was not part of the focus group guide. Such detailed questions would have been impractical in the focus group format. We recruited focus group participants by posting notices throughout Dexter. Forty-six parents, 14 men and 32 women, participated in a total of eight groups. Five of the focus groups were co-moderated by Kottak and Descartes, and Descartes moderated three alone. We audio-taped all these groups for later transcription. The software program AtlasTI allowed us to manage the transcriptions and organize the data.

Ethnographic Observation

The individual interviews and focus groups were just the beginning of our research. We knew the information they provided would be useful, but that they would not capture the detail and social context of media use in which we were interested. We thus asked all the parents we interviewed individually and in the focus groups if they would be willing to participate in ethnographic observation. Twelve women signed up. Since Descartes had conducted all the individual interviews and moderated or co-moderated all the focus groups, all but one of the women knew her from at least one meeting. The 12th signed up because her husband had been interviewed, and she thought the experience would be interesting. We feel this "foot in the door" approach was useful: the prior encounter had established some familiarity, which likely made the presence of Descartes somewhat less unsettling than it might have been otherwise.

All 12 of our ethnographic observation mothers had at least one child in elementary school. Descartes spent time with nine of these families (due to the constraints of finishing her dissertation, another graduate student, Mollie Callahan, worked with the remaining three). Since ethnography is such an intimate experience, we had parents direct the form and length of the visits. They invited Descartes to come at a time and day they deemed convenient, and she stayed as long as they wanted to have her with them. If they wished to invite her to their home again, they did so. If they did not volunteer such an invitation, she did not press. The minimum time Descartes spent on one visit was three hours, and the maximum was 12. Three families invited her to come for just one session, and six had her come for two or more. The maximum was five sessions. Since visits were at the parents' convenience, time with any one family was spread out, over periods of up to a year.

When Descartes spent time with mothers, children usually were present, as sometimes were fathers. Descartes participated in family activities, accompanying the women as they went through their daily routine. She rode in their vehicles as they transported their children between home and school, volunteered in the schools, attended soccer games, folded laundry, watched videos, ate meals, read to children, and so on. She was a participant in families' daily lives, but also an observer. Paying attention to the media they watched, read, and heard, she was exposed to the same work and family media content as the research participants. She observed type and frequency of media exposure, situations in which media messages emerged, attention paid to media content, and discussions of it with others. By participating in families' daily routines, Descartes gained insight into how media were used, such as to relax while folding laundry, or to entertain a child while a parent fixed dinner, as well as a more immediate sense of how parents balanced work and family responsibilities.

We used no recording devices during ethnographic observation. Instead, Descartes wrote up detailed notes after each visit, including information about what had happened during her time with the family, who had been present, what was said, what the surroundings were, what she perceived the mood to be, and how she had felt about the events and interactions. The procedures Callahan followed in her fieldwork were similar.

Media Content Analysis

We monitored media content during the period of our study, from 1999 to 2002, paying particular attention to presentations of work and family issues, both in fiction and non-fiction. We video-recorded every episode of the top ten Nielsen rated television shows in the 1999–2000 television season. In the 2000–2001 and 2001–2002 seasons we paid most attention to those top ten programs that we knew regularly had some type of family-centered content, for example, the situation comedy *Everybody Loves Raymond* and the hospital drama *ER*. We systematically examined local newspapers, primarily the *Ann Arbor News*, for family and work content in 1999 and 2000. We also looked at several popular magazines that seemed likely to contain work–family content, including *Redbook, Ladies' Home Journal, Harper's Bazaar*, and *Working Mother*. As noted previously, during our ethnographic encounters we experienced firsthand the same media messages on work and family as our informants. During the period of our study, and less systematically than with the steps discussed above, we also took note of work and family images that happened to come to our notice from day to day.

Multiple Methods: Integrated Data

Each method we used provided different kinds of information that contributed to our final analyses. Our analytic approach was similar to that of Jo Moran-Ellis and her associates (2006), who also had multiple datasets generated via several methods. They call their strategy "following a thread": "We picked an analytic question or theme in one dataset and followed it across the others (the thread) to create a constellation of findings which can be used to generate a multi-faceted picture of the phenomenon" (54). To illustrate, we offer an example from our own research regarding the radio advice show of Dr. Laura Schlessinger, colloquially known as Dr. Laura. Dr. Laura is a conservative talk show host who advocates traditional family configurations in which one parent stays home full time. Our individual interviews produced easily categorized and comparable data. We could determine, for instance, what percentage of parents in our sample listened to Dr. Laura's program, what work and family content they recalled hearing in it, and what men as opposed to women thought of that content. Responding to our open-ended questions, several interviewees also gave accounts of what Dr. Laura meant to them and how they used her advice. For example, some women who had withdrawn from the work force to care for their children spoke of how they appreciated Dr. Laura's public support for decisions like theirs. A few talked about how feeling supported in that way gave them strength to defend their choices when they felt they were being challenged, as some had been, by spouses, family members, or neighbors.

Focus groups yielded a different type of information, as participants engaged in dialogue and built on one another's comments. Such interchanges allowed us to hear more detail than we tended to get in the individual interviews. One person's remarks would lead another to react, or to recall something and chime in. Conversations about Dr. Laura usually were animated, full of humor, and went on at length. They allowed us to see where the group came to consensus—usually disapproving of Dr. Laura's brusque manner, and where it did not— usually on the utility and appropriateness of her advice. These interchanges gave us insights into cultural norms involving gender, work, and family.

Finally, ethnographic observation gave us a first person sense of how people actually listened to and used Dr. Laura's broadcasts, which several parents tuned to regularly. By spending time with mothers, Descartes could observe their interest in different parts of the program and listen firsthand to Dr. Laura's prescriptions about work and family. Parents commented to Descartes, and to others present, about aspects of the advice they agreed or disagreed with and why. Often discussions ensued about their own work and family choices, with some women explicitly linking messages in Dr. Laura's program to their own decisions. Being present for the media consumption itself turned broad recollections such as "I like what Dr. Laura has to say about being a stay-at-home mom" into much more specific data.

THE RESEARCH PARTICIPANTS

Almost all our research participants were middle class. We use "middle class" broadly to mean that the family owned or was buying their own home and that one or both parents had a college degree and worked at a professional job. Many of the men in our study were doctors, lawyers, scientists, and engineers. Their wives tended to have less professional training, with degrees in fields including dental hygiene, nursing, and social work.

All but two of our interviewees were married (Appendix E, Tables 1 and 2). None cohabited without marriage. Most had two or three children and were part of two-parent families. In these families, there were very few infants or teenagers. Besides the first or second grade child who provided our initial parent contact, most other children in these households were at least three and under 12 years old. All but one of the interview participants was non-Hispanic white.

Most of the eight interviewed men worked full time; many worked more than a standard 40-hour work week. Seven of the 28 women stayed home full time with no formal paid employment. Most of the women worked part time, many of them from home at least some of the time. Six women worked full time, but three of them worked at home for at least some of their hours. Most men we interviewed, along with most of the husbands of the women we interviewed, worked full time in an office or other business setting. The only father who worked full time entirely from his home was a single custodial parent. The only male interviewee who did not work full time previously had done so; he reduced his work hours for health reasons.

Our focus group participants were recruited separately from our individual interviewees. The parents who attended the eight focus groups had children of varying ages, unlike our individual interviewees, who, as a result of the recruitment process, had at least one child in first

32 • Media and Middle Class Moms

or second grade. Most of the children of our focus group parents were school age or preschool age.

Two of our focus groups were with men (Appendix E, Table 3). Twelve of the 14 fathers who participated were non-Hispanic white. Eleven were married to the woman with whom they lived; two were not, and one man was divorced. Eleven of the men in our focus groups worked full time. The wives of five of our focus group men were employed full time. Nine of the men had two children each, three had one child, and two had three or more.

We held six focus groups with a total of 32 women (Appendix E, Table 4). More groups were held for women than men because there was greater female response to our recruitment efforts. Our first focus group included both employed and stay-at-home mothers, but we segregated subsequent groups by work status. The mix in the first group seemed to inhibit free discussion of work and family choices. For example, one stay-at-home mother apologized before saying something she thought an employed mother might find insulting, and several silences, we concluded, suggested a wish not to contradict or offend others. Subsequently, we held two groups for women who stayed home full time and three for women who worked outside the home at least part time. Of our female focus group participants, all but one were married or partnered to men who worked full time. Thirty of the women were non-Hispanic white. Most had two children. Thirty were married, and two were cohabiting. The women in our employed mothers groups tended to have more complex marital pasts than did the women in the stay-at-home groups, most of whom were in their first marriages.

The 12 families who volunteered to participate in ethnographic observation were recruited from our interview and focus group participants. Only one of the women was employed full time (Appendix E, Table 5). No doubt there was a selection effect at work: full time working mothers probably had less time available that they felt like sharing with an ethnographer. All the women's husbands worked full time. Only two of the families had one child; the other ten families had two or more. One woman who was partnered when she participated in our initial focus group had separated by the time of our ethnographic observation. She was the only one of our ethnographic participants who was not non-Hispanic white or middle class. The other 11 women were white, middle class, and married.

The Dexter residents who participated in our study were representative of the town's demographic profile. Most were white and middle class and lived in a two-parent family. The man was more likely than the woman to work for pay, and the woman was likely to work part time if she did work outside the home. All coupled parents in our study were in heterosexual unions.

REFLECTIONS ON ETHNOGRAPHY IN DEXTER

In this section we reflect a bit on the fieldwork experience: what it was like to conduct ethnographic research in Dexter with its residents. Ethnographic research is a personal, intimate experience affected by the identity of all the participants. Ethnographic relationships are characterized by different types of power, boundaries, and ethical considerations. The comments below mainly reflect the voice of Descartes, who conducted the interviews and most of the ethnographic observations.

Issues of Power, Identity, and Representation

Ethnography originated in the study of small, homogeneous societies, and this trend continues among anthropologists today. A researcher working in such a setting typically offers resources that facilitate rapport and serve as incentives for local people to answer questions and allow the researcher to be present in their daily lives. Such resources can include food, medicine, or less tangible commodities, such as the ability to read and write or having useful contacts. Access to such resources usually indicates a power difference between the ethnographer and the research participant. This is not to imply that informants have no power in the ethnographic relationship, but that there may be inequalities in degrees and kinds of power. This disparity carries over into the realm of the academic voice. After fieldwork ends, researchers return to their home institutions and publish about their experiences in the field. In doing so, they establish themselves as experts on the group they worked with, with the authority to speak about, describe, and analyze it. Some ethnographers do ask informants for their input on data and analyses, but even so, the final authority lies with the researcher.

In an increasingly literate and electronically connected world, even people in nonindustrial societies now may have access to the materials written about them, and may be able to critique them publicly (e.g., see Lee and Ackerman 1994). Such access and feedback remain relatively uncommon, though, as are instances in which members of nonindustrial societies become voices with academic authority themselves. The power of representation thus tends to lie in the hands of a non-native researcher.

Even when ethnography is done in industrial and postindustrial societies, including the United States, the balance of power still has tended to reside with the researcher. This has reflected the structural constraints shaping the lives of the population under study, which often has been a group in some way marginalized from the mainstream. Most anthropological studies of families, for example, have been done with minorities. In such cases, the researcher, usually from a middle class background, may carry class privilege to the ethnographic experience, and often race privilege as well. Additional authority comes from the academic institution he or she represents. All these factors affect the research participants' interpretation of the legitimacy of the ethnographer's presence, questions, and writings.

By contrast, our study of work, family, and media took place neither in a nonindustrial society nor among a marginalized group. Our research participants, middle class white professionals, were very different from the people typically included in ethnographic studies. Descartes' relationships with them therefore were atypical of ethnographic encounters. The "privilege gap" between ethnographer and informant was reduced dramatically. Uniformly white and well educated, our informants were much like Descartes, who had no special material resources to offer in exchange for their participation. Nor was our research topic of nearly as much interest to them as it was to us. Indeed, many of our informants expressed incredulity that we were taking media messages on work and family as seriously as we were. Some of them really could see little significance to the topic. Eventually, we became intrigued with this tendency to downplay the importance of the media in their own lives, which our study, like numerous others, supports.

The primary resources Descartes had to offer were her companionship and status as an extra adult to help with the children and around the house. Eleven of the 12 women with whom we worked ethnographically did not work full time, in contrast to 38 of our 60 total female interviewees and focus group participants. The 12 women who allowed Descartes into their homes probably felt they had time available during the day and may have wanted adult company. Our interest in the particulars of their everyday lives may have been flattering too, even if our informants did not consider the research topic very important. Taking part in a study sponsored by a well-known nearby university probably also was attractive to some. When Descartes was with women in public, a few introduced her as their friend, but most explained that she was a researcher from the university.

Descartes' identity and role as the principal fieldworker undoubtedly also impacted the research process. As a graduate student during most of the fieldwork, she was markedly less privileged financially than the families she was studying. Also, she was single, childless, and younger than most of the participating parents. She carried far fewer status markers than most of her informants did. This situation also can apply to young ethnographers in nonindustrial societies, where having a spouse, children, and advanced age may be cultural measures of power and authority. However, fieldworkers in such settings often mitigate the effects of having few claims to locally defined status simply by being outsiders. As such, they are judged by different standards. For example, some female ethnographers have been allowed access to men's ceremonies normally forbidden to women (e.g., Caplan 1993). In our case, however, other than the (admittedly perhaps substantial) status conveyed by our university affiliation, there were few extenuating factors to excuse Descartes from expectations governing relations between Americans of differing social status.

Married couples with children tend to socialize either with family members or with friends who also are married with children. It is unusual for a single, childless woman to spend much time with a married couple unless she is a relative, nanny, or babysitter. Descartes' presence seemed to cause some discomfort, for men in particular. One evening, for example, as she accompanied a family to their son's hockey practice, the daughter grabbed Descartes' hand as they walked across the parking lot. The daughter then took her father's hand on her other side, and swung between them. Her mother walked behind. The father seemed uncomfortable to be paired with Descartes in this family-like configuration and soon released his daughter's hand.

Further, by agreeing to participate in our research, our informants gave Descartes the license to analyze and write about their lives. Granting such authority to someone of lower social status can create discomfort. Some of the parents, on meeting Descartes, did question her experience and seemed reassured when told that the study was headed by Kottak, an older, male faculty member.

On the other hand, Descartes' childlessness had some benefits. Because she was not a mother, her female informants may have been especially careful to offer complete information in describing the issues they had considered in making their decisions about balancing work and family. Most of the original individual interviewees and all nine families with whom Descartes worked ethnographically asked about her family and thus knew she had no children. Had Descartes been a mother, her informant might have assumed common ground and offered less explication of their situations, feelings, and choices. Another possible benefit relates to the fact that Descartes, an employed woman, was working with a number of stay-at-home mothers. Generally

36 • Media and Middle Class Moms

speaking, these women were committed passionately to their choice to leave the paid labor force, and many had learned to be wary of the judgments of working mothers. Had the researcher been a mother, and thus by default a working mother, that might have resulted in perceptions of greater threat by our informants. Such a situation more than likely would have harmed the research relationship.

Consider one more challenge related to our informants' middle class standing, the fact that our study was open to their scrutiny, personal interpretations, and potentially their comments. Most of the parents had computers at work and/or at home. They could log on to the university-sponsored website where we provided links to the working papers generated during our two-year fieldwork period. Our research participants could read exactly what we were saying about them while we still were doing the research. Although our writing has obscured personal identities with aliases, the descriptive details would have made self-identification easy. Few people actually commented on what we wrote, but the fact that they could do so was another reminder of the realities of ethnographic research in the contemporary United States, and Descartes did feel some inhibition in expression. Belonging to the same cultural group as our informants, she was well aware that our interpretations of their values, beliefs, attitudes, and behaviors could be construed as disrespectful or patronizing, even if they were not meant to be. We did not wish to hurt our informants or seem ungrateful for the time they had given us.

Space and Time: Private and Public

Unlike many nonindustrial societies, much of American family life takes place in the home, quite specifically in seclusion from outsiders. Even extended kin typically are not a regular part of a family's home environment. Few Americans can enact the ideology of private family space as effectively as the white middle and upper middle classes can. Generally speaking, the higher someone's socioeconomic status, the greater control he or she has over the incursion of outsiders into private space. Dexter's rapid growth itself is symptomatic of a middle class drive to maintain clear boundaries delineating home and family from the larger community. The acres of agricultural fields that predate recent housing developments allowed the construction not only of large homes but also of expansive yards and long driveways. Many of our informants had chosen to buy and occupy such homes. By definition they were people who had sought out the privacy of personal spaces contained within clearly bounded zones. Their norms governing family and privacy may have been disrupted by having a relative stranger spend extended periods of time in their homes. Concern about disruption and invasion of privacy helps explain the low assent rate to our requests for ethnographic observation. As noted, most of the women who did sign up for this stage of our research were stay-at-home mothers. The appeal of adult company during the day may have overridden any desire to keep family life separate and private. Even those families who did agree to participate, however, showed some initial discomfort about roles and boundaries. One man, for example, called his wife during the first session to see how it was going and to remind her of his instructions not to give out any financial information.

Our ethnography also faced challenges related to the American construction of gender, space, and time. The home still is construed as a female domain (Nippert-Eng 1996), and the male role in the home still is seen as one of protection and defense from the outside world (Andrews, Luckey, Bolden, Whiting-Fickling, and Lind 2004). Men generally were not eager to offer access to their homes and families. At all stages of our research, mothers were more willing to participate. Half of our initial contact letters had asked specifically for fathers, but only eight men agreed to be interviewed, with 14 more men joining our two focus groups for fathers. Furthermore, when women granted Descartes access to their homes, their husbands often seemed ill at ease, even after multiple visits. One man's position was that it was fine to have Descartes spend time with the family during the day, as long as she was gone by the time he got home from work. This injunction remained in place even after several visits.

Another fieldwork challenge involved issues of time, particularly in relation to our focus on the interconnections of work, family, and media. Media use is an amorphous phenomenon. A television may be on at any time of the day in conjunction with varied activities, including eating, doing laundry, or changing a diaper. A radio may be background noise while driving or cleaning house. Someone may browse a magazine while in bed or waiting in a doctor's office. To understand how people use media and what messages are transmitted and received necessitates spending significant time with informants.

It is a truism, however, that time is commodified in American society. Numerous studies have demonstrated the time crunch for middle class families—exactly our research population (see, for example, Hochschild 1989, 1997, Arendell 2000, Jacobs and Gerson 2004). Time, Americans think, has intrinsic value. Illustrating the law of supply and demand, the scarcer it is, the more precious it becomes. Giving away non-work time to strangers may seem senseless. Recognition of the tendency for middle class people to protect their space and time from outsiders may be one reason why ethnographers have shied away from this population. Although white middle class people are well researched in family studies, they have not been investigated much by ethnographers, who, as noted, have tended to study minority groups.

Consider, too, that much media consumption takes place during periods of the day defined as especially private family times, such as right before going to sleep and immediately on waking. Most of Descartes' access to families was granted for the more public daylight hours. Only rarely could she spend time with informants during the more intimate times of day when non-family members normally are excluded from the home. In fact, the only family who readily agreed to participate in the project in this way was headed by a single mother, who had no husband with whom to negotiate her decision. Otherwise, the most success Descartes had in gaining permission to be present in normatively private times was with one family with whom she spent a number of full days over the course of nearly a year. The closeness of that relationship allowed for a blurring of the outsider/insider boundary and resulted in an invitation to do ethnographic observation immediately on the family's waking.

We do not intend to characterize as negative the reduced ethnographic authority we experienced during and after our fieldwork. We feel that the ease with which our informants could protect their privacy, and their lack of incentive to do otherwise, is ideal in terms of preventing informant exploitation or misuse of authority. Further, in this case the lack of data supplied us with valuable information: we learned which spaces and times were off-limits to us, and who it was that made those determinations. With this knowledge of our methods, research population, and research experiences in mind, let us consider next the media available to the people of Dexter at the time of our study.

3

MEDIA REPRESENTATIONS: CONSTANCY AND CHANGE

A Fathers' Focus Group, Talking about TV Dads:

Most shows on Fox. The dad's dumb.
> —Kendall, full time working father of one, married to a stay-at-home mother

Most comedies, the fathers, men are the buffoons.
> —Raymond, full time working father of two, married to a stay-at-home mother

Yeah . . . The older ones where the father was better were *Leave it to Beaver, Father Knows Best.*
> —Butch, full time working father of two, married to a stay-at-home mother

My Three Sons.
> —Raymond

If, as we argue, media representations play a key role in shaping behavior, attitudes, and expectations, we need to know the nature and content of those representations. This chapter surveys, and provides a content analysis of, media sources available to the people of Dexter during the time of our study (1999–2002). We recognize, however, that people derive meaning not just from current media sources but also from ones from the past, including those of their childhood. Media representations were among the "scripts" and comparative narratives our informants used to understand and evaluate who they were, and what they might or should be and do.

40 • Media and Middle Class Moms

This chapter addresses several of the orienting questions listed at the end of Chapter 1, including key questions about how media messages and representations involving work, family, and gender accord with current social reality. To what extent are such representations mired in 1950s images? What has changed, and what has remained the same?

Over time anthropologists, historians, and other social analysts observe both constancy and change. In any society, including the United States, fundamental cultural models, including beliefs, values, and expectations, can persist despite significant changes in society and the economy. Any study of American media representations over time would reveal both continuity and change. For example, through a comparison of the original *Star Trek* with *Star Trek: The Next Generation*, one of us (Kottak 1990) illustrated how American TV portrayals have changed over the decades to reflect an ever more specialized, differentiated, and professional society. The greater role specificity and diversity of *Next Generation* characters, compared with their earlier prototypes, reflect this. *However, fundamental and enduring values were just as obvious as change.* Both versions of *Star Trek* conveyed a message reflecting a core value of American culture: although individual backgrounds, qualities, talents, and specialties may divide us, people still must be able to function as members of groups (the core value is *teamwork*). Such groups include starship crews, but also teams, businesses, families, and, most generally, society. The core value of teamwork still reverberates in contemporary American programs that require individuals to live or work together with a common goal. This theme remains fundamental in popular shows of the twenty-first century, from such medical and crime dramas as *ER, House, Grey's Anatomy*, and the *CSIs*, to such competitive "reality" shows as *Top Chef, Survivor, Big Brother*, and MTV's *The Real World.*

Another constant, and one more directly related to our Dexter study, is a persistent media interest in the workings and well-being of American families. Our content analysis of recent media representations, as described more fully later in this chapter, showed that while beliefs about the sharply gendered division between work and home have changed somewhat, fundamental ideologies about gender, work, and family do endure. Although, today, home is not seen as women's *only* role, it still is portrayed as their *primary* role. Similarly, work is not seen as men's only role, but still as their primary role. 1950s images do survive in current media representations.

POPULAR TV SHOWS FROM THE 1950s TO THE TWENTY-FIRST CENTURY

Specific media presentation and content do reflect (albeit imperfectly) the cultural preoccupations, values, realities, and technical achievements of a given time. In this section, we adopt a decades-long view of constancy and change in theme and content in the most highly rated American television programs (as measured by Nielsen ratings [Nielsen Media Research 2000, 2001]), starting in 1950. Although we think of the 1950s and 1960s as the heyday of the family-centered sitcom, much of this image is based in idealized memories and later syndication. *The Adventures of Ozzie and Harriet*, broadcast between 1952 and 1966, never reached the Nielsen top ten. *Father Knows Best* barely escaped cancellation after its first year on the air, 1954–1955. The iconic series *Leave it to Beaver* never made it into even the Nielsen top 30 during its original broadcast years, 1957–1963. Only one family-centered show (*Mama*, shortened from *I Remember Mama*) appeared in Nielsen's top ten list for 1950 (that list also included four variety shows; one sports show; two playhouse or "theater" type shows; and two westerns). Comparing 1950 and today, dramatic increases in scale, production values, and degree of audience participation separate *Arthur Godfrey's Talent Scouts* (number 8 in 1950 and number 1 in 1951) from *American Idol*, the most popular program of the first decade of the twenty-first century, but variety, sports, and drama have been popular in both eras.

Family-themed shows were better represented in the top ten programs of 1960, although western-themed shows were even more popular. *The Andy Griffith Show* portrayed family relations in a rural setting, as did *The Real McCoys*. *The Jack Benny Show* was a domestic sitcom set in suburbia. Most shows of this era highlighted white families without any discernible ethnic background. The Norwegian *Mama* of 1950 was an exception, as was Cuban Ricky Ricardo in the immensely popular *I Love Lucy* (1951–1957).

The westerns of that time were about establishing law and order on an unruly frontier—the early West. An emphasis on order and control, perhaps reacting to a society embroiled in civil unrest and Cold War tensions, continued into the next decade. The top ten programs of 1970 included police, medical, and western dramas. Two popular family-centered shows that year were *Bonanza* and *Here's Lucy*.

Douglas and Michaels (2004) observed that media attention to mothers and working women increased significantly during the 1970s and 1980s, as American women entered the work force en masse. The percentage of married women with children under age six in the U.S.

work force rose from 19 percent in 1960 to 59 percent in 1990. The major change took place between 1970 and 1990; the latter year's employment figure of 59 percent has not risen much since then. Contrary to popular belief, it is the 1980s—not the 1950s—that best qualifies as the golden decade of the TV family. Not only did family-oriented programs dominate Nielsen's top ten, there was a revival of interest in family shows of the 1950s and 1960s, such as *Leave it to Beaver*. In the mid-1980s, *Beaver* reappeared in syndication, a reunion telemovie, and a sequel series. The desire for and consumption of idealized media representations of traditional nuclear families increased in tandem with the subversion of that structure by socioeconomic fact. The TV programs available during the 1980s played a prominent role in the enculturation of many of our Dexter informants.

During the 1980s, family programs found a receptive audience and dominated the television lineup. In the 1980 top ten were *The Jeffersons* (an upwardly mobile African American couple), *Alice* (a working class white widow and her son), *Dallas* (a wealthy white extended family), *Little House on the Prairie* (a homesteading, white, nuclear family), and *The Dukes of Hazzard* (working class white siblings and their uncle). Considered together, these programs also illustrate a new willingness to highlight diversity in race, class, and family type.

In 1990 family shows in the top ten included the comedies *Roseanne* (a working class white nuclear family), *The Cosby Show* (a professional black nuclear family), and *Empty Nest* (a widower and his adult children). Reflecting an ever more mobile postindustrial society, a new type of program also had emerged—shows centered around family-like groupings of largely unrelated people, some with workplace settings, including *Cheers*, *A Different World*, *Murphy Brown*, and *The Golden Girls*.

The popularity of such family-like ensembles continued into the twenty-first century. The top ten shows of 2000 included *Friends* and *ER*, and workplace settings (often as sites where work/family tensions were represented) were becoming increasingly common. Besides *ER*, other workplace-centered dramas in 2000's top ten were *Law and Order* and *The Practice*, underscoring the ongoing appeal of programs focused on highly skilled professionals, especially doctors and lawyers. Like TV's early westerns, and comparable as well to the more recent *CSIs* and the medical drama *House*, the characters in these dramas constantly strive to establish order in a chaotic and unpredictable world. Today, reflecting changes in American society, the mechanisms of agency have been transformed from the rural or small-town rancher, marshal, or sheriff to the urban lawyer, detective, surgeon, and forensic specialist. Just one family-centered show made it into the top ten in 2000, *Everybody Loves Raymond*, a comedy focusing on a working father, a stay-at-home mother, and their family members.

In 2006–2007 (as in 1950, but with different content and presentation) the top ten show titles included variety (*American Idol, Dancing with the Stars*) and a sports program (NBC Sunday Night Football). Two shows had notable family content (*Grey's Anatomy* and especially the primetime soap opera *Desperate Housewives*). Two *CSI* programs, *House, Survivor*, and a game show (*Deal or No Deal*) rounded out the top ten titles for 2006–2007 (zap2it.com 2007). Note, however, that the marriage and family dynamics of *Desperate Housewives* and *Grey's Anatomy* are as different from 1950s shows as Ozzy Osbourne is from Ozzie Nelson.

CHANGING TV FAMILIES AND FAMILY ROLES

[My husband and I like to watch *That 70s Show* because we both had [a] very good upbringing, traditional family lives. Traditional doesn't exist any more, I don't think. But the old fashioned family, where the husband works and the wife stays home and takes care of the kids, those are both the kinds of families we grew up in.

—Johanna, part time working mother of three, married
to a full time working father

The changing American household organization described in Chapter 1 has been reflected in television and other mass media. During the 1950s and through the mid-1960s, such shows as *Father Knows Best, The Adventures of Ozzie and Harriet*, and *Leave it to Beaver* portrayed "traditional" nuclear families. Idealized middle class and upper middle class nuclear families survived on TV through the succeeding decades, as portrayed on *Family Ties, The Cosby Show*, and *Everybody Loves Raymond*. However, changes in family dynamics and in the roles of parents and children have evolved in the media and in "real life." For example, TV fathers have become much less omniscient, and we have seen more working class families, such as that shown on *Roseanne*, as well as the often dysfunctional and chaotic families of *Married with Children, The Simpsons*, and *The Sopranos*. It would be impossible to accuse Homer Simpson of "knowing best" most of the time.

Through the years, the diversity of TV families and households has continued to grow, as it has in personal social reality (see, for example, the third quotation at the beginning of Chapter 1). Recent and current media representations include coresident friends; roommates;

44 • Media and Middle Class Moms

unmarried couples; singles; single parents; unrelated retirees, "survivors," and castaways; nannies, housekeepers, and swapped wives; working mothers and caretaking fathers. Cable networks provide even more variety: HBO, while offering a demographically traditional, albeit conflicted, nuclear family in *The Sopranos*, also introduced a more atypical (extended) family with adult children, including a gay couple and their adopted children, in *Six Feet Under*, and an even rarer (polygamous) family in *Big Love*.

Despite the increasing diversity of TV families, the tendency continues—especially in popular sitcoms and soap operas—for the fictional families depicted on television to be white and materially successful. Researchers Hal Himmelstein (1984), George Lipsitz (1990), Stephanie Coontz (1992), and Debra Chambers (2001) observed that the continuing mass representation of such families (despite a social reality in which they are decreasingly common or representative) both naturalizes and legitimizes this family type. The media validate middle class families in more subtle ways as well, such as by depicting higher rates of conflict in working class families than in middle class families (Douglas and Olson 1995). The desirability of the nuclear family in particular is underscored implicitly when—and this is the rule—less conflict is portrayed in nuclear families compared with other family forms (Skill and Wallace 1990). Also validating the nuclear family are media representations of the ongoing quest of the single parent for a partner (Himmelstein 1984).

Media representations have normalized and universalized patterns of gendered care and work roles that are neither modal nor universal. One example is an episode of *The Waltons*, "The Deed," which first aired on February 8, 1973. In it a Depression-era southern mountain family nearly loses its land because they can't afford to go to court over it. The husband/father repeatedly refuses offers of help from other family members, including his teenaged children, explaining that it is his role alone to provide for the family. Representations of such rigid family roles, supposedly reflecting those of 1950s white suburbia, are presented as givens that extend back through time and across geographic and cultural variation.

Despite the idealization of the nuclear family, Thomas Skill and James Robinson (1994) contend that the extended family actually has been the most frequently occurring type of household on American television overall since 1960 (think of *Bonanza*, *Dallas*, *Full House*, *Frasier*, and *Six Feet Under*). Such extended configurations frequently are linked to a parent's single status. Single fathers in particular have been common TV representations over the years, especially in family sitcoms, some of which have been very popular. Examples include *My Three Sons* (1960–1972), *The Courtship of Eddie's Father* (1969–1972), *My Two Dads* (1987–1990), *Full House* (1987–1995), and *Two and a Half Men* (2003–present). As Richard Taflinger (1996) has observed, the men in such shows either live with relatives who help them with home and child care tasks, or they hire outside assistance, including nannies, butlers, and maids.

Single fathers have been a sitcom staple, according to Taflinger, because of the presumed incongruity of a man's handling domestic tasks and child care. Single moms are much rarer than single dads in sitcoms and family dramas—in contradiction to the proportions actually found in society. When fictional single mothers are shown, they rarely are portrayed as requiring the same degree of help as single fathers. (One exception was *Judging Amy*, which featured a professional woman in a position—that of judge—more typically held by men than women.) According to Scott Coltrane (2000), the persistent representation of bumbling TV fathers enacts a basic cautionary tale. It underlines the desirability of a man's having a woman to take primary responsibility for home and children (cf. Walzer 1998). Analyzing children's favorite television programs in 1989–1990, Katharine Heintz (1992) found three times as many parent–child conflicts when the parent in question was a man, again reinforcing the idea that women are better suited to deal with children and their needs than men are.

Although, as noted, TV representations of female extradomestic roles have become more common over the years (Signorielli 1999), there are significant differences between portrayals of women and men in the workplace. Women tend to be depicted in lower status occupations than men are (Signorielli 1999, Vande Berg and Streckfuss 1992). Female employment is represented as requiring less decision making, and as involving more interpersonal interaction, than men's work (Vande Berg and Streckfuss 1992). Unlike in the 1950s and 1960s, when female TV characters tended to be married and homebodies, single women have become more common in recent portrayals. Analyzing TV content from the 1992–1993 season, Michael Elasmar, Hasegawa, and Brain (1999) observed that twice as many single as married women characters were shown as holding professional, white collar positions. Nancy Signorielli and Susan Kahlenberg (2001) reported similar results from their examination of primetime programming from 1990 to 1998. Even married women with jobs rarely are shown at work (Chira 1998, Blodgett 1990). The centrality of women to home life and the assumption that their primary energies should be domestically oriented has been reinforced by many other media, from popular film (Makarushka

46 · Media and Middle Class Moms

1995), to child care manuals (Chira 1998), to parenting magazines (Hays 1996, Douglas and Michaels 2004).

A constant in TV depictions through the decades thus has been for men to experience difficulty and conflict in domestic roles. The complementary counterpoint is the representation of conflicts that women face at work and involving their employment. An increase in such images illustrates one of the most significant changes since the 1950s and 1960s, when many fewer women worked outside the home either on TV or in reality.

Although our discussion so far has focused on fictional depictions of families and work, we suggest that the distinction between fictional and non-fictional media is at best a blurry one, with considerable overlap and self-referential feedback. The content of non-fictional media also is created and manipulated, whether it be the choice of a topic for the *Jerry Springer Show,* or the writing and editing of a piece for *Fox News* or the *New York Times.* Each step of the process is shaped by the contributors' cultural values and structural positions, just as it is for media more easily characterized as make-believe.

HARD TO COMBINE WORK AND FAMILY

[On *ER*] I think with the several working mothers that have been on there, I'm thinking of Carol, the one with the twins, and then, a long time ago there was the other one who had adopted the sister's baby and still continued to work there and use the day care at the hospital. So I think both of those have been really positive, showing that women can go back to work, and especially Carol with the twins, and can be successful. I think she was fairly successful, up until the time that she left, but that was more, I think, that she couldn't manage work and home life. So I think it's been positive, on that show.

—Kylee, part time working mother of two, married to a full time working father

As our fieldwork proceeded from 1999 through 2002, we conducted content analysis of diverse popular media in order to identify the types of work/family representations in circulation at that time. We paid special attention to popular TV content, particularly of the shows, such as *ER,* that our informants mentioned most often. We focused on media used by or readily available to our informants. We were most interested in media sources with clear work/family content. Because our research methods were mainly qualitative, and because we did not plan any elaborate statistical analysis of our data, we did not attempt to choose a random sample of all the media that might have been available in the United States, or even southeastern lower Michigan, at that time.

Our content analysis revealed several patterns, of which one of the most obvious was an overall emphasis on the difficulties of combining work and family, especially for women. Consider some examples from TV representations. For several years, including the period of our field work, *ER* consistently ranked in or near the Nielsen top ten. Continuing through 2008, the show's characters have been involved in balancing work–family pressures, which frequently are presented as problematic (cf. Newitz 1998). Sometimes these conflicts were with older parents: one character took time off to care for his dying father; another did likewise to deal with her psychiatrically impaired mother. In both cases the care issue became a crisis when the parent's problems intruded on the adult child's job performance, implicitly underlining an ideal state of separation of work and family.

Similar patterns have been seen in the *ER* staff's work/family conflicts centered around children. A male surgeon, for example, juggled shifts in order to cope with legal issues concerning his small son; eventually, threatened with losing custody because of his long work hours, he took a different job. When a female surgeon was pregnant during the 2000–2001 season, her supervisor (a generally unsympathetic character) taunted her about not performing up to standards, specifically because of her pregnant state. Comments by other colleagues also hinted that her work was incompatible with pregnancy. Even her husband, an internist, worried about her ability to keep on working. She was portrayed as experiencing more and more difficulty on the job, accompanied by otherwise atypical emotional behavior. Eventually she accepted the limitations her co-workers and husband indicated were appropriate, saying, "Why do I have to prove anything?" and decided to go on early maternity leave, at which point her husband approvingly kissed her.

Another popular and frequently mentioned program in the early 2000s was *Everybody Loves Raymond*, a comedy featuring a traditional nuclear family, albeit one closely connected to other relatives. Ray Barone, the young father, worked as a sports writer. His wife, Debra, stayed home and cared for their three small children. Other family members lived nearby and were prominent cast members. A thematic thread running through the show was Debra's feeling unappreciated for her labor in the home and Ray's corresponding lack of involvement with the children. When one of their sons had trouble in preschool, for example, Debra told Ray that perhaps if he were around more, the child wouldn't be having problems. Ray's reply was, "I should go to work,

48 · Media and Middle Class Moms

and raise the kids? And what do you do all day?" Although many possible responses might have underscored the varied and unending tasks of a stay-at-home parent, Debra instead simply apologized to her husband. On a subsequent episode, during a conflict over disciplinary techniques, Debra advised Ray to read a (child care advice) book once in a while, to which he replied, "I make a living; that's why I don't read a book."

Like dozens of other recent programs, both *ER* and *Everybody Loves Raymond* present storylines that deal with questions of mothers, fathers, family responsibilities, and paid employment. On the one hand, women are represented as fully capable of engaging in paid labor, including highly skilled professional work, while also assuming family responsibilities. Caring for children and home is represented as important work, although the interactions between Debra and Ray highlight the ambiguous valuation of unpaid domestic labor in a society that stresses individual success and measures it monetarily. Such programs also offer representations of men as able, and even expected, to act as care givers as well as breadwinners. Still, media representations express an ongoing cultural tension about just how far such role permeability should go. This tension shows up in the mixed nature of the work/family outcomes in both shows, which question and explore just where boundaries should be drawn.

ENDANGERED CHILDREN

One of the most common representations of the problematic nature of trying to balance work and family is the trope of the troubled or endangered child. For example, a single parent family was the focus of a TV show that appeared regularly in the top ten lineup of 1999, the sitcom *Jesse*. In the first episode, Jesse confidently proclaimed herself a "superwoman" as she embarked on a new course of study and a new job. In the next half-hour, however, Jesse forgot her son's age, neglected to pick him up, and ended up quitting her job in frustration, although she later regained it. Highlighted here is the media tendency to represent the children of working parents as disadvantaged, and even endangered, by the lack of a stay-at-home parent (cf. Chira 1998). (The persistence of this theme is easily illustrated in present-day media, one example being ABC's popular Sunday night show *Desperate Housewives*, on which, however, even stay-at-home mothers are quirky enough to endanger their children's well-being.) Jesse merely forgot to pick up her son. More dramatic events await such children in other programs. On *Law and Order*, for example, the children of working parents frequently are either witness to, harmed by, or instigators of criminal behavior while their parents are away from home. On *ER*, the situation is similar. One episode featured a little boy who had been left alone at the soccer field because his parents, like Jesse, forgot to pick him up. When later taken to the hospital for a medical need, he noted matter-of-factly that his parents "work a lot. Sometimes they forget."

Non-fictional media, including news programs, and especially cable news, routinely transmit messages suggesting that working parents endanger their children. In one example, a November 7, 1999 *60 Minutes* episode focused on Nathaniel Abraham, an 11-year-old boy who was convicted of a firearm murder. After describing the crime, the story shifted to exploring the causes of his actions. Viewers were told that Nathaniel's father had left the family when the boy was small and that Nathaniel had been raised by a mother who worked the night shift, leaving him home in the care of his older siblings (which actually is a common and accepted child care arrangement in much of the world). Chira (1998) also observed this theme in news reporting, including the widely broadcast story of Louise Woodward, the British nanny convicted of murdering her employers' young child while his parents were at work. The child's mother was the focus of much of the media commentary, for, as the wife of another professional, she did not "have" to work.

Researcher Sharon Hays (1996) found that women discussed their fears about day care with frequent reference to stories they had seen on TV about day care neglect. Many of the parents we worked with in Dexter did likewise.

Corporations sometimes hone such risk perception to sell products, demonstrated, for example, in an ad insert from the Outdoor Fun Store, which featured the caption "Keep the Kids Safe at Home" and showed a glossy image of large, elaborate, obviously costly backyard play structure.

The radio call-in host Dr. Laura Schlessinger, whose program was popular among our informants, also invokes the theme of child endangerment as she tells callers their young children need a full time, stay-at-home parent. She labels the decision to put children in day care an act of "abandonment," and calls it letting "somebody else raise" your children. Her book *Parenthood by Proxy: Don't Have Them if You Won't Raise Them* (2000) recommends that couples purchase parakeets rather than have children if they are unwilling to have a parent stay at home full time. For Schlessinger, working outside the home is a morally valid option only during the hours when children are in school. Any other work–family arrangement, she contends, is a selfish choice made by parents to obtain luxury items.

50 • Media and Middle Class Moms

Schlessinger's pronouncements illustrate a common contemporary media message (one that contrasts with the 1950s) that American children exist in a state of persistent danger from parental selfishness, thoughtlessness, and resultant neglect. Such concerns arise in manifold contexts. In the nationally syndicated newspaper column "Dear Abby," for example, the columnist responded to a question about children and social problems with the comment "the majority of families these days have two working parents, and consequently many children are virtually raising themselves" (Van Buren 2000). At a more local level, similar sentiments were expressed by the editor of the Dexter newspaper, who wrote sarcastically that:

> If our kids are performing poorly or behaving badly, either the schools are falling down on the job, the government hasn't allotted enough money, or the teacher has a predisposition against the child in question. It can't possibly be that mom and dad are too busy pursuing their own ends to actually interact with the child, to converse with them, play with them, read to them, give them a sense of belonging and love. (Fischbach 2000)

This recent media preoccupation with child endangerment emerges from a persistent cultural model of motherhood as a moral status achieved through culturally approved sets of activities. Here we can answer one of Chapter 1's orienting questions—how contemporary media depictions of work, family, and gender accord with social reality, and to what extent such representations are mired in 1950s images. On the one hand, the increased frequency of working mothers in contemporary media accords with the fact of greater employment of wives and mothers in the United States today. On the other hand, the cultural model of motherhood remains much closer to the 1950s. A persistent component of the American ideal of motherhood is the expectation that a woman sacrifice herself for her children; her expected sacrifices extend to her personal career and aspirations.

Even magazine celebrity stories that focus on a woman's career accomplishments usually return to the coda of family being the single most important aspect of her life (cf. Douglas and Michaels 2004). A *Redbook* article, for example, began "Family First: Tipper Gore gave up a career to support her husband, Al, and their four children, but she has no regrets. It was a choice ... that saved her marriage and her sanity" (Conant 1994). The suggestion that career women need lessons on what truly is important in life often is the framing device for such articles, as in one called "Jamie Lee Lets Go" (Wolf 2000), in which Jamie Lee Curtis confessed to how much she learned by relinquishing notions of control and career and focusing instead on enjoying her children.

COMPETING DEMANDS OF WORK AND FAMILY

Although contemporary media do represent family responsibilities in terms of both parents, the issues surrounding work, home, and children most frequently are telescoped to working mothers—again reflecting the persistence of the 1950s cultural model despite a changed socioeconomic context. In contemporary media representations, working fathers remain an unmarked category; and stay-at-home mothers, an idealized one. This pattern also is illustrated by advertisements, including one for the Merry Maids company. One ad campaign included a mailing insert with the caption "No time to clean?" and an accompanying illustration of a woman wearing a business suit and looking at her watch. She has an expression of dismay on her face, as she holds both a briefcase and a toddler. This ad also exemplifies how media frequently represent family and work as opposed, competing forces, as does an illustration for a newspaper article entitled "Sizing Up Employers—What Job Candidates Really Want to Know: Will I Have a Life?" (Shellenbarger 1999). The cartoon accompanying the article shows a young woman in a cap and gown with two separate thought bubbles over her head. One bubble holds a baby; the other, a desk laden with paperwork. Work thus is represented as something that is not life; life is defined as family, and work and family again are modeled as occupying two separate spheres.

Managing the competing demands of those spheres is commonly represented as a complicated challenge—one that creates considerable stress for marriages and families. *Redbook*'s editor-in-chief describes balancing work, family, and time for oneself as "the everyday struggle" (Seymour 1999). A *Wall Street Journal* column on work and family by Sue Shellenbarger often emphasizes the need to avoid working too much, implying that to do so will jeopardize family life. "Job Stress Can Kill Marriages" is the headline of one such piece. In "Columnist Learns a Lesson She Already Knew," Shellenbarger discusses her regrets about letting work interfere with her father's final days. The media tend to frame the value of caring for others as a lesson women need to remember—else they regret not having done so. In our content analysis of media, representations of similar issues for men were much rarer.

Contemporary media thus represent family welfare as a complex task of female juggling, with working mothers constantly exhausted by the process (Fouad and Tinsley 1997). Advertisements in particular foster

52 • Media and Middle Class Moms

an image of mothers as harried, and working mothers as particularly so. Not surprisingly, the sponsoring companies pose their products as the solution, whether those be fast food, breakfast bars, beef, or even, in one example, royal bee jelly. In 1999–2000 the National Cattlemen's Beef Association ran an ad in many magazines, including *Working Mother* and *Parents*, of a rubber doll female figure with all four limbs being stretched by different hands. The caption read: "The bendable-stretchable-pulled-in-all-directions modern mom. Go to the game. Go to the client. These days, you have to do it all."

Media routinely reinforce this image of the would-be supermom or superwoman, usually with a negative connotation of frenetic activity and overstrained time resources. There are exceptions: *Ebony* (Randolph 1998), for example, published a piece called "Superwomen: How They Manage to (Almost) Do It All," which reported on how women may find it satisfying to have a balance between personal and professional lives. That this magazine targets an African American audience is not coincidental. African American women worked outside the home long before middle class white women did (Landry 2000). The overall tendency, however, across media types and genres, is to represent an incompatibility between paid employment and raising small children.

The representation of families as overscheduled and short on time is fairly uniform across media genres. The *Detroit News*, as an example, one week ran a feature article called "The Family Juggling Act" (Hodges 2000), and the next week a column by Cokie and Steve Roberts titled "Parents Need Help Fighting for Time" (Roberts and Roberts 2000). Lack of time is a refrain that recurs repeatedly in media discourse on work and family, as well as in social science research (See Jacobs and Gerson 2004). Media sources often propose as a normative solution that women trim their work hours. Women's magazines frequently feature mothers who have made such changes "for their children" (cf. Keller 1992). "Work at Home: How to Make the Dream Happen" (Holcomb 1998) is one article in which a mother who began telecommuting from home two days a week is quoted as saying "Before, I was always rushing and I was always late, either to the office or to pick up the kids. Now I'm so relaxed, my husband wants to know why I don't do this five days a week." *Real You*, a J. C. Penney publication, featured an article titled "The Balancing Act: Real-Life Survival Tactics for Working Mothers That Are Guaranteed to Inspire" (Milgrom 2000). The author described how she worked from home when her child was young. Of three interviews featured in that article, two were with women who altered their careers when they had children. One of them is quoted as saying, "I am not a superwoman. I can't be the perfect mother, the perfect businessperson." In the media we examined, no man ever was quoted as saying anything like "I am not a superman. I can't be the perfect father, the perfect businessperson."

HOME WORK

We found frequent media reports about women choosing to work for pay from the home, such as "Working at Home: Can It Work for You?" (Chatzky 2000) published in *USA Weekend,* and "How I Work at Home and Make $50,000+" (Goad 2001), in *Redbook.* A number of articles featured women who had left the workforce outright. A *Redbook* piece titled "The New Nesters" (Paul 2001) saw women across the country as changing their career goals, asking themselves "Am I working because I want to or because I've been told I want to?" Another piece, "My Balanced Life: Career Switch," focused on a mother of four who "proved that being a stay-at-home mom doesn't have to derail her career" (*Ladies' Home Journal* 2000). *Redbook*'s "Why You *Don't* Need a Balanced Life" (Smith, 2000) advocated that women conduct their careers and child-raising in series rather than in parallel (Jacobs and Gerson [2004], along with many other researchers, describe the damage to long-term career advancement that results from such deferrals.)

News media coverage resonates with similar themes, often with little basis in fact. One report describes "Career Mothers: Trend of Mothers Going Back to Work After Having Baby Has Reversed" (O'Crowley 2002). It turned out that the "reversal" (in mothers returning to work) referred to a drop of just four percentage points, from 59 percent to 55 percent. The headline of an Associated Press outed "The Babysitter Club: Massachusetts Lieutenant Governor Under Fire for Using State Resources to Help Care for Child" (Miller 2000). The article described how then-Lieutenant Governor Jane Swift thought she could balance career and family, while "others weren't so sure." It chose to quote the Executive Director of the Christian Coalition of Massachusetts, who said, "You can have a career and children, but normally you cannot have them both at the same time without a trade-off." The "you" in that sentence presumably is a female one, as men routinely and normatively combine career and children. Either way, the selection of the citation source itself illustrates how choices made in the writing and editing of non-fiction media frame the presentation of the material.

Books about women staying home to raise their children full time include *Team Work: How to Help Your Husband Make More Money, So You Can Be a Stay-at-Home Mom* (Watson 2001) and *There's No Place Like Home: Steps to Becoming a Stay-at-Home Mom* (Larmoyeux and Pope 2001). The first is a personal finance guide that avers that "a growing number of women feel that it is better for children to have their mother at home, and many women are finding that needing to work full-time outside the home is a source of stress in their relationship with their husbands" (2001:15). The proposed solution is for the wife to help her husband make more money by sending him back to school, networking, and helping him ask for raises. The authors of the second book begin by stating that it "is about helping moms fulfill their God-given role at home by providing them with biblical and practical information about how they can move from the marketplace to the home place. Or, for some moms who are faced with tremendous financial pressure to go out and find a job, how they can still remain at home" (2001:3). The book offers an unflattering portrait of the mental state of the working mother.

> If you are a mother who works outside the home, I'm sure you have experienced the pressure of juggling home and work responsibilities—especially if your heart longs to be at home with those you love. You know so well those signs of a stressful day—when you can't remember the names of your own children or whether you unplugged the curling iron. And when you put the newspaper in the refrigerator, watch out! Too often we moms act as though we are supermoms, and many in society say that we can be everything to everyone. You and I both know that supermom never existed and never will. But a lot of mothers are working today, and many are trying to do it all. (Larmoyeux and Pope 2001:16)

TRADING PLACES

> [*Daddio*] was pretty funny because he was your basic clueless dad . . . they did all your stereotypical male inadequacies in dealing with stuff, at least in that one episode that I watched. And the girl came in to help him, so it was almost like the helpless male, which is not sending a good message, I'm sorry.
> —Johanna, part time working mother of three, married to a full time working father

The 1950s model persists not only in media messages about women's difficulties at work, but also in portrayals of men in domestic settings.

Stay-at-home fathers rarely are featured in the media. When they are, the representation usually foregrounds difficulty and role clash, expressing the same type of cultural discomfort observed in discourses over working mothers. Some headlines that caught our eye included "Dads in Charge: At-Home Fathers Step Out to Find They Are Not Alone" (Marin 2000) and "Identity Issues Haunt House Husbandhood" (Tawa 1999). Although these examples demonstrate a lingering unease with changes in family roles, they also highlight escalating expectations that men actively participate in home life. An entire, albeit short-lived, sitcom, *Daddio*, aired in the 2000 television season. The plots revolved around a father's adjustment to staying home with his children while his wife, who previously had stayed home, began a career as a lawyer. Much of the comedy again arose out of clashes in gendered expectations, as a man performed what typically is considered a female job.

What has changed since the 1950s? The fact that *Daddio* even made it to TV as a plausible social script for a sitcom illustrates changes in perceptions of work and family. As we have seen, sitcoms featuring fathers making do domestically without a wife have been TV staples since the 1950s, but such men never were stay-at-home fathers whose wives worked outside the home. They were successful, unmarried, professionals (usually widowed) who could afford to hire help—or had relatives to help with home and children.

Despite the persistence of the 1950s model, we had no trouble locating media messages that encouraged male involvement in home and family. A *New York Times* editorial proposed that men need to be more active in asking for child care leave in order to make work and home more gender egalitarian (Levine 1999). A *USA Weekend* story led off with "2 Million U.S. Dads Now Stay at Home with the Kids" (Rubin 2000). Another reported that " 'Webcams' at Day Care Let Mom and Dad Check in Any Time" (*USA Weekend* 2000). A *Ladies' Home Journal* article discussed work and family pressures faced by men (*Ladies' Home Journal* 2000). Redbook described housework division between spouses in "The Dirty Work" (Hubbert and Hubbert 2000) and "You Can Have a 50/50 Marriage!" (Gifford 2001).

There can be no doubt that American gender and family roles are undergoing significant change, and media are reflecting that, even if sometimes awkwardly, as exemplified by the titles of magazine articles such as "When Wives Earn More: He Works. She Works. But Her Paycheck's Bigger. How Much Does it Stress Their Relationship? Four Couples Confess" (Hoyt 2000), "No Time for Errands? Rent a Wife" (Minton 2002), and *Redbook*'s "Win a Wife for a Week" contest (Roach 2000). These titles acknowledge that both women and men are likely to

56 · Media and Middle Class Moms

work outside the home for pay, but the 1950s model of a male bread-winner supported by the unpaid labor of a stay-at-home wife endures.

MULTIPLE REPRESENTATIONS AND THREE THEMES

This book's central argument is that media representations are an important part of the cultural information that shapes people's behavior, attitudes, and expectations. This chapter, which surveys and analyzes the nature and content of media imagery available to Dexterites during the time of our study, also has addressed questions involving constancy and change. We have noted that current media representations of work, family, and gender do reflect a changing socioeconomic reality, in which increasing numbers of women, including wives and mothers, work outside the home. Compared with the 1950s and 1960s, recent and contemporary media depictions of women in workplace settings are much more common, as are portrayals of female work conflicts, male domesticity, and tensions (portrayed mainly for women) arising from the need to balance work and family responsibilities. However, these representations of change are mediated by lingering cultural models of motherhood and gender roles inherited from the 1950s.

Three major themes emerged from our content analysis. First, most media we monitored represented "worker" and "parent" as difficult roles to combine, particularly for women. Second, both fictional and non-fictional media portrayals implied that children were endangered by the absence or inattention of working parents. Several sources suggested that parental, particularly maternal, absence for the purpose of work was a choice, and a rather selfish one. Third, and most clearly demonstrating the tenacity of the 1950s cultural model in the face of substantial socioeconomic change, contemporary media still depict home and child care primarily as the domains of women.

There were exceptions to these tendencies, although the most unambiguous ones were confined to print media. Popular television programs were more ambivalent. Even they, however, included representations of women as successful professionals, and of men as competent caregivers. At the time of our study, as is true today, multiple media representations of work and family were available. Such representations allowed parents to perform social comparisons (e.g., to get a sense of what others think and do, and to identify with or against), to establish common ground (e.g., by sharing and discussing media accounts with family and friends), and to connect to a larger world (e.g., by experiencing, accepting, reworking, or rejecting external scripts). In the next chapter we begin to present the results of our fieldwork, showing how our research participants took in messages such as these, how they felt about them, and what they did with them.

4

PARENTS' MEDIA USAGE, CONSUMPTION, AND REFLECTIONS ABOUT MEDIA

We watch *Barney* all the time . . . My son, he watches *Baby Bach, Baby Mozart*. Have you heard of it? It is God's gift, he gave me something wonderful. I could sink that tape in there and my son will stand there for a half an hour, watch that whole tape. I can do laundry, I could take a shower, I could clean the house, make dinner. If he starts fussing, I stick that in.

—Bridget, part time working mother of two, married to a full
time working father

I don't depend on the media for what my ideas of work and family are. I don't depend on the media for anything except entertainment. But that's just me. [My husband] relies on them for the news. He wants to be up on the current stuff. No matter how awful it is. And so I'll usually hear the main highlights from my husband. I listen to the weather and then I'm gone.

—Chantelle, part time working mother of two, married to a
full time working father

This chapter continues our examination of how varied media, and the representations they offer, contribute to people's behavior, attitudes, and expectations about various aspects of work and family. The previous chapter surveyed media content available to the people of Dexter during the time of our study. Recognizing, however, that people derive meaning from past as well as present media sources, our research also focused on television programs available to our informants as they grew up. Asking about the extent to which current media representations accord with today's social reality involving work, family, and gender, we found that media representations of change are mediated by lingering cultural models of motherhood and gender roles inherited from the 1950s.

This chapter addresses several of the other orienting questions listed at the end of Chapter 1. In determining how media normalize expectations involving work, family, and gender, we must recognize the role that gender itself plays in the selection, use, and evaluation of media. The first half of this chapter describes how parents in Dexter use media, including how mothers' and fathers' media consumption overlaps and diverges. Our informants' media usage was shaped quite strongly by gender. This was due in large part to how gender influences who is most likely to be with children on a daily basis. The work/family patterns that shaped the typical day and week were the most important factor determining media use by women and men. Because women most often were responsible for home and child care, they were exposed to a great deal of children's media. Gender also influenced how media fit into the daily routine, such as being used to distract children while doing household chores (women) or while relaxing and as a way to enjoy time with the family (men).

Gender shaped how media sources were chosen, and in what circumstances (cf. Morley 1986). Overall, men, when at home, seemed to have more influence in selecting media content, by controlling the remote, for example, but women had "veto power" over material they considered unsuitable for children (cf. Seiter 1999). Women tended to be more fearful about potential adverse effects of media on their children than men were. Gender shaped how parents saw their role as either media guardian or mediator. Mothers tended to want to protect their children from the outside world by limiting media, whereas fathers preferred to introduce their children to the world by sharing the media experience with them.

The second half of this chapter addresses the social functions of the media in connecting people and in creating common ground— functions to which we return often in subsequent chapters. This chapter also focuses on the paradox of why people deny media influence on themselves while also fearing possible media impact, for example, on their children, and blaming the media for their perceived effects on others. Dexterites' own words and choices will show how media images and information do shape their behavior and expectations, despite their denials.

DEXTER PARENTS' MEDIA USE: HOMES AND MINIVANS

What media selections and judgments did Dexter parents actually make? Popular TV programs among our informants included *Who Wants to Be a Millionaire?* (which some parents said they'd started watching after schoolteachers suggested it to their children), *ER, Friends, Frasier,* and the news magazine show *20/20.* Also fairly popular were the dramas *The Sopranos, Ally McBeal,* and *Seventh Heaven,* and the news programs *Dateline* and *The Today Show.* Several parents commented that the cartoon show *Arthur* was enjoyable for both parents and children. Syndicated comedies cited fairly frequently were *Home Improvement* and *Seinfeld,* and many mentioned *The Cosby Show* as a family-centered show that they missed.

For those who listened to radio, most said they tuned in to NPR and a local AM talk radio station, followed by a local light rock station and other music-oriented stations. Many reported listening to the radio mainly when driving, either to and from work, or while running errands and transporting children. Most of our parents did listen to music for enjoyment. During our ethnographic visits we observed, in homes and vehicles, a range of musical tapes and CDs, including Celine Dion, Shania Twain, and Pink Floyd.

Most of the parents in our study read the *Ann Arbor News* at least occasionally, as well as their town's weekly paper. *Reader's Digest* was popular, with several parents citing its condensed ("short and sweet") content as something they appreciated. Several parents read books for pleasure, with Stephen King a frequently mentioned author.

Most of our informants used the Internet, mainly for work, but also for information on health issues and consumer products, or to buy tickets or plan vacations. Parents talked about visiting such websites as eBay, along with sites specific to their own interests, including crafts, breastfeeding, and religion, and family members' websites. One father, Clancy, had turned to the Internet for "bedtime issues, and our youngest son has had separation anxiety, and we've gone on there and gotten some good information that's talked about that."

In the time we spent with the parents in our study we were able to observe that a fair amount of their media consumption was on the fly, accompanying other activities in their busy lives. Women listened to talk radio or music in the car or while doing household chores, read newspapers while waiting in line for their children at school, and watched TV as an accompaniment to nursing a baby or folding laundry. Only one mother actually sat down with intent to watch a specific program—*A Baby Story*, a reality-type show that was a particular favorite of hers.

Our informants also fit computers and the Internet into their work/family routines. One woman checked her email while her daughter napped. She sent out messages about her son's soccer team, of which she was a parent manager. A father in a different family did the household accounting, checked email, and looked up recipes while his wife prepared a meal. Another mother used the Internet to look up online degree programs to help her with an upcoming career change. Several parents used their computers to work from home. Descartes observed one such woman, an engineer who worked part time from home, using her laptop to email her workplace and to work while her infant daughter played on the floor beside her.

Parents consumed a great deal of children's media. Some of this was structured by the school: for example, a child's version of *Time* was distributed at school; children did homework projects using its articles. Any parent who helped with or reviewed the homework ended up reading through the articles. Some of this was less formal: it was common for parents to read their children books throughout the day to calm or entertain them. Bedtime reading was a ritualized part of the day for many families, with parents reading to their younger children, or being read to by older children. One family, for instance, had made J. K. Rowling's *Harry Potter* books a significant part of their lives. The three children and their parents not only read the books together, they also created Halloween costumes based on characters from the series. The mother organized *Harry Potter*-themed crafts for her daughter's Brownie troop. Her eldest daughter owned all the *Potter* books as well as the books on tape. The family even made up *Harry Potter* trivia games to pass time in the car on their vacation. Reading aloud from the latest book in their camper one night, the family was so interested in hearing the end of a chapter they all stayed up late together to finish it. Our informant remembered this occasion fondly as a special time with her children.

Parents also received media exposure through faith-centered activities. Descartes accompanied one mother and her children to their religious education class at the town's Catholic church, and observed a rack of religious books available for parents and children to check out and take home. These apparently changed with the season; that spring all the readings were about Easter and Lent. She went with another woman to a mothers' Bible study group, coordinated by a church. Weekly meetings were held on a weekday in the late morning. The timing made these seem designed for stay-at-home mothers, and there

62 • Media and Middle Class Moms

was no corresponding fathers' group. At the meeting, the women read the Bible and a discussion workbook. The week Descartes was there the workbook topic was family conflict. The module posed questions such as "Do you yell when you get angry?" and "Do you tell other family members about your marital problems?" Relevant Bible passages were suggested with each set of questions. The women read the questions out loud and shared and commented on situations they'd experienced, primarily with their husbands. They described how they had tried to negotiate those situations and what moral reasoning had gone into their decisions. Topics that arose included gendered differences in arguing and in attitudes toward housework. Two women described how they had decided to let small battles with their husbands go, such as those over picking up socks, in order to focus on the issues they considered more important to the family as a unit, such as male leisure time spent apart from the family.

Often, exposure to one media source had a ripple effect, leading our informants to others. For example, a TV program about families of her own ethnic group led one mother to buy a magazine about women sharing that identity. Other mothers mentioned getting books from the library after encountering references to them in print or on the radio. Several parents had visited websites recommended by magazines, television, or radio shows. One father's appreciation of James Dobson's radio broadcast led him to Dobson's Focus on the Family website, which he bookmarked and revisited frequently. Our informants' considerable knowledge of media personalities had been garnered from magazines, newspapers, and television programs about media. When discussing Brett Butler's cancelled situation comedy, for example, one informant, who previously had mentioned reading the *National Enquirer*, said, "That probably would have lasted if she hadn't hit the bottle."

In our ethnographic observations, we observed the physical environment that contextualized media use, considering that to be as informative as the actual media type or message. The placement of media equipment in the home varied from family to family. The living room was the most common location for televisions, VCRs, DVD players, and stereos, although families in larger homes frequently put them in a family room or den, sometimes located in the basement. Most families had racks of videotapes and/or DVDs next to the television. Usually, children's programming dominated these selections. Some families had smaller TVs, with or without VCRs, in their kitchens, bedrooms, or children's rooms. These rooms frequently had radio clocks and/or combination radio/tape/CD players as well. The placement of computers varied considerably, from kitchen to living room to home office to bedroom. Although books on display were rare, many families had magazines, placed either in racks or in piles on tables or floors. Newspapers, often seen in homes and vehicles, ranged from the *New York Times* to the *Ann Arbor News* to Dexter's community paper.

All vehicles we observed had radios, some had tape players, and most had CD players. Minivans usually had dual sound controls, permitting the driver and passengers in the back to listen to different programs. These parents used media to entertain their children during car trips and while waiting in line. At least one family had a video-player in the back of their minivan. We observed this mother listening to Dr. Laura as she drove, while simultaneously playing *Muppet Treasure Island* for her three-year-old daughter.

MOTHERS AND FATHERS

Although mothers and fathers shared many elements in their media consumption, as noted above, we did observe a number of gender-based differences. For one, gender dynamics influenced choices about media equipment and its placement. TV sets in male-oriented locations (e.g., dens, basements) tended to be larger than those in such female domains as the kitchen. One husband/father had his own separate media room, where a large easy chair, remote control at hand, stood before a big-screen TV. Sports memorabilia had been placed throughout the room. Ordinarily, neither the mother, Jennifer, nor the children watched this set. They had this setup, Jennifer said, because her husband, a coach, enjoyed watching sports broadcasts on the bigger screen.

Gender also influenced control of the media. On one visit, as the ethnographer chatted with a couple in their living room, the husband sat in a recliner, grasping the remote, even though no media device was being used. The woman said her husband did this all the time, whether he was watching TV or not. He simply liked having the remote control device in his hand. He would even get up and take it to a different room, often misplacing it, providing a source of amusement for this couple.

On the other hand, women tended to monitor their children's exposure to media, and in doing so influenced what their husbands viewed. Several mothers said they were more aware than their husbands were about what children should not see. They complained they had to watch their husbands to ensure they did not display inappropriate content to the children. Some mothers actually described themselves as "media monitors," telling their husbands when to change the channel because of overly explicit sexual or violent content.

64 · Media and Middle Class Moms

Men, however, offered a different view about exposure to content that their wives might find objectionable. Fathers tended to see it as their duty to introduce their children to the real world (this is a key concept in Parsons and Bales' [1955] theory of the role of the family in the socialization of the child). Rather than shielding their offspring, the fathers saw their role as watching and discussing material that their wives might find problematic. This was heard in a fathers' focus group, for example:

VAN: I really have only somewhat limited my oldest daughter's access to the stuff about the [9/11] terrorist attack. Because I kind of want her to know what's going on. This is especially after one day, she came up from school with 18 wild stories about what the hell was going on . . . I also kind of want to see what . . . conclusions they come to without talking to me. You know, talking to them after they watch television . . . So yeah, I think sometimes you have to give kids a little bit of room. I think that certainly their ages, it's dependent . . .

ROGER: The thing about giving kids a little bit of rope . . . I am more permissive in the type of shows I'll let my children watch than my wife is.

VAN: Right, me too.

STU: Yeah, same here.

ROGER: But I also will talk to my kids about what we're watching.

VAN: Right.

And consider this exchange from the same group:

CY: My wife doesn't understand why I'm still listening to rock 'n' roll and top 40, but it's like, she doesn't know who Kid Rock is, she doesn't know who Nine Inch Nails is. When my son starts listening and wants to go to concerts, I'm going to want to know who these groups are, what kind of lyrics they have. She's off listening to country music. That's fine for her, but . . .

ROGER: Yeah, I'm exactly the same way, trying to stay current on terms.

Although mothers tended to be more fearful and vigilant media monitors than fathers were, we noted no significant gender difference in the belief that the media had greater impact on their children than on themselves. Parents frequently complained that their children mimicked behaviors or words from television. Regulating how children of different ages had access to media was a continual concern in many families. This could take the form of simply monitoring content appropriate to a child's age group (a difficult task for those families with children of different ages), or it could take the form of seeing that a toddler did not have access to an older sibling's more fragile non-board books. Some parents of younger children used V-chip devices to restrict access to certain channels. Many had house rules banning media with violence or sexual content.

We confirmed many expectable gender-based disparities in our informants' specific media consumption. Men were much more likely than women to say they watched and listened to sports. Women were much more likely than men to watch daytime TV programs such as *Oprah*, *The Today Show*, and soap operas. Women also mentioned enjoying home-oriented television channels such as Home and Garden Television (HGTV), and programs about cooking, gardening, and home design. In one focus group comprised of working and stay-at-home mothers we asked them what they liked to watch:

POLLY: Anything on HGTV. HGTV, the Home Garden Channel.
VICTORIA: I like the Discovery Channel.
BRIDGET: Mine, it's Lifetime.
POLLY: I like *The Baby Story*.
[All laughing and talking]
BRIDGET: That's my favorite! I watch it every time, every time. And *The Wedding Story*, that's always nice. I always just cry at the end.
VICTORIA: That's all I watched, right after the baby . . . I'd just sit there and watch [the bride] cry.

Women were much more likely than men to say they avoided TV news. Many said this was because they didn't want to hear negative reporting. As one woman put it, "I know there are wars and shootings going on, but I don't have to have it in my face. It upsets me."

More than one woman commented that her nighttime viewing was determined by her husband's domination of the remote control. Women described male channel flipping with some exasperation and occasional amusement. However, in our fathers' focus groups, men told of having to view what their wives watched, as is revealed in this exchange:

STU: I guess we watch a lot of HBO. My wife does, and I kind of just watch what she watches. I'm thinking about *The Sopranos* and *Sex in the City*.
VAN: I'm pleased to hear that I'm not the only one that has to watch HGTV or whatever it is my wife is watching. When I come in, I'm watching television. She comes in, she grabs the remote. She goes, "Can I watch a show?" I'm like, "Mmm." I go get my book.

66 • Media and Middle Class Moms

CY: When I got sick of watching what my wife wanted to watch I bought her her own TV.

VAN: We have one TV, that's what I think my big problem may be.

Women also were more likely than men to say they did not read a newspaper, usually because they were too busy, or again because they didn't like what they described as negative news content. Women were more likely than men to read magazines, although many said they didn't often find the time. A few reported that they flipped through various magazines while waiting for appointments at doctors' offices. The magazine titles the women mentioned differed from the men's, with women regularly reading *Family Fun, Parents, People, Working Mother,* and others dealing with cooking, fitness, and home issues. Men preferred politically oriented, religious, sports, and outdoors magazines, such as *Field and Stream.* Our question to men in one focus group about what magazines their wives read elicited some amusedly disdainful responses. One man, Clancy, said, "She likes *Oprah,* she likes that magazine, but it just looked to me like mainly women and family issues." Amused disdain went both ways: in a women's focus group, when enumerating their magazine subscriptions, one mother said, "We get *Sports Illustrated.*" Another woman replied, "I don't count that one."

Mothers were more likely than fathers to read books on child development, along with mystery, romance, and novels in general. Women also were more likely to say they enjoyed movies that dealt centrally with women and relationships. Several women mentioned Julia Roberts' films as particular favorites. Men were more apt to cite action movies as a favorite genre. Several people commented that they rented videos or chose movies to accommodate this male–female contrast. One woman, for instance, described how she might rent something like the action film *Con Air* for her husband and a Meg Ryan movie for herself.

COMMON GROUND: WITHIN FAMILIES AND BEYOND

Exposure to a given media source or representation can provide shared experience, common knowledge, and a basis for animated discussion, within the family and beyond. Parents shared media with other family members, especially with their children. Most parents mentioned their children when they spoke about media, even when answering a question about the parents' media consumption (cf. Hoover, Clark, and Alters 2004). Beau, for example, was asked, "What about print media? Do you use any newspapers, magazines, or books?" He replied, "My kids read, not as much as I like, but it's for entertainment for the most part."

Parents used media to create a special treat or shared time with family members. More than one parent, for example, mentioned watching programs such as NBC's "Must See TV" lineup on Thursday evenings with their spouses. For one woman this was a "date night" with her husband. Another described how she and her boyfriend watched a lot of television at night: "It's our common ground. We can sit there and relax together." Several parents described ritualized "movie nights" with their children. The family watched a video or two, frequently accompanied by a special food such as pizza or popcorn. One mother called her and her son's viewing of cartoons and Animal Planet "doing a family thing together." Media thus provided a connection among family members (Hoover 2001, Hoover, Clark, and Alters 2004) and a way to feel connected to the outside world. Consider Polly's comments about a favorite radio experience:

> We listen to a lot of NPR too, and *Prairie Home Companion*. I don't know what it offers our family, other than it keeps my husband and I in touch, because he can be listening to something when he's in his car in the day, and then I'll hear it again later and "Yeah, I did hear that. I'm a knowledgeable stay-at-home mom. I know exactly what you're talking about."

Our informants' narratives illustrate how media also provide points of common reference beyond the family. For example, one focus group participant, Noreen, described her parents' lifestyle as "Laura Ingalls Wilder," assuming that the other women in the room would know what she meant, as indeed they seemed to. Later, she used a scene from a then-current Rice Krispies commercial to illustrate to the group the idea that people sometimes present themselves as more virtuous than they are.

The Internet provided a place for many to share common ground even with others they'd never met. One husband of a stay-at-home mother said she belonged to Formerly Employed Mothers at the Leading Edge (FEMALE). He related that the women in that group use the Internet to exchange information, interact with each other, and provide mutual support. Another man said his wife belonged to an online coupon trading circle that used the Internet similarly: "It's amazing what they talk about and share . . . about their families . . . It's like they're old friends." Men also interacted online. Stu, who worked from home, got social contact from an online stock chat room: "They're like me, but yet they're someplace else. And it's just kind of nice that I can vent in a way that I couldn't to a good friend face to face."

THE MEDIA ONLY INFLUENCE OTHER PEOPLE

Again and again our research encountered informants who were quick to deny media influence on themselves while readily perceiving media influence on others. Parents routinely voiced concern about the potential effects of media exposure (e.g., television, video games) on their own and other children, or blamed the media for negatively influencing people (usually errant teenagers in the news or parents with different work/family configurations than their own). Other studies confirm the tendency of Americans to discount the impact of mass media on their own lives (Tiedge, Silverblatt, Havice, and Rosenfeld 1991). American culture attaches substantial stigma to excessive televiewing, summed up by the image of the passive, impressionable "couch potato." Americans tend to think of media influence mainly in negative terms. The positive aspects of media exposure (e.g., providing a conduit to a wider world and new information) may be obscured by the very ubiquity of mass media. Americans don't realize the benefits of wide media exposure until those benefits are taken away, as when there is a power outage, the wireless is down, or the computer is on the blink.

For our informants, deriving ideas or information from fictional entertainment was seen as a particularly negative thing. When we asked Mitch, the husband of a stay-at-home mother, to comment on the work–family content of one of his favorite TV shows, *Law and Order*, he replied rather shortly, "It's just purely entertainment to me, okay." One woman observed similarly, "If you don't see it as fantasy, then you're viewing TV as real, and there's something not quite right there."

Ginny rejected the idea that media could be used to think through real life issues:

> Sometimes when I see these women who are, like a Special Agent or something, and can do all these things, and all of a sudden they have this family at the end, I think "That's so stupid." I guess I don't take movies or media, unless it is real-life, I kind of keep it separate. I don't really connect them.

It is telling that Ginny saw it as far-fetched for a female character to be successful in a demanding career and also have a family.

Many of our informants spoke of media—television, in particular—as something to be consumed only in measured moderation. When we asked people what media they used, many were quick to say they watched very little television and lacked time for much other media: "We don't watch a lot of TV. I mean it's there but we don't watch it. We are more into listening to what the kids have to say or what's happened at school . . . between that and their sports we're very busy." However, parents' words regularly illustrated their familiarity with mass media, despite their denials. Nicole, a stay-at-home mother of two, proclaimed at the start of her focus group, "I don't really look at the media." But once the women began discussing portrayals of stay-at-home mothers, Nicole brought up specific TV content. She mentioned *Oprah* segments on mothering, characters on *The Brady Bunch* and *Arthur*, contestants on the *Amazing Race*, and the hosts of *The View*. When the group turned to magazines, Nicole stated that she received *Family Fun* and *Simple*, and used to read *Parenting*. She also knew of Dr. Laura's radio program and helped explain Dr. Laura's messages on work and family to the rest of the group. She was familiar with the content of child care manuals and able to discuss "supermom" imagery in the media. She cited books distributed by FEMALE and the sad details of the Andrea Yates case, in which a mother of five drowned her children. As the focus group concluded, Nicole mentioned that she viewed news broadcasts, naming *Dateline*, and was a fan of the reality programs *A Baby Story* and *A Wedding Story*. Some of her final comments were about an article in the *Ann Arbor News* and letters to the editor that appeared in response to it. Despite her initial denial, Nicole clearly consumed a wide range of media, and with some regularity. She was alone neither in her discounting of, nor in the fact of, her media consumption.

Even people who did not underplay their media usage seemed to feel they needed to justify it. Consider this exchange from one of our focus groups of working mothers:

SHIRLEY: We watch TV a lot at night.
JOELLEN: It's okay.
SHIRLEY: Because it's our common ground. We can sit there and relax together, you know.
MARTA: I watch TV from nine to eleven, just so I can . . .
MARCI: I use it to forget about things.

Parents offered different valuations of particular media sources. They freely disclosed familiarity with PBS and NPR—probably because these public media have a reputation for being respectable sources that educated people use for information. Other media fared less well. Media consumed solely for entertainment, as opposed to information, often were discounted as unimportant. When we asked one mother what she listened to while driving, she replied, "Just the audiotapes from the library, books. But nothing high level. Just murder mysteries or something." Daytime TV was especially disparaged. Several inform-ants mentioned "people," not any they knew, who watched soap operas

70 · Media and Middle Class Moms

and talk shows. They seemed to be using this as shorthand to indicate character flaws, especially if the phrase "all day long" was tacked on.

Our informants frequently asserted that they didn't let their children watch a lot of TV. Instead, their sons and daughters played outside and participated in sports and other activities. Letting children watch "too much" TV seemed to signify poor or overburdened parenting. Some couples in single-income households saw their dual-income fellows as most prone to let their kids watch too much TV, using it as a "babysitter." Noreen, a stay-at-home mother, offered this image of life in a family with two working parents: "They come home at the end of the day and they're tired, so they put the children in front of the TV, they make their dinner. They're still not parenting, because Barney's parenting." As well, some married parents saw single parents as more likely than others to use television to help cope with work/family pressures.

Researching the impact of television in Brazil, one of us (Kottak 1990) found that when directly asked, "Has television changed your life?", most respondents said no. However, people were twice as likely to answer "yes" when asked, "Can TV change someone (else)'s life?" Something similar goes on in Dexter, and in the United States as a whole (Tiedge, Silverblatt, Havice, and Rosenfeld 1991). While denying that mass media influenced them personally, our informants had much less trouble seeing media's effects on others, whom they saw as more impressionable and gullible. According to Penny, "People believe a lot of what they hear, and the news media and the magazines play a big role in that." In one of our focus groups of stay-at-home mothers, participants echoed Penny's perceptions:

STACY: The people I know, the media doesn't affect them that much.

ANNAMARIE: I would agree with that.

CHLOE: But that might be because the groups that you're in might be smarter than the average bear.

ADA: The average bear's not very smart.

CHLOE: That's what I was going to say. The average bear is not very smart, so the media could have a profound influence. And the media does have a profound influence on them. And they're all voters.

Parents, especially those in single-income households, often blamed the media for fostering (over)consumption. Several stay-at-home mothers and their husbands described the media as manipulating other couples into thinking that both should work, thereby sacrificing their children's health and happiness for superfluous additional income. Mitch commented: "The media is teaching us that we have to have four

TVs or six TVs or three cars or a big home. That kind of pressure I think undermines the traditional family because you can't have what you want without having both people work." According to Tom, the father of one child, "You have a lifestyle, and you don't realize what's the difference between needs and wants, and of course advertising helps to blur those lines tremendously." This idea was passed back and forth in a focus group of employed and stay-at-home mothers as well:

JENNIFER: I also think the media puts out these images that make us want more.
KATRINA: That make us want more.
JENNIFER: That make us feel like we should take that summer job, we should work overtime, we should do all these things to have more money . . .
KATRINA: It definitely is the media in this country, they make us want more and more and more. To get that you have to work more and more and more . . .

We asked one focus group of working mothers how they thought a stay-at-home mothers' group might view them. One woman forecast accurately that single-income couples would see dual-income parents as overly influenced by images of consumption. Yet, she felt that the media she saw tended to support stay-at-home mothers: "They'll be like, all the advertising makes us feel guilty, that we should be out there working. And we're all like 'It makes us feel guilty, like we *shouldn't* be out there working!' "

DISCOURSES *ABOUT* AND *OF* THE MEDIA

In Chapter 1 we drew on Hoover's (2001) categories of media discourse: those *in, about,* and *of.* To recall that discussion, discourse *in* the media refers to the intended meaning, the message the media want to convey. Discussing a program with friends or family is discourse *about* the media. A comment such as "TV is trash" is a discourse *of* the media, one that reflects the speaker's perceptions and attitudes. Chapter 3 reflected upon the discourses *in* the media about work and family that were available to the people of Dexter during the time of our study. This section begins a more specific consideration of how Dexter parents spoke *about* media and *of* media.

Everyone in our study used multiple media sources, both for information and pleasure. Many spoke of actively seeking information on work and family, or at least noticing the messages that were available. Many parents said they sought out media that supported views they

72 · Media and Middle Class Moms

already had, while avoiding sources that did not. Bridget, a stay-at-home mother, discussed her affection for the child-rearing advice of Drs. Brazelton and Leach, two media personalities: "Sometimes you listen to people and they say stuff, and it either rings true or it rings false in your ear. You tend to agree with what they're saying, so you want to hear more, or you go, 'I don't know about that, it's a little too far off for me.' And they made sense for me."

Some parents managed to tolerate discordant messages by analyzing the motives of the messengers. Thus, Stu observed about talk radio hosts: "They just have this canned, extreme view . . . The purpose is to invoke the listenership to call in and get excited, and not for everyone to say, 'Oh yeah, I agree totally with that and that's great,' because then that would be boring." One mother, speaking of Dr. Laura's on-air technique, which many in her focus group found abrasive, said "I think it's a game." Another woman called Dr. Laura's program a "little talk show con-game." A men's focus group likewise discussed radio, labeling Howard Stern's dismissive way of addressing his mother, as "theater." "It has nothing to do with reality."

Our informants also speculated about the circumstances that resulted in media content. One father, Van, saw the media as necessarily limiting the range of work and family messages:

> I think Dr. Laura is consistent with other media in a sense that media . . . seems to try to make such a limited use of time to make a point or get across a message. They want to do it quick, and that apparently is what we desire. And so a stereotype of a traditional family model is something that's so quickly recognized and understood by people that it's easy to get that message out.

Noreen made a similar connection when commenting on how advertising uses idealized visions of home life to sell products: "Who would buy Pillsbury cookie dough if the house was like [makes screeching noise]. They're asked to portray everything as great . . . You buy Pillsbury, get this great scenario."

Parents were well aware of the television trend of focusing on people in higher socioeconomic brackets, and how that affected media portrayals. One group of employed mothers pondered a *Sex and the City* plot line involving an attorney, Miranda, who had just become pregnant:

SHIRLEY: She's just been named partner in her law firm.
JOELLEN: It will be interesting to see where they take that.
SHIRLEY: Successful.

DESCARTES: How do you think they'll portray her?

JOELLEN: Probably like she has a live-in nanny and that life is wonderful.

SHIRLEY: Life is never wonderful on that show.

MARCI: They definitely have the money to have those type of things.

SHIRLEY: I get that too, she does have the money, she's very successful, so she'll probably have someone help her.

MARCI: Right, exactly.

Mothers in a focus group of employed women considered whether wealthy media personalities could really relate to people with more modest incomes:

LUCILLE: We watch [*Oprah*] sometimes for a lunch break. They had this woman on there the other day that was trying to survive on minimum wage, and [Oprah's] just "Oh, yes, honey, I know how hard it must be." You're sitting in your millions and million-dollar mansion. How do you know? You don't know what they're going through. I can't even get into it.

MARNIE: That happened with me and Martha Stewart. If I had that much money and I could pay people to do anything, then yeah, I'd have tons of time to make crafts.

JEANETTE: Yeah, paint your whole house and you make the furniture.

LUCILLE: I think it's great that these women all got to achieve this, but they can't really relate to the rest of us.

Some parents could be quite savvy about their own use of and reactions to media. As Hannah put it, "My son says I filter what I pay attention to based on what's really on my mind at the time." Other parents spoke about how they thought anyone, including themselves, could feel supported or not by diverse messages in the media, depending on what they chose to consume. As Jaime, a focus group participant, put it, "I would listen to Rush [Limbaugh], and I believed a lot he had to say, but I know he was only presenting one perspective."

ADMITTING MEDIA INFLUENCE, ADMITTING MEDIA USEFULNESS

Although initially dismissing the influence of media on their own lives, most parents actually had a great deal to say, and seemed to have strong feelings, about aspects of media and media content pertaining to work and family. And, despite their initial denials that media affected them, many informants ended up discussing their own lives as indeed

74 • Media and Middle Class Moms

influenced in some ways. Stu, for example, discussed the sacrifices he and his wife made so she could stay home full time, with reference to "a cover of a *Time* magazine about 'raising your kids'." Several women spoke of finding good ideas and tips about family and work in parenting and women's magazines. One woman recalled reading life-altering advice about domestic violence in a "Dear Abby" column. Her comment prompted others in her focus group to recount instances of the media providing useful information and resources to deal with various problems. Constance, a retired military officer, stated that when she and her husband were raising their family abroad, the military paid too little attention to its members' family concerns. The day care, for example, was not high quality. However, Constance noted, "When we started having the *Army Times* and the *Stars and Stripes* overseas, and the different venues of being able to discuss these issues, there was a turnaround."

Of the parents in our study, Curt was the most explicit about the impact of media on his life. This was a topic he had considered before, and he was able to talk about it at length. A father of four, Curt was a born-again Christian. He placed a great deal of emphasis on the media and its effects on people. Part of his religious awakening had to do with seeing *The Exorcist* in college. The movie frightened him enough that he became involved in a Pentecostal church, which helped him overcome many of his concerns. The most avid consumer of Christian media in our study, he received Christian magazines, used Christian websites to obtain information on marriage and family life, and listened to Christian radio. Curt particularly enjoyed Dr. Laura: "I really like what she has to say. She cuts through the fog. She cuts! (laughs)". Curt also appreciated the radio program of James Dobson, and his organization, Focus on the Family, saying, "I get a lot of my teaching from them." He described Dobson's broadcast as "captivating" to him, saying it talked about "the importance of dads spending time with the kids." He credits his wife's and his decision to have her stay home in part to the messages on that program. When asked about those messages, Curt replied:

> I would think they would say that the feminist movement has tried to put on women that they need to work outside the home, in order to feel relevant, or important, or [of] any value, and they would say that's not true. That just being a mother, like Dr. Laura would say, being your child's mom, is very important. It's a higher priority than say being a doctor, if that's what your career goals are, or a lawyer, or anything else. To invest yourself in that child,

that's a gift from God, and you invest in that and that's more important.

Some parents drew on media to reinforce their opinions to others, citing a media source as bolstering their own views. Eloise, a part time working mother, said that listening to Dr. Laura gave her the courage to say things she might not say otherwise, because she felt supported. Abigail, a stay-at-home mother of five and fan of that same radio program, used Dr. Laura's opinions to support her own. To her daughter, who disagreed emphatically, Abigail cited Dr. Laura's opinion that young teenagers should not date. Abigail used Dr. Laura's words, along with her own rules, to set limits for her daughter. Abigail said her daughter hates Dr. Laura "because she's always right!" An unmarried father, Toby, made a practice of finding articles to give to his child's mother to support his own perspective on issues on which they differed:

> She's really big on "I have to see the article or I have to have the facts." So I try to give her [articles], "Well, just look at that." It doesn't mean I'm right but it means that someone else is saying it. It's out there. You look out there yourself for some information, what you think you should do.

ESCAPISM AND ALTERNATIVE IMAGES

Many parents said they used media for pure escapism. Marta and her husband were fans of *The Bachelor*: "That gives us a break from reality." Joellen related that she listened to music radio in the car, saying, "I do listen to it very loud, and that's my escape." Several parents (particularly the more adventurous ones) drew attention to media's role in providing vicarious pleasure, portraying lifestyles, characters, and situations that differed from their real lives.

A number of mothers reported enjoying soap operas and romance novels because they portrayed lavish lifestyles and sensitive, romantic men. Ginny, a part time working mother of two, explained her fondness for *The X-Files* due to its contrast from her own circumstances:

> I like the way they're independent and I guess I like their characters because they're so much not me. You know what I mean? (laughs) [Agent Dana] Scully doesn't have kids, she's independent, she's not married, and she has this career, and it's like total opposite of what I am. So it's nice to watch and think about things like that. But I'm glad of the choices I made. And it's all pretend, it's just TV.

Shirley, a fan of *The Osbournes*, liked viewing the extreme lifestyle of the featured family, which was so different from her own: "I'm always amazed to watch that show. It's funny though, but I don't have to live that life."

For some parents, television presented scenarios or challenges with which they could identify somewhat, even if at a distance. They enjoyed seeing how other people dealt with such situations. Nicole, for example, a fan of the *Amazing Race*, said "I just sort of enjoyed it, because it's real stressful, and I'm getting excited for them, and somebody else has this stress." For some informants, such shows were a guilty pleasure. When asked about her viewing habits, Amber initially said she watched *Dateline, 20/20* and news content on MSNBC. Much later, at the end of her focus group, she admitted, "I watch mindless reality shows. Those just kill me. Everybody in my family thinks I'm insane. *Temptation Island, Big Brother*. I just find those so mindless. Everybody in my family is 'What do you see in this?' To me it's just funny."

CONSUMING MEDIA

American culture stigmatizes excessive media use, summarized in the stereotype of the passive, gullible "couch potato." Not surprisingly, then, parents in Dexter typically underestimated their own media consumption and discounted the impact of media on their own lives, while readily admitting that media could influence others, especially children and other perceived social inferiors. Nevertheless, our interviews, and particularly our focus groups, revealed considerable shared knowledge of media, and our ethnographic visits allowed us to observe directly where and how families used media in their daily lives.

Our informants lived within an ever more media-saturated world. Despite their frequent disclaimers about the significance of media in their lives, most were habitual and even enthusiastic consumers. Media entertained and informed them, and, as became especially evident in our focus groups, let them participate in a shared culture. Exposure to the media and their representations provided a basis for common ground within and beyond the family. Men and, especially, women worried about the influence of the media, specifically on their children, and blamed the media for an array of social ills. Tensions related to media use occasionally erupted in some informants' homes, often involving the father's wish to enlighten, as opposed to the mother's wish to protect, the child.

Our research confirms the need to take media seriously even if and when informants deny and discount their importance. Media were an ongoing, regular, and significant presence in Dexterites' lives. After an examination of the actual work/family choices made by Dexterites in Chapter 5, we will see in Chapter 6 specifically how media representations offered an array of work and family content that our informants were aware of and reflected upon. Chapters 6–8 will document the place and role of media in our informants' lives, while also showing how individuals and groups in Dexter used media creatively, deliberately, and selectively to fit, support, and reinforce their pre-existing knowledge and beliefs.

5

WORK–FAMILY CHOICES

I think there are a lot more working moms on TV [than stay-at-home moms]. I think it's changing, I think that people are realizing that stay-at-home moms are important and especially in light of all the tragedies that have been going on with kids, and people are wondering who's watching the kids, what's going on with the kids, and is it really worth it to have everything?

—Dina, stay-at-home mother of three, married to a full time working father

I think [media] totally support people who work— two-income families. A lot of people don't have the choice. So I think that's where the media leads itself . . . articles on the housing market, there's a lot of stuff on travel, and I think kids are growing up a little different now, they expect more things, that parents are kind of pushed into a position to bring in two incomes to pay for them. Extra stuff. Toys are expensive, toys are kind of ridiculous . . . a lot of people are buying their way, and the media plays on that.

—Giselle, stay-at-home mother of five, married to a full time working father

[When I was newly married, media] portrayed the working moms as a kind of supermom. I really felt a lot of that. I really felt like I was trying to be a supermom. And decided "I'm not going to be a supermom, I'm going to be an okay mom who's not so tired." And now I think in the media, [they're] looking more at finding balance hopefully. I've seen a couple more programs or talks or news items talking about working moms or families.

> —Eleanor, part time working mother of three, married to
> a full time working father

If we wish to understand the relation between media representations and social reality, we must consider the latter as well as the former. Chapters 3 and 4 examined media sources and representations available to and used by the people of Dexter during, and before, the time of our study. This chapter is mainly about social reality. If, as we argue, the media influence behavior, attitudes, and expectations, it is equally true that life experience and circumstances influence how people use and perceive media. This chapter, although still citing media references used by our informants, focuses on the social reality of the work/family choices of people in Dexter. We also consider here the nature and impact of social comparisons with real people—other community members, parents, relatives, friends, and co-workers.

Employed mothers, stay-at-home mothers, supermoms . . . If the media offer varied images of work and family, our informants had made choices that were equally diverse. What were the actual work/family patterns of the men and women in our study? What were the contexts in which work/family decisions were made? How did parents feel about those patterns in relation to those of their own parents, friends, and other community members? The 60 women who participated in our study (combining individual interviewees and focus group members) were divided fairly equally among mothers who stayed home (32 percent), worked part time (32 percent), and worked full time outside the home (37 percent). This distribution is very close to the censused proportions for Dexter in each category. According to 2000 Census figures combining Dexter village and township, 33 percent of mothers with children under six years were not in the labor force, and slightly more than half of employed women worked full time compared with part time. There were 22 direct male participants in our study, including 8 interviewees and 14 focus group members. However, we also have information on the husbands of our female participants (along with the wives of the male participants).

Most of the men in our study (research participants plus husbands) worked full time before they had children and continued to do so after their children were born. Those (very few) men who did not work full time either were retired or had health problems. Two men, a self-employed accountant and a contractor, worked from a

80 • Media and Middle Class Moms

home office. One father telecommuted from home to an out-of-state corporation.

Nearly all the women in our study had worked full time outside the home before the birth of their first child. The advent of children produced much more variation in the employment status of wives than of husbands. While virtually all the husbands kept working full time, some of the wives—now mothers—worked full time; some, part time; and some stayed home full time—as we have seen, about a third in each category.

EMPLOYED MOTHERS

I like working. I'm not a Suzy Homemaker. I'd rather be out working than stay here and do laundry and dishes, that's for sure! I need a Rosie Robot [referring to the maid from the animated futuristic series *The Jetsons*], that's what I need.

—Cassidy, part time working mother of two, married to a full time working father

Many mothers kept on working full time after childbirth, or returned to full-time employment after spending a few years working part time or having no paid employment. One reason for pursuing two incomes was financial need. Marisa, a mother of one, "didn't want to go back to work after the maternity leave, but had to for financial reasons . . . We both have to work in order to make it right now." Many parents spoke of needing two incomes to provide nice homes for their families and opportunities for their children. According to Jack, a father of three, "Two-income families now are pretty much what you have to have . . . if you don't want to live in the bowels of Detroit." Sandra, who worked full time, had considered cutting back, but her husband thought, "It doesn't make any sense . . . think about it. If you work now, we have more money for our retirement. [And], for sure, [our daughter] is going to go to college." Indeed, their daughter was contemplating an Ivy League school. Sandra concluded, "We can do a lot with that extra money and provide for our kids, or make different opportunities available to them."

Some women made it clear that they personally could not be stay-at-home mothers. Nor would their children benefit if they tried. Paid employment, they felt, made them better mothers than they would be otherwise. In one of our focus groups of working mothers, Jeanette, for example, asserted, "I think I'm a much better mother working." Daisy agreed, "I know I was."

Cassidy was a mother of two who worked part time. She was seeking a second part time job, and was explicit about why she chose to work, despite her husband's preference that she stay home:

> I don't want to just stay home. It drives me crazy. It was one thing when they were little, and I had to stay home because there was constant business, there was diapers, and there was all this stuff, it was a whole different stage of life. But now when they're in school and I'm just here, I don't like it, and I want to be working.

In *Weaving Work and Motherhood* (1999), Anita Garey underlined the importance to many women of their lives at work as well as at home. The self-concept of many of the women in our study included a work identity in addition to their mother identity. Consider Marci, mother of two:

> We both put so much into our careers, and we were a little bit older when we got married and started with children. And then you get into a lifestyle where you have that two-income family. And the thought of going to just one, or one and a half, would be life altering. And to be honest, I love my children to death, but the thought of being at home all day . . . I'd pull my hair out.

Echoed Daisy, another mother of two, "I was 37 when [my daughter] was born. By that time work was a real important part of my identity and not something I was willing to give up forever or for a bigger chunk of time than I did." Tegan, a mother of one, observed, "for the first couple of years, I was a stay home mom, and I nursed. That was important. I had to be there. But I did want to work. I wanted to get back into the routine, and I honestly don't think it was really healthy for me. I needed a bit of balance."

At a working mothers' focus group the following exchange took place, highlighting the centrality of work to many women's lives, aiding their self-concepts, material circumstances, and overall well-being:

JEANETTE: I never really thought about not working.

MARNIE: I really couldn't think about not going back to work. [My son] turned six weeks old today, and I went back to work three days ago. With the jobs we have, neither one of us could afford to not work and still pay rent.

DAISY: The balance issue was something I was aware of when the girls were much younger. I suppose it would have been nice to have infinite money and not have to work, but even so, I think I appreciate aspects of the world of work that would have made me want to

82 • Media and Middle Class Moms

go there. Because as much as I do, and did, love being a mom, there's a lot to be said about hanging around with grownups.

JEANETTE: Taking a break when you want to.

DAISY: Exactly.

ROBERTA: Or just being productive and having some other place where you're getting some input and being part of something else.

DAISY: Yeah, a kind of flexibility and privacy that you literally don't have at home with two little ones.

MARNIE: I enjoyed being back at work even these last three days. I can actually get out of the house for a few minutes and do a little bit on my own.

For many women, work outside the home was not only satisfying but empowering. Fiona, a mother of one, put it this way: "It was never an option for me to not go to work because I'd had my job forever and ever, and I'm not willing to give that security up." Women who had experienced marital difficulties were especially likely to voice pro-work sentiments. Consider Roberta: "When somebody doesn't let you work, your self-esteem and everything . . . It's like somebody ripped something away from you and says you can't have it, and that's not fair." Then Tegan: "I agree with you. I almost went into depression . . . with the postpartum and having a newborn and being . . . in an unfamiliar area, and then finding out the person I was with was somebody else . . . I had to get back to . . . some kind of working environment."

Some women who were working full time would have preferred part time employment. Although they valued the work experience outside, they also wanted more time at home with their children (such sentiments have been expressed by women in a number of other work/family studies, including Fuchs Epstein, Seron, Oglensky, and Sauté [1999], and in a recent survey conducted by the Pew Research Center [2007b]). For example, in another focus group of working mothers, the following exchange took place:

CONSTANCE: I've always loved to be working part time . . . because that part of yourself gets out in the community and an adult person is alive.

MARISA: I'm hoping that by the time the second child is born and it's time to go back to work, I can think about going back part time again and not have to go back full time. Just like Constance said, I think I always want to be out there working. I don't want to be home permanently all the time. I think that just keeps yourself going, and still out in the community.

Work–Family Choices · **83**

Part time employment offered the possibility to these women of maintaining their ties to the world of work but maintaining a primary presence at home.

LEAVING THE WORK FORCE

People are neglecting, when they look at us as stay-at-home moms, that probably not a lot of us have Alices [referring to a character, a paid housekeeper, in *The Brady Bunch*] at home with us, and if we do she probably only comes once a week, not every day.

—Noreen, stay-at-home mother of one, married to full time working father

After the birth of their first child, some women immediately shifted to part time employment or staying home full time. A number of our informants, however, returned to full time work after the birth of their first child, then were unhappy about leaving that child in someone else's care, and/or felt overworked and harried. As one mother remarked, "I didn't like having to juggle, trying to get ready for work, and then getting the baby ready, and then rushing to work, and then rushing home." Some complained that their job kept their time with their children from being what they wanted it to be. Grace, for instance, was a mother who had gone from full time to part time hours, but this arrangement still didn't feel right to her, so she decided to stay home full time:

I felt that on my days off I was just running and doing errands and doing laundry, and it wasn't really time spent with [my children]. They were there, but I wasn't spending time with them playing games, reading books, and so on. It was just more of a "Here, you play here while I do this." And it bothered me because I didn't feel like I was really there for them.

Women who wanted more time at home employed different strategies: some cut back their outside work hours; some found a job with more flexibility; some left paid employment altogether.

How did couples decide which spouse would work full time? Typically, the women in our study who had reduced or relinquished external employment explained that their husbands held higher-paying jobs and/or weren't comfortable taking care of babies. It simply had made more sense for the woman to be the one to make the change. For Amy, one such mother, her withdrawal from the work force was "kind of the way it fell out naturally." Very few women who had reduced or abandoned paid employment said they had found it difficult to do so, except in terms of adjusting to the lower household income. Most of these mothers expressed pleasure at being able to spend more time with their young children, and at having the financial wherewithal to do so. As Madge, a mother of two, put it, "I had the flexibility of staying home. That was good, because [my husband] always worked and always had a good job." Men also spoke of being happy if they were in a position to be a single wage earner. Mitch, a father of two, commented, "I'm in a lucky position because I'm able to support my family and let my wife stay home." Mitch was especially committed to doing this. If his family were struggling financially, he said he'd work extra hours to keep his wife from having to work at all. Nicholas Townsend's research (2002) found that, to men, this urge to be the breadwinner demonstrated their commitments to their families: it was part of the "package deal," a gendered cultural expectation linking marriage and fatherhood with male employment.

A few women who had left outside jobs mentioned having to adjust to a non-work identity, as well as missing social relationships with co-workers. One stay-at-home mother recalled that when she first left the paid work force "All of a sudden I turned into an unknown person. I didn't have any identity, other than now I was a mom. That wasn't a whole lot of fun." The women who missed their work friends said that as their children got older they made new social contacts, the parents of their children's friends.

Most of the women in our study who were not employed full time reported that they were happy with their current work/family arrangement and said they would prefer to keep things as they were even when their children were older. They would only want to work for pay during school hours, if at all. Some women who worked full time said they wanted to cut back as their children got older. All these mothers expected their children's schedules to become even more packed with age; mothers wanted to be available to attend events and provide transportation. As one mother said, "I often say it would be easier to not work . . . because so many things are right after school." Amy, a mother of three, agreed: "I don't think I'm ever going to go back to full time until they're gone. Because I've heard other moms say, 'You think they're busy now in elementary school, just wait until they're in high school.' "

Another reason to stay home with older children was concern about the trouble adolescents could get into if left home alone after school. One woman with teenagers and younger children cited Dr. Laura: "At three-thirty the kids come home, no parents; guess what time the kids get pregnant. Three-thirty." This mother continued:

If I had to go out and work, I'd have to take a job where I could be home with my kids still in the morning and come home when they got home. That's the only way I would work it. That's it. Because I know that the kids, they need an adult, they need some-body because they don't always make the right decision on what to do.

INSTITUTIONAL BARRIERS TO COMBINING WORK AND FAMILY

I wish [work] were more flexible. Just more flexible. It's important to go to your parent–teacher conferences and be there for your children, and I've chosen my career and the flexibility isn't there, but it's nice to see the flexibility that is there for some people who can cut out for an hour or two there.

—Elaine, part time working mother of two, married to a full time working father

A combination of institutional and cultural factors made it difficult for the women we studied to combine employment and motherhood. One factor was an inadequate social infrastructure for family care. As one retired, formerly employed, mother commented:

One of the most important lessons that I learned [when I went from full time to part time work] . . . was the need for kids to have some adult in their life. And I don't think that [family care] is being supported . . . it's getting thrown around, the last couple of administrations . . . said . . . "We really support parents . . . and we'll give them maybe some tax credits." Depending on how the tax code's written, you may or may not see that credit actually come back to your purse. But it's not happening at the corporate level fast enough. There's a lot of us that are struggling, trying to do the best we can. We're not getting a whole heck of [a lot of] support about this.

While there may be some corporate support for family-friendly policies, such policies are far from universal and do not have strong government backing (Gornick, Heron, and Eisenbrey 2007, Hartmann, Hegewisch, and Lovell 2007). Many employers still function as if their workers have no family care responsibilities. Indeed, as Kathleen Gerson (1991) noted, most employers continue to penalize workers, regardless of gender, for parental involvement that interferes with the job.

86 · Media and Middle Class Moms

Hannah, a working mother of three, commented:

Our work roles primarily have been defined by what the work environment has been for men. For professional women my age who went into the workforce, we simply went in and occupied exactly the same roles that men occupied, with exactly the same expectations and then some, because we were women. And to change that, it's going to take a redefinition of work, in my opinion.

In the world of paid employment, men still earn more on average than women do, and "male" professions continue to pay better than "female" ones do (Rose and Hartmann 2004). This economic fact makes it rational for more women than men to fill the stay-at-home or part time working parent role. Kelly, a nurse, for example, was married to Dean, a physician. As the arrival of each of three children made the family schedule more and more hectic, Kelly and Dean decided that having one of them cut to part time hours made sense. Who that parent would be wasn't even discussed: "He makes three times the money I make! [The decision] was easy. We didn't even think about it."

The nature and scheduling of work constitute another key structural factor making it difficult for mothers to work full time for pay. Generally speaking, the less power and prestige the job has, the less autonomy and flexibility the individual has. This became very clear from our working mothers' focus groups. Three women who worked at lower prestige jobs—at a day care center, a restaurant, and a grocery store—complained about having very little flexibility in their schedules and little ability to control when they worked. Even in higher prestige jobs, workers who are lower in the company hierarchy can face similar difficulties. Audrey, for example, a mother of two, worked three days a week following the births of her first and second children, but then decided to stay home full time. Given the hierarchical structure of her medical workplace, Audrey had little control over her schedule beyond that allowed by her boss. This worked well when her boss was sympathetic to her needs for flexibility, but when a new, less understanding, supervisor was hired, Audrey's carefully coordinated plans were thrown into disarray. Further, social comparison with others in the workplace hierarchy (which is common when that hierarchy offers unequal flexibility) highlighted the difficulties Audrey felt her employment was causing:

I know some people who really do have a nice schedule, and they don't realize they have as many freedoms. It's interesting when you're in the hospital setting where somebody in administration has more freedom, whereas if you're [in my former position], you have to be there. You can't just leave . . . so you don't get the same freedom or the same schedule to go off and be part of your kids' life in the middle of the day. I think just within a structure there's inequity in there, too. And I think that's partly why I left my last job . . . when I left I said, "It's very hard for me to make sure I have day care and to rearrange my schedule and for my husband to leave home and do all this type of thing when I'm sitting next to somebody that can go home in the middle of the day."

The issue of autonomy was important to many parents, as is demonstrated by this exchange in one of our focus groups comprised of employed women:

HANNAH: When I left my last company I definitely decided I was not going into an environment where other people had control of my time and control of my life. And it's not really the hours that matter to me, it's the flexibility and control.

JOELLEN AND MARTA, SIMULTANEOUSLY: Yes, I agree.

Another work policy that reinforces traditional gendered patterns of work and family is that many women get a paid maternity leave, whereas most men do not get a comparable paternity benefit. Because women give birth and are viewed culturally as the primary child care givers, men tend to get less employment flexibility for family issues than women do. None of the fathers in our study had used the Family and Medical Leave Act, mainly because they worried about how a request to do so would be perceived in the workplace (and indeed, in her 1997 study of a corporation with "family-friendly" policies, Hochschild documented that even there, most men avoided paternity leave and, when a few did try to take it, difficulties ensued in their relationships with bosses and co-workers). When men in our study did take time off at childbirth, or for various events in their children's lives, they usually used sick leave or vacation time (cf. Rudd 2004, Wisensale 2001).

Employers seemed more supportive of women's than men's needs for flexibility for family care. Penny, a full time working mother, said that she and her husband tried to divide the responsibility of caring for their twins. Her husband's employer, however, wasn't as understanding as hers when someone needed to stay home with a sick child. Nonetheless, "They dealt with it. Employers are realizing . . . that dads are taking a more active role in their children. And that it is not just a woman's thing to do. So they would make comments, but [my husband] was

88 • Media and Middle Class Moms

never disciplined or anything like that." Bryce, a father of one, had a much less accommodating experience with his employer. By arranging an early start to his working day at an auto manufacturer, Bryce had managed to keep his commute to one hour. However, despite what he bitterly referred to as his company's professed commitment to "family values," Bryce's hours suddenly were changed to a later shift. This caused him to hit rush-hour traffic, which added an hour to his total commute each day—time he regretted not spending with his family.

Throughout the United States, the school system poses additional institutional barriers to combining paid employment with family responsibilities. School days do not match the conventional hours of most full time employment. And typically schools begin and end at times that vary with children's different age groups. In Dexter, as elsewhere, the parents of two or more children may face difficulties coordinating their children's departures from home. Audrey, for example, was a stay-at-home mother of a ten-year-old daughter and a seven-year-old son. She previously had worked in a medical profession and wanted to return to that. Audrey's daughter, however, was entering a grade in which she had to arrive at school an hour before Audrey's son. Scheduling issues, as Audrey noted, made it difficult for her even to contemplate paid employment. She couldn't simply get both children on the bus, then leave for seven hours. Because her children left and returned home an hour apart at each end of the school day, Audrey had no easy way to coordinate a work/family schedule.

Also, in Dexter, as across the United States, children take part in numerous activities for which there usually is little or no public transportation. Parents must arrange for transportation if their children are to participate. Both Audrey's children were involved in sports and musical extracurriculars, and Audrey wanted to be the one to get them there and home again. In part this was because she wanted to know personally who the children's coaches were, and who else was around her children. This was a common wish among the women we interviewed. Many discussed their desire to observe and monitor their children's non-parental adult influences, whether from coaches, teachers, or child care providers. They could do this by being available during the day to attend school events, volunteer in the classroom, and drive children to and from various activities. Stacy, a stay-at-home mother of a kindergartener, commented:

> If I couldn't be involved in his school, to know exactly what kinds of things they're teaching him, what kinds of interaction he's having with the children, how . . . they handle discipline on a daily

basis, and I could[n't] pop in there and just be there to observe it rather than hearing what the theory is . . . I don't know if I could do it, I don't know if I could allow myself to give up that responsibility to them. But because I'm not working I can.

Garey (1999) noted how this intensive presence of mothers in the school and at extracurricular activities is part of the way mothers communicate to others and themselves that they are *good* mothers. Similar involvement is not expected of fathers.

DECIDING WHO STAYS HOME: WORK/FAMILY ADJUSTMENTS

[My husband would love for me] to get one kick-butt job, and he could just stay home and be Mr. Mom. He would love that, he's got his gardening, he loves to bake pies, he's actually more domesticated than I am.

—Cassidy, part time working mother of two, married to a full time working father

Gendered norms about marriage, child care, and breadwinning obviously also influence parents' decisions about work and family. Audrey, for example, said when she and her husband had both worked they had experienced conflict about who would stay home when one of their children was sick. It was a relief for her to have that behind her once she stayed home full time. Several women reported that their husbands happily endorsed their decision to stay home. Ginny, a stay-at-home mother for several years, had worked full time until her second child was born, then went to part time, then stopped altogether:

Financially we didn't want both of them in babysitting, and financially it wasn't worth me working three days a week. I needed to work full time, and we never wanted to do that. [My husband] has always wanted me just to stay home anyways. And I did, too. I really wanted to be here for the girls.

Some parents said they had discussed having the father rather than the mother stay home, and many phrased this as "being Mr. Mom" (after the Michael Keaton movie of the same name) (cf. Deutsch 1999). Few, however, seemed to have considered it seriously. Viewing such an arrangement as a possibility seemed to meet a need to express ideologies of equality between the spouses. Not actually doing it fit with ongoing structural realities and cultural norms of female caregiving and male breadwinning. There were some exceptions. As noted, a few fathers stayed home when they suffered from health problems, and their wives took on more or all of the breadwinning burden. There also were some men who seemed genuinely frustrated with the narrowness of contemporary gender roles. Bryce was married to a woman who, because of a disability, could not work outside the home; she therefore served as primary caregiver for their child. Bryce said he would prefer a different situation: "I wish I could stay home and that [my wife] had the career. I would do it in a second . . . there's nothing that has given me as much pleasure as my son, nothing that I have done." Bryce described his impatience with standard gender roles regarding child care and work:

> There's one woman [at my old workplace], who [said], "I want to get married, I want kids, but I want to work. My husband doesn't, but it's the husband who should work." . . . It's just so caught up in roles that they think they should be doing. Here's a case, she doesn't want to stay home, her husband does. I don't understand. I'd stay home in a heartbeat.

For most parents, however, earning the principal family income still was seen as a man's responsibility. In our Dexter study sample, this pattern was nearly ubiquitous, as it is nationwide. Our informants, both men and women, spoke of wives' incomes as "helping out" the family finances, or as "extra" or "additional" (cf. Potuchek 1997, Townsend 2002). Jaime, for example, was a father of four. His wife previously had stayed home full time, but when the family moved to more expensive housing, she began working part time:

> So it's basically a matter of her income allows us to have little extras or the quick grocery run or all of a sudden the kids need some shoes, those types of things. It was really more for the extras. My income still goes to pay the basics, the house, the car. But hers just kind of gives us that cushion.

Such a breadwinning ideal can cause strain. One relationship ended during the course of our fieldwork, reflecting conflict over money and housework. Toby described how he listened to talk radio in part to hear about the causes of problems like those he and his girlfriend were having, and to hear about how other people coped:

> I try to get my girlfriend . . . to understand that the problems going on with her and things going on, it's not just her. It's not just us. That everybody has those problems. I'm not going to have some job that she's going to be able to stay at home and not work.

She has a degree, but she chooses to stay with the kids because she wants to raise them and I respect that. But we have a lot of problems . . . now she's spending all the time with the kids. And I'm working, I'm doing all I can to bring home what I can.

Few of the men in our study had changed their jobs or schedules when their children were born. Those who had done so either took a job with less overnight travel or arranged to work closer to home. At least one father turned down a promotion that would have meant more travel. A few sought different jobs that meant less time away from home. One such father was Clancy: "It took a complete career change to try and get more time with my family. There was no way to change the type of career that I was in to really get a lot more time." Some men arranged their workdays so they could spend time with their children at one end of the day. Gene, for example, said, "When I'm the busiest I try to leave as early as possible in the morning so I can get home in the evening to spend time with the boys out in the yard. I just make the sacrifice in the morning and get stuff done and get home."

HOUSEHOLD DIVISION OF LABOR

The ratio of female to male housework and child care was highest for women who were stay-at-home mothers, next highest for part time working mothers, and lowest for full time working mothers. (Similar patterns have been found by other researchers, such as Coltrane [1996].) No matter what their employment status, however, women reported doing the lion's share of both housework and child care, including transporting children to and from activities. This included both the actual labor and the planning of it, another pattern found in prior studies (Hochschild 1989). Women who worked for pay from their homes unanimously spoke of combining housework with their cash employment throughout the day, such as by doing laundry while working on the computer. The few men who worked from home did not report such a pattern. Women who traveled for their work all spoke of doing housework ahead of time, including laundry, laying out clothing, and preparing and freezing meals. No man or wife of a man who traveled for work reported anything similar.

Men did outside chores (e.g., yard work), some child transporting, some dishes, and occasional cooking. One woman, Bridget, called the division of labor in her household "kind of Old World. He does the outside, I do the inside." Parents reported more fatherly involvement with the daily routines of child care as the children got older; infants

92 • Media and Middle Class Moms

and toddlers were primarily the purview of women. Men who did little else in terms of child care often did participate in bathing and bedtime routines.

Cleaning and laundry were two tasks that almost all the mothers performed exclusively (this model is predominant, even among couples actively seeking to divide household labor equitably [Coltrane 1989]). Many men and women said that women were more exacting about those tasks, frequently using the words "compulsive" and "obsessive." If left to the men, neither would get done to the women's standards, and therefore, the women did them (cf. Hochschild 1989). Penny, a full time working mother, said of her husband, "When he was at home he would do the laundry, and it just got to the point that I preferred that he didn't." Madge, another full time working mother, laughingly said of the laundry, "I wouldn't trust my husband to do it!"

As a corollary to women's income being framed as a "help" to their husbands, much of men's work in the home was described by both members of the couple as being done to "help" their wives (cf. Coltrane 1989, Hochschild 1989). Kate, a stay-at-home mother, for example, said of her husband: "He's an engineer, so he's always fixing things that are broken, doing projects for me, whether it's helping me build my cornice boards or helping me hang wallpaper, and he's really terrific that way." Elaine, a mother of two, worked part time. On days when she worked, her husband altered his schedule to "help her" when she "couldn't do it all" herself.

Many women presented their husbands' contributions around the house, no matter how minor, in a positive light. Some even seemed to overestimate what their husbands did, perhaps in order to convey a picture of an egalitarian division of labor that they might have felt was socially desirable (Deutsch [1999] found a similar pattern among her research participants, who estimated their division of child care labor as 50/50, revising that figure only when asked to break down the tasks one by one). Willa, for instance, said that her husband cooked "almost all the meals, pretty much on a daily basis." When asked to go through the schedule in detail, however, Willa related that she prepares breakfast, because her husband leaves for work before the children waken, gets about half the week's lunches together, and makes approximately three of the seven weekly dinners. Thus, although the couple shared the cooking, Willa's husband didn't actually seem to cook almost all the family's meals.

It was rare for husbands to overestimate their housework in this way. Nate, for example, ran a business from his home with his wife. They both worked full time. An accountant, Nate was numerically precise as he tabulated their respective contributions to housework. He related that although they "try to keep it 50/50," his wife actually does about 80% of the laundry, 60% of the cooking and general cleaning, and 80% of the bathroom cleaning. He gave himself an 80% for yard work. One father, Brad, did seem to inflate his contributions by saying child care in his marriage was "split down the middle." Since he was away from home eleven hours a day, while his wife was only away for five, this seemed unlikely.

Some women spoke with resigned amusement about their husbands' (lack of) participation in housework. We spent time with the family of Elaine, for example, on a night when her husband was scheduled to make dinner. He left home for an errand and was gone so long Elaine fretted he wouldn't get back in time to prepare the meal. She framed this as an issue of being male, saying that women "thought things through" more, making sure to allot time for meal preparation, child homework, and so forth. Elaine complained that her husband could leave home with both children at 11:30 a.m. and never think that at some point the children would need lunch. When her husband finally did arrive home that night, he didn't end up making dinner: Elaine helped him to fix leftovers. Another mother who worked part time said that even if she didn't work, she didn't see what else she could do around the house, since she already did so much more than her husband did. She'd just have more time to do it.

At one focus group of working mothers, the women discussed their husbands' (in)attention to housework and their own roles as household overseers. Like Elaine, they framed men's lack of participation as an innate characteristic tied to their gender:

JOELLEN: My husband grew up in a home where his mother didn't work and did everything, and she apologizes to me all the time. And . . . he will help, but I always have to ask him. So I always feel that I'm the one in charge. I'm the organizer and if I don't remember it . . . He'll do anything I ask. But it's like, one time it'd be nice not to have to be the one.

SHIRLEY: Is it unanimous? We all feel that we are in charge?

HANNAH: It's true. Every woman I know, whether or not she's working, feels that that is her responsibility, and it's the number one complaint, because there's only so much energy that you want to put into the management, the remembering, the clocking, the assignment.

TAMMI: And we just can't let it go. Even if you are at your job, you're thinking, "Brownies. Is he going to get her there or not? I'd better

94 · Media and Middle Class Moms

call." And I'm grocery shopping on my lunch hour to get something for dinner . . . Men don't have that. I don't know if they don't have it, or they haven't honed into it.

MARCI: They're just totally different from women . . . He doesn't think of the finances, he doesn't think about what's for dinner, he doesn't think about the dirty laundry, he doesn't think of the dirty diaper . . . Bless his heart, he's very good, he'll help, but like Joellen said, you have to ask.

Some women did speak with real frustration about their husbands' lack of participation in the home. Julie, for instance, was a mother of two who worked part time. Her husband worked full time. Both were professionals. Julie did nearly all the housework and child care. Her husband had trouble staying on top of the children's activities:

> The other day [my husband] came home and he said, "I didn't know [our son] had a conference." And I said, "Well, check the schedule." I am tired of reminding my husband, who is an educated, mature adult, when everything is. It's on the calendar. If you miss a game, you miss a practice, I'm not every morning going to leave a note. Because I do all the juggling. When I work, if I don't get home in time, I do all the planning of where my kids are going and how are they going to get here. He does none of that. That is a lot of work. It's a lot of frustration. So I just will not any more remind him of events. If he misses them, he misses them.

Shirley, one of the few single mothers participating in our study, had separated from her child's father, in part due to housework issues. Both worked full time, but he had not contributed to the upkeep of their home or to the care of her two children in ways that she felt were fair. Nor was he supporting the family financially in a way that Shirley could see as justifying the other gaps, so she asked him to move out. Another woman who had separated from her husband told it this way:

> [He] just wants to work and come home and doesn't think about things too well, he's not very organized. That's what broke us up. I do all the thinking on that stuff, so I get used to it. I do the bills and budgeting and the spending and dealing with teachers at school and all that.

Most of the women who expressed discontent with their husbands' share of the housework and child care ended their narratives by saying, "But he's a great dad." Julie, after detailing her husband's shortcomings about scheduling, did the same: "He's a wonderful dad, but horrible at trying to organize and plan." And indeed, in what seemed to be an implicit substitution, fathers seemed to be more involved in doing things with their children than with keeping the house in order. Greg, however, explicitly recognized and drew upon this tradeoff in his own marital negotiations. A father of two, he had cut back on his job after a medical incident, and thus was doing more of the after-school care and transportation than his wife, who worked full time. Of their arrangement he said, "I think I do so much of the child-rearing that [my wife] really appreciates that and at some point, three or four years ago, she just stopped badgering me about the housework."

Few couples diverged from the pattern in which men were less involved in child care, and much less involved in housework, than their wives (this is a common pattern nationwide; see, for example, the 2004 U.S. Department of Labor Time Use Survey). One couple that did differ to some extent was Eloise and Kent, who had three children. Eloise worked part time as a nurse, while Kent worked full time as a police officer. His schedule was unusually flexible, in that he worked 12-hour shifts and had a number of days at home each week. Eloise and Kent reached their work/family arrangement specifically through gendered norms of division of labor: "We decided it really is better when Mom's home and Dad works." Despite this, Eloise was one of the only women in this study who talked extensively, with pride, about her husband's involvement in both child care and housework. In part this reflected social comparisons that Eloise made with her co-workers, by whose standards Kent's participation was extraordinary. Although Eloise might prefer that he do more, she seemed content with what he did do:

> [My husband is] quite an updated guy for having traditional values. So we kind of have a contemporary marriage, but it's kind of skewed a little bit. But I complain about him at work . . . "Oh my husband, you know, I can't believe it, when he did the wash or when he cleaned the floor, he left this there." "Your husband will clean the floor?" they say, or . . . "When he did the laundry . . . he never puts it away." "He'll do the laundry?" So I shouldn't complain, because he does do quite a bit, but he doesn't do as much as I do when I'm home.

Kent was well aware that his household participation was greater than most other fathers'. During one ethnographic visit, while making breakfast, he commented upon that. During this and another visit, Kent attended to all the children, including his infant daughter, undirected by his wife. He was familiar with the children's care and school routines, and, unprompted, completed a number of household chores, including

96 · Media and Middle Class Moms

the dishes. Kent's involvement in child care and housework, which was exceptional in our study, was facilitated by his unusual work schedule. However, he also managed to stay home to nurse his wife and care for the children when she was on extended bed rest after a difficult birth. Kent was the only father in our study who had done anything similar.

CHILD CARE CHOICES: WHO'S FORMING THEIR PERSONALITY?

LARRY KING: This book is going to be controversial, *Parenthood by Proxy: Don't Have Them If You Won't Raise Them.* Are you saying if you have to send your child to a day care center, don't have a child?
LAURA SCHLESSINGER: Yes.
KING: That's what you're saying?
SCHLESSINGER: Yes . . .

—*Larry King Live* excerpt, May 3, 2000

Not surprisingly, parents in dual-income families differed from those in single-income families in their opinions about the best way to care for children. Parents who had made choices and sacrifices to have one parent stay home were far more likely to express negative feelings about non-parental child care, saying they did not want their children to "have to go" to day care, and they did not want their children to be raised by other people. Care providers, these parents felt, would not love and understand their children as parents would (among a number of other researchers, Hays [1996] heard identical sentiments expressed by her research participants). Nor would they provide them with the attentiveness of a parent, or instill the parents' values. Said Dina, a stay-at-home mother of three:

> I think [having a stay-at-home parent] helps. I think it helps [children] to make good decisions, if you're the one teaching them to make decisions rather than a day care worker . . . Who's forming their personality? And who's helping them to know what's right and what's wrong? And teaching them that love is important and their feelings are important and valid?

Like many other parents who felt this way, Dina did send her children to nursery school for the purpose of socializing them in a non-familial context. For Dina and parents like her, a crucial variable was the number of hours spent in day care: her children spent comparatively little time there, usually one to three afternoons per week. Kendra, a stay-at-home mother of five, reported that she sent her children to preschool a few half-days a week for "socialization . . . more structure, school structure, learning how to follow rules from somebody else, making friends that aren't family members."

Some stay-at-home mothers asserted that the children of dual-income couples were not as well behaved as the children of single-earner couples. Consider Noreen's comment as she took part in a focus group consisting of stay-at-home mothers:

> When you go to school, and you go on field trips, you can almost pick out the kids that are home with their mom all the time, and the ones that are maybe part time with their mom, and the ones that basically grew up in day care . . . The very first time my husband went on a field trip he came home [and] he said, "Anything that I have doubted for the first five years, I will never, ever doubt again. There is no way that we have made a wrong decision." . . . Their kids are just, they're different.

Several mothers spoke with concern of the "six to six" or the "twelve-hour" care child. This child was used as a point of contrast to their own children, who were depicted as more fortunate. Alison, for example, was a stay-at-home mother of two who said:

> Sometimes I feel real bad . . . I see some kids that get dropped off at my son's school at six in the morning and don't get picked up until six at night, the before and after kind of care at school. I feel bad for the kids, but I don't know that they're suffering from it really. I personally would never put my kids in that situation.

Cammie, a part time working mother, expressed similar feelings about children whose parents couldn't come to school parties:

> It's hard on the child when they see . . . [During] the parties at my elementary school . . . [it was school policy that] if your parent was at a party you could leave school early. And there were always just the group of maybe five or six kids . . . It was always the same kids, they had to stay and help clean up and wait for the bus. You just always felt sorry for those kids because their moms were never there.

Meredith had three children and worked part time. When discussing why she chose not to work full time, she said it was because she knew how much effort it took to be a good mother and to be involved as much as she thinks is right. She also didn't like seeing children in after school care programs, involved in a series of activities to keep them occupied until 6 p.m. Interestingly, her own children were heavily involved in

98 · Media and Middle Class Moms

activities, participating in sports, Cub Scouts, and other extracurriculars. The element of "having to" participate was key in Meredith's discomfort with the activities scheduled at the care facility.

Julie, a part time working mother, felt strongly that children shouldn't be raised in families with two full time working parents:

> What will the children be like? Are they just going to be workaholic adults who want to buy all this stuff? . . . So I'm really concerned about all these kids that are shoved out to different day care centers, and they don't get the hugs when they need them. They're put in front of computers in the evening because mom and dad are so busy doing all the things that they need to do to run a home.

Gerson (1991) noted that the erosion of the structural and ideological supports for domesticity has left domestically oriented women feeling embattled (contributing, we note, to an army of Dr. Laura listeners). Increasingly, homemaker mothers feel they must defend a personal choice and family arrangement that once was considered sacrosanct. In reaction, many domestically oriented women view employed mothers as either selfish and dangerous to children, or overburdened and miserable, or, in the case of childless women, unfulfilled.

A frequently heard sentiment among our domestically oriented informants was expressed rhetorically by Kate, a stay-at-home mother of three. "Why did you choose to have kids if you weren't going to spend time with them?" (Probably uncoincidentally, phrases like these mirror those frequently used by Dr. Laura.) Many partners in couples where the woman stayed home full time or worked part time said they wanted to be the ones to "raise" their children. One stay-at-home mother of one wondered how working mothers could even communicate with their children. She felt that her comprehension of her toddler's baby talk was dependent upon being with him throughout each day. Mothers who stayed home sometimes imputed a lack of caring to parents in dual-earner families: "Their business or their workshop is more important than their own kid. And I disagree." "You want that boat? You want that vacation? You want that second home? You want the Explorer and the sports car? I think there are some sacrifices you make when you decide to have your wife stay at home [and] the husband work all day."

In an analysis of *The Time Divide: Work, Family, and Gender Inequality*, Jerry A. Jacobs and Gerson (2004) discuss Juliet Schor's (1998) idea (shared by many of the stay-at-home mothers in our study) that parents in dual-income households are influenced by an ethic of competitive consumption, which leads them to strive for bigger houses, nicer cars, and other symbols of material affluence. Jacobs and Gerson do not attempt to locate the sources of this ethic, but our informants readily blamed the media. Parents in single-income families criticized the media for propagating a culture of consumption that manipulates parents into thinking both should work, thereby sacrificing their children's health and happiness for superfluous additional income. As James, the husband of a stay-at-home mother, put it, "It's just a feeling I have that people are trying to move their way back away from two-income families. Cutting back. The two-income family gets you a lot of nice stuff. And there are people that are saying, 'Maybe I don't need all the nice stuff. I'd rather have one stay at home.' " This idea was passed back and forth in a women's focus group, as well:

BRITTANY: I could see, on just the right day, reading an article on ... how to achieve that perfect Montessori-educated child and going "I'll get a job during the summer. Oh, that's a great idea." If it's communicated well, ideas like that can be snapped up in a heartbeat.

DARCIE: By people who want to be the best parents they can possibly be.

BRITTANY: So I think it makes childbearing and childrearing even materialistic.

Dual-income parents were very likely to talk about the benefits to their children of non-parental day care, although they often qualified this by saying that their day care providers were exceptional or that their children enjoyed going to care. Most parents seemed happy with the child care they had found: "I had a great day care lady who was like their second mother." "I had a great sitter. She loved my children dearly, took great care of them, they loved her." Many parents who used child care mentioned what they saw as positives of the experience, especially adaptability. Gwen, a full time working mother of two, stated that she thought children did better when they spent some time away from their home:

They become more diversified, they're not shy, they're social, they're able to adapt to different situations. Where a child that stays home is kind of limited. They've not experienced other things that a child [does] who goes to day care, comes home. That's my opinion. And I've noticed it with my children. My children adapt very well to change, which is extremely important nowadays. Because things change quickly and if you're not ready for it ...

DO PARENTS' CHILDHOOD EXPERIENCES INFLUENCE THEIR CURRENT WORK/FAMILY PATTERNS?

You see on TV where they have these horrible situations in day care, which may or may not be true, but the media plays to that, they want to take and make parents who choose to work seem to be put in situations that are no-win. I don't know if that's the case or not because I never had to go that way. My experience growing up was with parents not at home, there were problems. And then that's reinforced by the media, the way they play to the emotion.
—Mitch, full time working father of two, married to a stay-at-home mother

We found no clear relationship between the work history of a woman's mother or mother-in-law and her own work status. Several of our dual-income parents had had stay-at-home mothers. One full time working mother, for example, stated that "My mom was able to stay home with us. She got part time jobs when we were in school." Other dual-income parents, however, had been raised in dual-earner households. One such woman said, "I came from a two-income household, so it just never really occurred to me not to work." The same range of responses was heard from women who stayed home full time or worked part time, as well as their husbands.

Some people did report making work/family choices at odds with their parents' arrangements, on the basis of negative childhood experiences. Cassidy, for example, was a part time working mother whose own mother had stayed home full time. Cassidy felt strongly about working for pay: "I could see the stress in my parents, and it was all centered on money . . . I think it's just one of those things where we knew we all had to work, because my parents really struggled, being on one income." By contrast, Julie, a part time working mother, recalled that her mother went to work full time when Julie was in elementary school: "And I didn't like it. I remember that . . . I just remember in the summers, or from three to five, missing her. Coming home from school, empty house. So I always said, 'I'm working part time.' " Dina, a stay-at-home mother, had similar recollections. Her mother got home at 4:00 p.m. and Dina did not like arriving home from school and not having her mother there. In a focus group of stay-at-home mothers, Noreen recounted how she and her husband came to their work/family decision based on their observations of their parents: "We always knew when we had kids that I wouldn't work. My mom didn't work, and his mom did. And he could see the dramatic difference, and what it was like to be brought up with . . . when you got home nobody was there."

Many, like Noreen, made choices similar to their parents', based on positive feelings about how their parents had managed work and family. Ada, a stay-at-home mother, reported that "My mom stayed at home with us. It was very natural for me, that's what I know." Similarly, Penny was a full time working mother whose own mother worked as a bartender and was away from home into the night. Penny described herself as a "latchkey kid," but didn't have the same negative reaction as Julie or Dina. In turn, she did not seem to feel conflict about being a working mother.

In explaining current female employment and work/family orientations, Gerson's research (1991) also discounted the significance of childhood experience, including whether or not one's own mother worked outside the home. About two-thirds of her respondents who held domestic orientations as children ultimately became work-committed. Similarly, over 60 percent of women who had been ambivalent about childbearing or had career aspirations as children became committed to domesticity in adulthood. Adult, rather than childhood, experiences involving work and family predicted whether a woman's orientation was domestic or non-domestic. Gerson (1991) found that women's exposure to expanded opportunities outside the home (for example, upward employment mobility) and unanticipated insecurities within it (for example, marital instability or economic squeezes) tended to promote a non-domestic orientation, even among women who once planned for full-time motherhood. Exposure to a more traditional package of opportunities and constraints (such as constricted employment options and stable marriage) tended, by contrast, to promote a domestic orientation even among those who felt ambivalent toward motherhood and domesticity as children.

Gerson did not examine fathers' childhood experiences. In our study, two fathers with atypical involvement in child care did feel that their orientation toward family and employment had been shaped by their own parents' decisions. Greg's parents ran a business out of their home and were both involved in raising their children. Greg became his own children's primary caretaker, although he originally cut back on his work hours primarily for health reasons. Nate, a father of five, worked out of his home with his wife. He said their decision to build a home business together was at least in part due to their parents' influence. His parents had had flexible schedules, which allowed both to engage in child care. Nate and his wife similarly were both involved in their children's daily care.

SOCIAL COMPARISON INVOLVING WORK/FAMILY CHOICES

When our informants talked about how their parents' work and family patterns shaped the arrangements they themselves had come to, they were engaging in social comparison, using their parents as a point of negative or positive contrast to themselves. Their narratives tell a story in which they didn't follow their parents' examples because of bad outcomes, or they did because of good outcomes. When discussing their own work and family decisions, and how those impacted their own children, the parents in our study tended to cast their current work–family configuration as the best possible for their children. They often used examples of other people's families as a means of negative social comparison to illustrate how patterns other than theirs could go awry. Sandra, an employed mother, for example, contrasted her sister-in-law's family/work choices unfavorably with her own, saying that although that sister-in-law was a stay-at-home mother, she didn't do anything with her children, who now were plagued by drugs, depression, and obesity. At the other end of the work–family continuum, Sandra mentioned that another of her sisters-in-law was *too* career-focused and didn't want her children. Those children, according to Sandra, also had problems; one shy and not verbal, and the other hyperactive. Like Goldilocks, Sandra used these contrasts to show that neither sister-in-law's choice was ideal, and to provide implicit justification for her own decisions, because Sandra's children were free of the problems ascribed to the other children.

Kate, a stay-at-home mother of three, also used a family member's children as a negative example to highlight the rightness of her own choice. Kate's younger sister worked full time and had children with behavior problems. Kate recalled being influenced by her older sister's decision to be a stay-at-home mother, and being happy that she had done so. Both sisters who were stay-at-home mothers, and their mother, put pressure on the employed sister to stay home: "We just say, 'Oh, just stay home and spend some time with your kids.' But she doesn't. It's just really a bad situation." Similarly, one part time working woman, said of a full time working woman:

> It's fascinating to me to see some of these women and to see what they think. I worked for a woman who's a CEO of one of the largest health organizations in the country ... And when she presented who she was to us and how she balanced family and work, her commitment was that she had breakfast every day with

her family. And I don't know, I guess that's great, but everything doesn't happen at breakfast in your family.

This mother used the comparison with an overly busy woman to shed favorable light on her own work and family balance, which she felt was ideal. Some parents engaged in a different kind of social comparison, more upward than downward, by finding role models whom they felt handled things in ways they would like to. Tegan, to illustrate, was a mother of one. She was friends with a woman whom she called her hero:

I [know] this one woman who has 11 children and she's pregnant now and she walks around with a smile on her face and can carry everything . . . She's an inspiration. Sometimes if I feel upset about something, I can just use her as an example and think, all right, this is a better way to cope with life.

SOCIAL SUPPORT FOR WORK/FAMILY CHOICES

Our informants generally felt that their families and friends supported them in whatever work and family decision they had made. Most people had family and friends whose situations ran the gamut from stay-at-home to full time working mothers. Daily contacts, however, tended to be more with people who had made choices that were similar to their own. Volunteering at the coop nursery school or getting together for a weekday playgroup, for example, a stay-at-home mother was unlikely to spend time with a full time working mother. At work, full time working mothers were not in contact with stay-at-home mothers. Some parents in our study chose to socialize exclusively with people who had made similar work/family decisions, but this was rare. Ada was one who did surround herself with women who had made choices similar to hers: "I don't know a mom who's not home, and I couldn't relate to a child who was in day care. I don't understand that experience."

Although most parents reported feeling supported by their families in whatever decision they had made about paid labor and child care, not all did. Noreen, for example, a stay-at-home mother married to a man raised by two working parents, received negative feedback from them about her decision: "They thought I was taking advantage of him." Her own extended family wondered why she was going to stay home when she had just completed a graduate degree, commenting: "Well, that was such a waste. You're never going to use that. What are you going to do?" On the other side of the work/family spectrum, one full

104 • Media and Middle Class Moms

time working mother, Sandra, had had a stay-at-home mother, Joan. When Sandra's son started to lose his hair, Joan asked her if she thought it was because he was upset that she traveled for work. When Sandra was having trouble finding a quality babysitter, Joan told her that her (Sandra's) sister-in-law, a stay-at-home mother, said "Well, maybe if [Sandra] stayed home and took care of her kids, this wouldn't be a problem."

Although most mothers found community support no matter what their work situation, some reported uncomfortable situations involving teachers or other parents. When one stay-at-home mother told her child's teacher she felt distracted, the teacher asked what she had to be distracted about, since she stayed home full time. Another stay-at-home mother, serving as room mother for her daughter's classroom, found that working parents would not return her phone calls about organizing school trips and class parties. Other stay-at-home mothers also had negative feelings about their encounters with employed mothers, as heard in this exchange from one of our stay-at-home mothers' focus groups:

NICOLE: I feel really weird saying this, but, the working moms work. But they're lucky to have the stay-at-home moms to do this volunteer stuff.

NOREEN: They will never tell you that though. After I [made] 200 [craft items] last year, not one of the working moms [thanked me]. They were just like, "Well, I wish I had the time." No you don't, because you wouldn't sit at home night after night [making them].

NICOLE: When you said that, it reminded me. I did some work in the subdivision, we were trying to put a directory together, and it hadn't been done in years ... So these forms were sent out, and people had to follow up on them. I called this mom, she was a working mom, and she really snapped at me. She said, "I'll put it in your mailbox on my way to work tomorrow. I don't stay at home doing this." And I was really insulted by it.

NOREEN: I feel like a lot of working moms, they feel like we sit at home. Just like my husband, he was so disillusioned, like every day was just like going to the park.

NICOLE: And they think it's really fun too.

Working mothers likewise reported negative comments about their choices. One working mother, Joellen, was in a job sharing situation at a large automotive corporation. She and her job share partner were interviewed for a position in a different part of the company. The male interviewer said to them, "I'm just going to say this right out to you. Don't you feel guilty leaving those babies?" He also had young children. The women left without pursuing the job further.

Although working fathers escaped commentary about combining paid employment with fatherhood, men were sometimes on the receiving end of discomforting judgments based on gender stereotypes. One father who came frequently to his child's school kept getting stopped in the hall and his reasons for being there questioned. He thought the staff suspected him of being a pedophile because he was a man at an elementary school. This ended only when he became more familiar to the school's employees.

"PRACTICAL" CHOICES REPRODUCE CULTURE

Like all parents, those in our study needed both to support and to care for their families and homes. Structural and cultural forces, including the media, as we'll see more clearly in the chapters that follow, shaped their work–family choices and expectations. Inflexible workplace and school schedules made it difficult to combine full time employment with child care. Cultural expectations—derived from media as well as "real life"—that men should earn and women should nurture reinforce male–female inequality in career tracks and pay scales. In the context of cultural values and workplace realities, most parents in our study found a work-family solution that made sense to them. Yet, as both Marjorie DeVault (1991) and Susan Walzer (1998) have pointed out, such commonsense, "practical," choices tend to express and reproduce gendered inequalities. Most fathers worked full time, and most mothers worked part time or not at all. For mothers who had worked full time with one young child, the arrival of a second one often was a tipping point, making the coordination of daily activities too demanding for continued external employment (cf. Upton in press). Fathers, working full time and with gender norms on their side, contributed less to child care and much less to housework than their wives did, regardless of work status.

Some women stayed home specifically because they felt the available child care options were unsatisfactory and that they should be with their children throughout the day. Most working mothers, in contrast, viewed outside child care as beneficial to their children's development. It was common for parents to describe their own work/family choices favorably via vignettes that contrasted their situation with presumably less desirable circumstances and outcomes involving other families and children. No matter what their work–family decision, parents tended to report overall support from family, friends, and others. There were, of course, some negative opinions and incidents, often related to stereotypes of one camp—stay-at-home mothers or employed mothers—about the other.

This chapter has examined "real life" factors, including social and structural supports and constraints, that impacted our informants' lives, specifically their work/family choices. Chapter 6 will focus on how our informants received and processed media-borne work/family images and messages. The theme of social comparison will reemerge as an important one—whether through family and community examples, as has been considered here, or via the media—the focus of Chapters 6–8.

6

MIDDLE CLASS MOMS: YOU FEEL GUILTY IF YOU WORK, YOU FEEL GUILTY IF YOU STAY HOME

A Mothers' Focus Group, Talking about Dr. Laura:

Is anyone a regular listener [of Dr. Laura]?

—Descartes

No.
　　　—Poppy, full time working mother of one, married to a full time working father

My husband likes her.
　　　—Willa, part time working mother of two, married to a full time working father

Oh, Willa, I'm so sorry. Come here. I have to give you a hug!
　　　—Eveline, full time working mother of one, married to a full time working father

My sister listens to her, and my mom and dad listen to her, and they tell me about her.
　　　—Lissa, full time working mother of three, married to a full time working father

One of the managers at work listens to her really loud, all the time.

—Poppy

I am so sorry to hear that.
　　　—Rhoda, full time working mother of two, divorced

Yup. I make him stay in the back room, though. "Stay back there."

—Poppy

In *The Time Divide*, Jacobs and Gerson (2004) draw mainly on survey data to document changes in work/family patterns of American men and women over the past several decades, along with ongoing gender inequality. Although their study is very informative, they have little to say about where people might get the cultural models and scripts that propel their work/family choices. They do mention the proliferation of time management books (as a response to the culture of busyness and increasingly fast-paced lifestyles), and the conservative reaction (presumably spread in part via the media) to feminism and increased female employment. They do not, however, systematically consider how the media, community expectations, and other cultural forces contribute to Americans' work/family decisions. We see our study as complementing theirs (and others that focus mainly on statistics and socioeconomics) by concentrating on media as a central source for deriving self-supporting rationales (and counter-rationales). Through our study we have learned of, and will describe at length here and in the remaining chapters, the inconsistent and complex ways in which people use media sources as a basis or backup for their personal stories of work, family, and gender.

Dr. Laura Schlessinger's program, as discussed in the beginning quotes, is just one of the media sources from which parents in our study took in content on work and family. In this chapter we focus on one of the key orienting questions listed at the end of Chapter 1: How do people use media creatively, deliberately, and selectively to fit, support, and reinforce their pre-existing knowledge and beliefs? This chapter examines the work/family messages that parents reported receiving from the media, and what they made of them. Media depictions allowed our informants to discuss issues important to themselves, such as gender roles and ways of raising children, and provided points of comparison with their own lives. As was suggested in Chapter 1, media messages can be seen as texts that are creatively "read," interpreted, and assigned meaning by the different readers who receive them. The particular meanings that each person finds in a given text, such as *ER*, can be very different from what others, including the original creators of that text, imagined. As Fiske (1989) proposed, the essence of popular culture is the creative processing that each of us brings to such common messages. Although they may be constrained by dominant paradigms, it is not uncommon for people to resist the standard or accepted meaning of a text, by finding alternative meanings that support their own life choices.

FLAWED ROLE MODELS: DUNCES AND DAMSELS

Informants' own words show how they actively evaluate media images and messages—blaming or praising, choosing and using, avoiding and rejecting—in ways that make sense to them. The media provide fodder that enable people to validate beliefs, choices, and actions; indulge fantasies; and find empowering (or disturbing) messages. People use media to get information, make social comparisons, garner support, build or enhance images of self, relieve frustrations, chart social courses, and formulate life plans. They also, as we have seen previously, blame media for their actual or potential effects on others, particularly on children. Parents clearly saw a function for the media in providing role models. Often, however, they felt the examples that should be there were not, or that the ones that were there were flawed. To return to a stereotype discussed in Chapter 3, Dexterites were particularly harsh on media representations of incompetent fathers.

When we asked parents to tell us about their observations and perceptions of media family and work messages, many brought up gender. Some had paid particular attention to media depictions of men's roles in the family. Cassidy, a part time working mother of two, spent quite a bit of time discussing how television failed to show male household participation in a positive way. Recalling the plot of *Daddio*, in which a formerly employed man became a stay-at-home father, she observed, "They did all your stereotypical male inadequacies in dealing with stuff, at least in that one episode that I watched. And the girl came in to help him, so it was almost like the helpless male, which is not sending a good message, I'm sorry." She continued: "I think men could use a show that deals with men raising [children] . . . I think they need more shows like that now."

Several informants pointed out a stereotype of the bumbling father. Curt, for example, a father of four, complained that:

> One thing I do see on TV a lot is that they try to make the guy look like a dunce. Just really make him look stupid. Fathers, yeah. Probably some of that Disney stuff. The father's usually incompetent! They go on some camping trip and the father doesn't know anything about anything. Of course it's the mother that does everything.

110 • Media and Middle Class Moms

Stu echoed Curt's sentiments: "They always make the dad look stupid. And the kids always are the smart ones, and they always know what's going on. That's what people like to watch I guess." Ada, a stay-at-home mother, connected the bumbling male to difficulties maintaining traditional family roles: "I think a lot of the shows, that the men, whether or not they be husbands or not, always are playing the doofus. Which is unfortunate because I think husbands or fathers are struggling to be heads of households, and that doesn't help."

Some parents, particularly those with daughters, were concerned about female portrayals in the media. In a men's focus group, Stu, for example, said:

> I have a boy and a girl, and the boy I don't really worry so much about because there's enough role models. But the girls, I don't think there are enough good women role models, in my opinion. So when we're watching, it could even [be] women's sports or things like that, I kind of reinforce . . . "You can do this if you want. If you want to be a lawyer, you can do this. If you want to play basketball, you can do that."

Van agreed: "A lot of the people that are on the news shows are women. And to me, a father of two daughters, that's reassuring, because that's an extremely professional image. That's the kind of thing I want my daughters to see."

Women, whether employed full time or not, had similar concerns. In one women's focus group, Joellen discussed how differently she felt about her daughter's media exposure compared to her son's:

> Those types of things, talking about the advertisements for women, the media, the expectations. That's really bothered me more. I should worry about it just as much for my son, but for some reason, I just think the undertones towards little girls . . . It's just right in their face.

In another mothers' group, we heard the same sentiments: "Especially with my daughter in adolescence, we look at the way women are behaving, and in some cases it doesn't seem that women need to have a lot of intelligence, [but instead] they have looks."

STAY-AT-HOME MOMS: MY DAUGHTER WANTS ME TO WORK, LIKE ARTHUR'S MOM WORKS

In terms of staying home, I don't think there's as much as there should be in terms of the media, in my opinion. You know, that it's a good thing, that it's worthwhile.

—Ashleigh, stay-at-home mother of two, married to a full time working father

Some parents were perturbed by perceived gaps in media depictions of their own lifestyles, and linked their media consumption to their ability or inability to identify with media representations. Among those in our study, stay-at-home mothers were the most likely to say they were underrepresented: "I can't think of any TV program where there is a stay-at-home mother." Another stay-at-home mother, musing on the topic, said "maybe that's why we don't watch much TV anymore. Because there's no one to relate to."

Several women, however, recalled older programs that did include stay-at-home mothers, such as *The Brady Bunch* and *The Waltons*, and also the more recent drama *Seventh Heaven*. Many women mentioned enjoying *Everybody Loves Raymond*, a comedy featuring a stay-at-home mother and working father. Madge, for example, said of the characters: "She is a stay-at-home mom, and he works full time, and they have several young kids. I probably can relate to her the best of all, just some things that she'll say or that her husband does." Ada commented on the same program, "I love that show . . . It's real to me, it just captures a slice of life that I find so humorous. It's real. The house is a mess, oftentimes. So I can identify with her because she's a real mom, she doesn't have a perfect life."

Some stay-at-home mothers recalled feeling undermined by some media. One mother said she never read parenting magazines because she assumed they wouldn't support her decision to stay at home: "I wouldn't agree with what they had to say, that they would be too liberal, really biased. And I thought it would be a waste of money." Another woman remembered reading an article in *Working Woman* about the benefits of working: "I guess I took offense to it just because I thought, 'Oh, that's not necessary.' So and of course it was very one-sided because it was *Working Woman* magazine." She continued:

It was just the benefits of working, and one of the biggest benefits turned out to be financial of course. You know, the fact that you have a lot of money in your 401K, when you were done, if you started investing at the age of 35, and when you turn 65, if you put

112 • Media and Middle Class Moms

in so much and the company matches so much you'd have 1.5 million and blah blah blah and I thought "So?" (laughs) "So, you could do better on the stock market!" kind of thing! But at any rate it was just, it was mostly financial was the premise of it, and obviously the career-climbing ladder, but it was . . . for personal gain, more than family. So I didn't see it as the way family benefits.

Another woman felt a bit undermined by how her daughter used content from the children's cartoon *Arthur*:

[My daughter] wants me to work. I think, like . . . Arthur's mom works. But she doesn't realize that I won't be around like Arthur's mom. It means I will be at an office, and I will pick you up and be tired and cranky and we'll go home and we'll cook dinner and we will put you to bed and we'll have two hours at the end of the night to be with each other. But she was proud of me when I worked I guess.

Stay-at-home mothers often suggested that mothers who worked full time must face constant time pressures, with never enough hours in a day to get everything done. Consider comments in our only mixed focus group, which consisted of several part time working mothers and stay-at-home mothers, and Victoria, the sole full time employed worker. The group concluded that full time workers, such as Victoria, usually were too pressed for time to consume much of the media specifically aimed at them.

VICTORIA: I don't really read a whole lot of anything or watch a whole lot of anything. My husband and I just work out our own system. I guess I don't recall a tip that I've used out of a magazine. I'll grab them when I'm standing in line at the grocery store, but I don't really recall.

KATRINA: If you work full time there's no time to read about tips on how to get more time.

BRIDGET: It's us, the mothers who don't work, who are reading the tips on how to make your life easier if you worked . . . Here we've got Victoria, she can't read it because she's too busy.

JENNIFER: We'll call her and tell her, "Hey we've got a great tip for you."

KATRINA: Yeah.

EMPLOYED MOTHERS: HE WORKED, SHE WORKED, AND THEY ALL WERE A FAMILY

For the most part I don't think [commercials] show working women. It still seems commercials are lagging a little behind the time of working parents. That they're still June Cleaver staying at home cleaning the house all day.

—Elaine, part time working mother of two, married to a full time working father

Stay-at-home and employed mothers alike believed that media could offer support and reinforcement by providing models to which they could relate—although the specific examples cited by each group differed substantially. Echoing Jacobs and Gerson's (2004) comment on the proliferation of time management books, the employed mothers in our study were particularly likely to cull media sources for work/family tips and information. And just like stay-at-home mothers, they also sought out, and found comfort in, positive media depictions of family situations like their own. In addition, the use of media representations as a basis of social comparison was common to both groups.

Women who worked outside the home tended to speak of the media as supportive, although exceptions were cited. One mother, Marci, recalled that when she had her first child she thought women's magazines were more supportive of nonemployed than employed mothers. Employed women were particularly critical of advertising messages about gender, home, and work. Tammi recalled a commercial she found particularly offensive: "The worst one is the mom with those biscuits that are always ready. 'Oh, we have such different schedules. I'm glad my biscuits are always here.' It's like, oh my God."

Working mothers also talked of finding support in media content that offered constructive ideas on balancing work and family and positive role models. One employed woman reported:

I think they're trying to be supportive, is what I would say. It's always in there. I get *Crane's Detroit*, the business paper that comes out weekly. They always have the under-40 women that are most successful, as well as the under-40 men, and I think they do try. And they usually address family, and how they do juggle those things.

Ginny, a part time working mother of two, enjoyed media content that stressed family life, but that didn't exclude work. She liked reading or seeing items that provided stress-busting tips and time-saving hints.

114 • Media and Middle Class Moms

Of *Working Mother* magazine, for example, Ginny said, "There's a lot of great articles in there, especially how to juggle both [work and family] and little tips of how to do [tasks] quicker." Ginny especially enjoyed reading pieces from *Reader's Digest*, saying:

> There are true stories, and it's not some doctor saying "This is the way you should do it." It's actually real life people talking about events in their life and things like that. There have been certain stories about work and family life and what they did throughout their life, and you think, "Oh, I should slow down here." It does that for me, it makes me think about I should slow down on this part and watch this because [my children are] only going to be this age one time.

Joan also enjoyed media that provided work and family tips: "Because I am a working mom I probably look at the articles that are about keeping a balance between work and home and how you can do that, and . . . to encourage positives between you and your boss with working and balancing work and home life." Another mother mentioned that it was important to her to see articles about child care: "Maybe any time there's a little article [with the] headline 'Day care not as bad as once thought' or something like that. There occasionally are stories on somebody who works and takes care of her kids and makes it to all the soccer games, and you think, 'Wow, I can do that too.' "

Working mothers tended to enjoy fictional media that portrayed positive family situations involving dual-income families. One full time working mother recalled the show *Growing Pains*, saying, "I liked that show. That was a working family show in my opinion, and I liked the way they did it. She worked, he worked, everybody had a role, and they all were a family, no matter if they were working or not, they came home and it was a family." Another full time working woman commented similarly on the pleasure she derived from *The Cosby Show*: "All the kids get along and the mom and dad both work and yet they were home for the kids and they could talk to one or the other of the parents regarding something and everyone's always able to help out."

Employed women also mentioned news stations with regular working mother segments and specials. Bridget tended to watch one particular station, Channel 4: "I see that show, they're giving you tips on how to juggle your family and work and things like that." She added, though, "There was a lot, though . . . Channel 4 had it too, the big thing on your kids are going to be really bad if they go to day care and things like that. That was for a really long time. And it's died down a lot. New studies are showing that it's okay to send your kids to day care."

One employed women's focus group, however, pointed out the prevalent gendered norms of work and family that result in women rather than men being the targets of programming on work and family: "I think it's expected that the women have to watch TV to learn how to juggle."

The media tastes of the employed mothers in our study diverged somewhat from those of the stay-at-home mothers. In a focus group comprised solely of full time working mothers, when asked about their favorite shows, the women responded with some that nonemployed women also viewed, such as *Seventh Heaven, Friends, ER,* and *Oprah.* However, they also mentioned shows with high-powered career women, such as *The Pretender, JAG,* and *The Profiler.*

MATERNAL GUILT AND THE SUPERMOM IMAGE

Regardless of their work status, many women lambasted media images of female, and specifically maternal, perfection. One woman said that on television "Most of them, the moms, are portrayed as always being nicely dressed and their hair's done. They never show anybody that hasn't had a chance to shower in the morning with their tracksuit on, out getting the kids on the bus." Another said of magazine portrayals of women: "Everybody looks way too good there."

Several women brought up the issue of guilt. One working mother commented that media messages make working mothers feel guilty. Other mothers contended that those messages seemed aimed to create guilt feelings in women whether they worked or not. As one part time working mother put it:

> In the media one thing that I find is that women always feel like what they're doing isn't the right thing. You feel guilty if you work, you feel guilty if you stay home, and that's where I think a real problem is . . . It seems like women are always defending what they're doing, and Dr. Laura only feeds into that sort of mentality. Unhelpful. That you're doing bad by your children for working, yet if you don't work, are you exposing them to the social things that they need?

Audrey, a stay-at-home mother, expressed similar feelings:

> For a father it's expected that they work and then for a mother, again with moms, it goes both ways. Sometimes it's like you're damned if you do, you're damned if you don't stay home, or work, because you have to contribute type of thing. I still think

116 • Media and Middle Class Moms

with fathers that's something that's a positive thing and it's expected of them to do and that's their role, the stereotypical role.

Several informants brought up, usually to criticize, media images of the "Supermom." One stay-at-home mother, Greta, recalled reading an article in the *New York Times* about "Can you do it all?" Greta had taken away the message that one could not: "I remember thinking, this makes complete sense to me. I never was convinced by the Supermom idea. I always was like, you can't do everything, there are only so many hours in a day. And I feel that in order to do something well, you have to give it your full attention." Two other women discussed the Supermom ideal in the context of celebrity interviews about giving up employment for the family. One stay-at-home mother, for example, commented:

> Female celebrities are even doing it. And they're coming out and saying that they're not going to do it all, they're going to stay at home. That cute little blonde that was on *Melrose Place* all those years ago, I think they're on their second one now. I just read an article . . . how much she praises herself for leaving the TV industry and being home with her kids, and how important that is.

Another informant, a part time working mother of two, commented similarly:

> There was an interview with Maria Shriver, and I happened to be watching part of that, and it was very interesting. She said, "You know, this Supermom stuff is for the birds!" I'm like, "Yeah! No kidding!" It is so true. It's just like we're trying to be everything to everybody and you know, forget it. That's the hardest thing. Everybody wants you. Your kids want you, your husband wants you, the school wants you, the clubs want you.

Tegan, who worked full time, and whose own mother, she said, was a Supermom, had a different opinion:

> I think it's okay to be a Supermom . . . I don't find anything wrong with it as long as I know my limits and when I start compromising certain things and when things don't fall into place. So it's that balance issue for me again. It's okay to be a Supermom and to have all those things. I don't have to be perfect at it . . . It's about the journey and I enjoy making my life full.

"I AM MY KIDS' MOM," SHE BARKED

[Dr. Laura is] a working mom, she's a mom first. And she works when her son's in school. So it's not that she disapproves of moms working . . . I think Dr. Laura would say [my] values are right on track because they're what's most important for the kids, what the kids need.

—Elaine, part time working mother of two, married to a full time working father

The topic of Dr. Laura Schlessinger arose many times in our research. Sometimes our informants raised it spontaneously; sometimes we asked directly about it, knowing that Dr. Laura offers controversial messages on work and family. Schlessinger is very clear about her belief that a parent should stay home full time with children. As expected, some mothers felt supported by her messages, and some did not. Most had heard of Dr. Laura, even if they didn't actually listen to her. Several parents commented that their spouse, friends, co-workers, or family members passed on stories from Dr. Laura's program to them: "My mom [listens to Dr. Laura], and my mom's sure to pass everything along." "My sister listens to her, and my mom and dad listen to her and they tell me about her."

Most people who tuned in to Dr. Laura did not agree with her on every point, but stated that they listened anyway, if only for amusement. As one woman put it, "She's a stitch." Nearly all mentioned, some admiringly, and some critically, Dr. Laura's brusque style and black and white presentation of moral issues. These sentiments are expressed in this exchange, heard in a focus group comprised of both employed and nonemployed mothers:

VICTORIA: We used to have Dr. Laura on all the time at my old work. We used to listen to her every day, and then she switched her hours. So all of us working moms would sit there listening to Dr. Laura every day.

KATRINA: She's totally anti-working mom.

VICTORIA: Oh yeah, we listen to it for the calls.

KATRINA: Yeah, I don't know why people would call her, because she attacks.

POLLY: She scares me, just listening to her. I would never call . . .

VICTORIA: We just listened to her for entertainment value.

The men who were most approving of Dr. Laura's messages were not married to women who worked full time. We asked one Dr. Laura fan, a

118 • Media and Middle Class Moms

father of four whose wife worked part time, which of Schlessinger's messages had resonated with him. He replied: "I think she says, all the time, 'I'm my children's mom,' or something like that. About the priority of being the parent probably above work, especially for the mother."

Interestingly, few stay-at-home mothers were fans of Dr. Laura. One such mother said, "I don't know. There's a notion that you can parent your child better if you're with them more hours during the day. I'm just not sure that's true. And I'm with my children 24 hours a day." Another mother, Dina, however, related that she listened to Dr. Laura whenever she felt depressed about staying home. The program made her feel better about her decision.

Many women who worked part time outside the home listened to Dr. Laura and liked much of what she had to say. Most of them held professional or semi-professional positions. Most worked when their children were in school or after they were in bed. These women, many with careers that had involved advanced training, had either stopped working or cut back to spend more time with their children. They reported feeling supported and validated by Dr. Laura's messages. One part time working mother of three commented:

> I would say I've always agreed with her philosophy on the majority of things, so it's more just reassuring to know, yeah, what I'm doing is good and right for the kids . . . I think more or less it just reinforces what you're doing is a good thing, feel good about yourself and what you do, versus really changing anything just because she said it would be better to do this or that.

This mother was asked if she would always have agreed with Dr. Laura's messages on work and family, since she actually had worked full time after the birth of her first two children. She replied, "Well, no, see, I didn't know who she was when I was working full time. I think I would have maybe even changed sooner had I listened to her sooner. Although all along I felt like I didn't really want to work that much." Had she been asked directly whether media could change her own life, this woman might well have said no, but her comment reveals an assumption that a media source can influence (hasten) work/family decisions, including her own.

Julie, a woman who worked part time, was only a qualified fan of Dr. Laura's. "There are some real good things I like about her . . . she thinks mothers should stay at home. She's all for that. Mothers staying at home and families staying together no matter what . . . She believes in families." Julie felt that Dr. Laura would not approve of Julie's own decision to work part time, however: "She would tell me to quit work

Guilty if You Work, Guilty if You Stay Home • **119**

altogether. Yeah, she would . . . It's easier for her to say that. She's not in my shoes . . . Not everyone is in her situation."

Another part time working mother of two expressed more ambivalent feelings about Dr. Laura's messages on work and family, saying:

> I listen to Dr. Laura sometimes just because she's so funny, she's so black and white. It's like, if life were that easy! Some of her advice is useful and some of it's just a crock. You know, "I'm my child's parent." Oh, so I'm not because I work? I just feel like going, "Give me a break. Just because I don't agree with you, I'm wrong?"

A number of mothers who worked full time listened to Dr. Laura, even if they didn't concur with her work and family messages. One of them, asked if she had ever felt undermined by the media about work/family, specifically brought up Dr. Laura, saying: "You hear the fringe ones like the Dr. Laura, like 'You have to be home with your kids and if you aren't, you are a bad person.' I don't want to hear that. You know, I still listen, because I listen to the other stuff and I just say, 'Okay, well then, that's fine.' " Another woman, Marci, said she listened to Dr. Laura every day, and that "When I first had [my son] and I would listen to Dr. Laura, I'd feel very, very guilty, because working moms is just not what she thinks is good. And then I just thought, 'This is what I like to do, too bad what she says.' I just get a kick out of her."

Other employed mothers seemed to feel similarly. Victoria, one such woman, related:

> Her point was always that it's better for the kids to be at home. Which is funny, because in a room full of women working, we all just kind of agreed with her. But we were all in the same situation, that we had made some life choices, houses, whatever, that it would be a struggle to go down to one income. I think ultimately we all wanted to get down to part time . . . so we didn't disagree with that.

Some of our informants used Dr. Laura's pronouncements as starting points for discussions about morals and values, as they articulated why and how they agreed or disagreed with her stance. One example comes from our ethnographic observation of Pam, who listened regularly to Dr. Laura on her days off. Pam, who worked part time in a professional position, said she appreciated Dr. Laura's messages and that listening to Dr. Laura reaffirmed her own feelings. She and her husband frequently listened together when they were home at the same time. The spouses used Dr. Laura's calls as a point of departure to explore and communicate to each other their own ideas and norms about gender and family roles, and how to raise children. For example, Pam used a call that touched on teen pregnancy to discuss her fears for her own children as they grew older. Her husband seemed astonished that she had such worries and asked her to explain. Listening to Dr. Laura thus gave these parents an opportunity to think about their own child-rearing concerns and to learn about each other's.

Many parents, however, could not abide Dr. Laura. They tended to express themselves strongly, saying things like, "I hold her in utmost contempt." For some this was because they objected to her brusque, even harsh, way of talking to her audience and callers. As one woman put it, "I hate that woman. I quit listening to WJR because of her. She is strident and shrill, and if you listen to her for a month you've heard every one of her six opinions." "Arrogant" was a word used by a number of these informants. We also heard "egotistical" and "mean." Many complained that Dr. Laura does not listen to and cuts off her callers. ("She rarely listens to the whole questions." "Sometimes you can't even get two sentences out and she's barking at you.") We felt that some of this discomfort probably had to do with gender norms. Male radio hosts with equally abrupt mannerisms did not garner the same intense disapproval as Dr. Laura. Pam's husband, for example, used Dr. Laura's verbal style to illustrate his feelings about how women in particular should not conduct themselves.

Some parents criticized her for inauthenticity; for the fact that her doctorate is in physiology, rather than a counseling-related field. Said Sloane, a stay-at-home mother, "She makes me mad because she tells people what to do and she has no degree in it . . . I don't think she has any kind of psych. background and it's dangerous just telling people what to do like that." Jeanette, a full time working mother, similarly said, "Not even a Ph.D. in psychology, or something that, would be appropriate for counseling people." Some criticized her for actually being a working mother while telling other women to withdraw from paid labor. Some disliked her for what they perceived as being out of touch with the realities of contemporary life. As one man put it:

> I think it's easy for her to be arrogant when she's got millions of dollars and can have the best of everything, and I don't think she really understands the state of some people, middle class, lower middle class, people in this country, what they go through on a daily basis . . . I don't think she really understands what people go through where they have to work and try to make a living.

And some simply objected to her messages on work, family, and gender. Tom, a father of one, considered her "very narrow-minded, and I have absolutely no desire to listen to her." A full time working mother, Joellen, said that if she came across Dr. Laura on the radio, "I probably would flip it to something different because I just wouldn't want to hear it. If I don't agree, I wouldn't want to keep [it on]."

Many also said they agreed with some basic tenets of Dr. Laura's, such as that family should come before material things, but disliked the "one size fits all" approach of her and other talk show hosts' advice. According to Clancy, a father of three, "You can't tell another couple what the right mix and what the right balance is . . . What works for you does not necessarily work for someone else."

When we talked with informants about Dr. Laura, we also asked them about Dr. Joy Browne, another radio talk show host, and a real psychologist, who is less didactic. Even if they had heard of her, our informants rarely listened to Dr. Joy Browne, whose only broadcast in this area came from Canada. Victoria, a full time employed woman, said she and her work friends tried listening to Dr. Browne but stopped because she "wasn't as exciting" as Dr. Laura. "For some reason, all the calls we caught that week, her advice was bribing the kids with money or toys or some such thing. So she got kind of boring after a week, so we went back to vicious Dr. Laura. We had fun listening to her." Others who couldn't bring themselves to listen to Dr. Laura still did not listen to Dr. Browne, for different reasons. One woman stated, "She's much better [than Dr. Laura], but she's also a talk show hostess, and I've got to worry about the whole concept . . . It's like listening to an oral version of 'Dear Abby', what good is that?"

SOCIAL COMPARISON: OKAY, I'M NORMAL

One of my favorite shows has always been *Law and Order*, and I like that it just gives you a little more of what's actually happening out there, and how things are being looked at.
—Rosa, full time working mother of one and another on the way, married to a full time working father

In Chapter 1 we signaled three key *social functions* of the media: comparison, connection, and common ground. In the remainder of this chapter we will use our informants' comments and stories to highlight how the media facilitate social comparison. People in Dexter routinely used media representations as points of *comparison* with themselves and their families. The media (illustrating the second social function) served to *connect* Dexterites to a world beyond the local community, thereby enhancing the range of work/family models available for comparison. The discussion of Dr. Laura in the previous section illustrates the third social function of media—if not exactly *common ground*, certainly common knowledge. Although they judged and reacted to her radio program in strikingly different ways, most of our informants knew about Schlessinger's work/family message and what it said about contested social norms. According to John Fiske (1989), such selective and creative processing by different individuals of common media messages is the essence of popular culture.

Many of our informants said the media helped them keep in touch with what other people were thinking and doing. One father, for example, when discussing his radio habits, said, "Dr. Laura, I find her on the dial every once in a while just to hear what people are thinking. I know I'm not going to think that way, but I want to hear what they have to say." Nate, who ran a business with his wife at home, partly so they could spend more time with their children, regularly read the *Wall Street Journal*'s weekly column on work and family "just to see what other people are doing." That information helped him feel he was not alone in his work and family choices: "It seems like more people are doing things out of the home, as telecommuting gets more popular and easier to do with the Internet."

Social comparison via the media allowed people to evaluate their own situations and effectiveness in balancing work and family. Informants contrasted their own situations to those they saw on television or heard about on the radio. Kate, a stay-at-home mother of three, who had worked outside part time, decided to stay home full time when her third child was born. She liked to listen to a local radio station and got validation from it about her own choices. Some of its morning show hosts were working parents. She paraphrased them, empathizing with their situation, but preferred her own choice to stay home: " 'Gosh, I'm really tired today and it was a struggle, and so and so had this to do after school.' And I can relate, having gone through that with my other ones. 'Gosh, I'm so glad I'm staying home!' And it makes me kind of validate that whole idea of staying home." A working mother who listened to the same show took away a different message, but still gained positive reinforcement. "It's real, it's everything that we go through, they go through that as well, as far as getting the kids here and dinner, this and that. So it's nice to be able to listen to them and go into their life and say, 'Oh yeah. Okay, I'm normal.' " Knowing that others juggled work and family and felt the same pressures she did helped this woman feel good about the way she coped.

Our informants observed media characters facing situations similar to their own, and noted how they handled them. If they thought the situations were handled well, they could try to cope similarly with like circumstances. Jennifer, a mother of two, engaged in similar social comparison with the mother on the fictional children's program *Arthur*: "Every time I watch that show I think, 'Gosh, that's how I'd like to be.' Because she's always so patient and even, her voice always has this sing-songy sweetness to it, even in bad situations, like the kids have done something bad. So she's my role model."

Social comparison sometimes made parents feel somewhat bad about their own situations. When we asked about newspaper consumption in a women's focus group, one mother mentioned reading an *Ann Arbor News* article about a local woman with 14 children. Many women in that group had read the same article. The story produced a great deal of commentary, some of it revolving around how their own parenting compared to that of the parents of the 14 children:

JENNIFER: If she can do it, what's wrong with me?
KATRINA: And you wonder why you can't take care of only two. Why you struggle when someone's having 14.
VICTORIA: That's exactly what I thought when I read that. "Look how together those people have it, they have more than a dozen children." And I've got two.
JENNIFER: And they're wrecking the house.

In another group, Nicole heard Sloane say she received *Parenting* magazine. Nicole's response was, "Do you? Wow. I gave up on the *Parenting* magazine because they made me feel like I was doing everything bad. Like you're supposed to be doing good, you're supposed to be doing . . ." Another mother chimed in, "I know, like real elaborate Halloween costumes." Sloane, the *Parenting* subscriber, at this point stated, "Mostly I'll just flip through it. But it's almost better not to read too much." This topic came up at another women's focus group as well. Jeanette, discussing her media consumption, said she used to get *Parenting* because "It made me feel like I was going to be a much better mom if I cut [craft ideas] out and save them for a rainy day," but then she stopped because she never actually had time to do that.

Women in one focus group were very suspicious of what they saw as idealized images of parenting and family life found in parenting magazines, child care manuals, and pregnancy manuals.

GRETA: We're in a society that likes to read about how to do things. And I think that we sometimes don't trust our own internal voice. A lot of my friends have read almost every single book on "Your

124 • Media and Middle Class Moms

child's turning two and what to expect." Granted there are challenging moments, but you get through them ... I've had many people say, "Have you read this particular book?" ... No, I haven't read anything on this, I'm just sort of doing it from what I feel is correct.

NOREEN: Plus we're such a collaborative effort society. He's got a runny nose, you call four people before you say to yourself, "The kid's got a cold" ...

SLOANE: They make you nervous if you read too much.

NOREEN: It made me crazy when I was pregnant. And once I read all of it, when I had my son, it was not like anything I had read. I said, "I don't need to read another thing."

Sometimes, social comparison invoked negative examples of family life from the media. Consider these comments during a fathers' focus group:

CONNOR: I watch talk shows. I watch *Springer* [*The Jerry Springer Show*] once in a while. I can handle a little *Springer*.

TOBY: Yeah, every once in a while.

CONNOR: I don't know if it's just to make me feel better about my own life.

JAIME: Sometimes it's like, "Man, these people." You can just imagine how sick some people are, how stupid.

News media in particular provide extreme examples, giving parents marked points of contrast to their own lives, often involving danger. Mitch commented, "We're even finding out in our local news media that a lot of the problems are just presented by the fact that parents aren't available at critical times for their kids, or it's a hired situation." When asked to give an example, Mitch mentioned a house fire in Detroit, in which nine children were present without parents. Abigail, a stay-at-home mother of five, similarly said: "I see so many kids being left home alone and then a fire starting." When describing why she chose to stay home, Noreen, a mother of one, replied that a lot of it had to do with the negative things she's observed in working parents' children and on TV. When asked to expand upon this, Noreen replied:

When you see news stories. The one that freshly comes to mind is when the Columbine incident happened. Those were kids from working parents that were building bombs in their garage. My son's never going to build a bomb in my garage and me not know about it. I'm home every day. I go in and out of there. Just like you hear about kids on the Internet. And sure enough, they come home from school, they go to their room, their parents come home at six o'clock or whatever time . . .

Noreen then expanded upon the crime theme, comparing the work and family choices of criminals' parents to her own parenting: "If you look at some of the big crime figures, the Jeffrey Dahmers, they're not from a home where a mom was there every day when they got off the bus and raised them and nurtured them."

The Work/Family Struggle: Nurse Hathaway's Got Twins

NBC's long-running *ER* was the show named most often as regularly viewed by the parents in our study. Our informants used the show's characters, all emergency room doctors, nurses, staff, and patients, as points of social comparison. As Kate, a stay-at-home mother of three, commented:

> They have shown the struggles with day care and leaving your kid in a day care situation and then having to go get them when they're ill and then, "Now what do I do? I can't leave, I've got surgery scheduled." So they have covered that issue occasionally . . . And they also dealt with the issue of divorce and what to do with the child. At first [Dr. Greene and his ex-wife] were close, and it was a shared custody, and then they moved away and then here's a single man, working long hours and what does he do with his ten-year-old daughter? So certainly a struggle that makes people think. [It makes me think] especially how fortunate I am to have a husband that helps out and that is here, because I don't know what I would do if I didn't have that.

Similarly, when we asked Cory, a part time working mother, how *ER* did in portraying work and family, she stated: "They always tend to portray . . . such discomfort and agony . . . that balancing act, it's a terrible thing. I just can't imagine if I was a single parent."

The most frequent comment was that the show portrayed the combination of jobs and children as a struggle. Referring to a character raising her sister's baby, one father said, "This lady was trying to be a full time mom to this daughter and she was not doing very well, because she was not getting enough support." Many of these parents then went on to say that *ER* offers an unrealistic portrayal of juggling work and family in that the characters always seem to be at work, and additionally to have free time to eat out and be social. Ginny observed, "Supposedly they have these families, but they can go out to eat.

126 • Media and Middle Class Moms

Sometimes I'll watch it and they'll all go out across the street to the restaurant and I think, 'Man, they have a lot of money, they can have a babysitter stay that long.' " She followed this by saying, "*ER*, I don't think they spend enough time with their kids." Some parents described feeling a little exasperated at such depictions, since they knew from their own experience that raising children is exceedingly time-intensive. One father, married to a part time working woman, commented about Nurse Carol Hathaway and her twins:

> Nurse Hathaway's got twins, from a guy she's not married to, who just decided to wander off to Seattle, and she's just taking care of these twins, and going to work. Occasionally they might show a little bit of her having to deal with some conflict but for the most part I think it's not realistic ... She always looks like she's just ready to go, raising one baby is a hard task, raising twins, I think that it's not real.

In introducing the theme of social comparison in Chapter 1, we mentioned Festinger's (1954) discussion of how people draw on the experiences of others to gain information and to evaluate themselves. In citing such others—for example, Nurse Hathaway—from the media, some of our informants used her negatively, calling her situation unrealistic, or faulting her for trying to do too much. Others, mostly employed women, used her example positively, to support their own choices and solutions.

One working mother, Joan, had this perspective:

> Carol, the one with the twins, and then a long time ago there was the other one who had adopted the sister's baby and still continued to work there and use the day care at the hospital. So I think both of those have been really positive, showing that women can go back to work, especially Carol with the twins, and can be successful.

CRITICAL CONSUMERS OF SOCIAL COMPARISON

This chapter has addressed the key question of how people use media creatively, deliberately, and selectively to fit and reinforce their pre-existing knowledge and beliefs, and to support and justify their own life choices and identities. Fiske (1989) has asserted that the essence of popular culture is the creative processing that each individual brings to common messages. This process is clear from our study: the meaning that one parent derives from a given text, *ER* or Dr. Laura, for instance, can be very different from what other community members imagine.

As cited in this chapter, their comments and narratives indicate that our informants, in their media exposure, processed considerable work and family content and were well aware of the kinds of messages being transmitted and received. Their descriptions and analyses showed them to be critical consumers of media. Many, like communications scholars, had thought through issues of producerly intent and audience reception. Our informants had paid enough attention to media to be able to discuss, often critically, sometimes eloquently, depictions of men's and women's roles in families and the workplace. They expressed their concerns when they felt content did a disservice to real parents and children. Media personalities and messages often were cited in ways that highlighted the function of social comparison. By suggesting, depicting, or proclaiming what other people were thinking and doing, media provided an important means for our informants to think through and evaluate their own circumstances and decisions. In the next chapter we focus on six Dexter mothers to illustrate, in a more personal and individual way, the relation between media, life circumstance, and social reality.

7

ISOLATION, BOUNDARIES, AND CONNECTION: SIX CASE STUDIES

[I'm] not in popular culture, I'm kind of outside that.
—Jennifer, stay-at-home mother of two, married to a full time
working father

I don't watch any news, or any TV shows . . . Once in a while I'll
listen to Dr. Laura. She's a stitch.
—Julie, part time working mother of two, married to a full
time working father

[I like watching local news to] pick up on stuff happening, to do
with the kids or as a family.
—Penny, full time working mother of two, married to a full
time working father

There's just something I can relate to [about Ally McBeal] [a
fictional TV attorney].
—Gwen, full time working mother of two, married to a full
time working father

As one of us (Kottak 1990) saw clearly during his research on the
impact of television in Brazil, the typical media consumer is not the
passive "couch potato" that dominates our stereotypes of a TV aficion-
ado. Instead, people, whether rural Brazilians or Americans in rural
suburban areas such as Dexter, actively evaluate and use media in ways
that make sense to them. Program choices and preferences reflect social
contrasts, power differentials, and variant individual predispositions.
People continue watching, listening, or reading because they find

meaning in their texts of choice. In one town in southern Brazil, Alberto Costa (see Kottak 1990) found that women and young adults of both sexes were particularly attracted to *telenovelas* (melodramatic nightly programs often compared to American soap operas, usually featuring sophisticated urban settings). In the small community that Costa studied, those relatively powerless social groups used the more liberal content of *telenovelas* to challenge conservative local norms.

Even in a relatively homogeneous community such as Dexter, Michigan, people have different incomes, values, and social networks, find themselves in diverse work/family situations, and use the media in varied ways as they reflect on and evaluate their own personal, family, and social lives. In this chapter we describe six Dexter mothers with contrasting work/family situations and patterns of media use. Our goal here is to illustrate—in a more personal, contextual, and concrete way than in previous chapters—the relation between life circumstance, individual choices, and media exposure. Of the orienting questions listed at the end of Chapter 1, this chapter's focus is on how individuals (and social groups) use media differently. Our six cases will illustrate how particular Dexterites actively evaluate, choose, use, and avoid media sources, "scripts," and representations. Despite Dexter's socio-economic and ethnic homogeneity, we had no trouble selecting six contrasting cases to illustrate a range of ways in which different life histories and personalities influence media choices and effects. Let's meet those middle class moms.

STANDING APART: JENNIFER NELSON, A FULL TIME STAY-AT-HOME MOTHER

Jennifer is a young mother of two small children, only one of whom is old enough to attend school. Her husband, Jeremy, works full time in Dexter. In four visits with the family, Descartes never met Jeremy; he asked his wife to make sure ethnographic visits occurred only when he was not present. The family lives about 15 minutes from the village center in one of the town's older subdivisions. Jennifer seems to feel somewhat isolated, with only one other mother home during the day on her block. Nor does Jennifer's family of origin live within easy driving distance.

Although Jennifer's daughter, Bethany, goes to school, her son, Steve, remains at home full time. The fact that he requires a considerable amount of Jennifer's attention sometimes seems to embarrass her. In public settings she does her best to distract him, usually without much success. Steve, Jennifer comments, is happy to stay with her at home, unlike Bethany, whose vivacity and sociability sometimes seem to overwhelm her mother. Jennifer decided to send Bethany to preschool at age three because of the girl's eagerness to enter a social world. Recently Jennifer has become intrigued with the possibility of home-schooling her son. She got this idea from a book she read, which claimed that public education fails boys by emphasizing competition, tolerating bullies, and encouraging (usually female) teachers to impose feminine standards of restraint on energetic boys.

Jennifer often helps out in her daughter's classroom. In this volunteer work she has contact with some full time working mothers, who irritate her when they fail to return her calls about classroom business. Jennifer expresses sympathy for mothers who work full time and "don't have the flexibility to do the things that your kids want you to do," such as go on school field trips. During her volunteer work at the school, Jennifer does not interact very much with the other mothers. Indeed, we observed some tension between her and one assertive mother prone to giving advice.

Sometimes Jennifer seemed to doubt her own abilities. When her mother-in-law sent her a subscription to a cooking magazine she viewed it "as a hint." "What's wrong with me?" she wondered after reading a newspaper story about the parenting skills of a woman with 14 children. Jennifer views the mother of the title character in the children's cartoon *Arthur* as a role model, someone who has the patience Jennifer would like to have.

Jennifer says she always wanted to be a stay-at-home mother, just like her own mother. She could not bear the idea of working and having someone else care for her children. Had she done so, her anticipated constant worry about her children' safety and happiness would have prevented her from working effectively. Jennifer, who never was career-oriented, only went on to college because she wasn't seriously involved with anyone at the end of high school. She says she enjoys staying home and doing as she pleases during the day, and not having to get dressed if she chooses not to do so.

What messages about work and family does Jennifer wish to transmit to her daughter? She states firmly that she wants Bethany to stay home with her own future children, but then notes that she seeks out female physicians and dentists so that Bethany has professional role models. Upon further reflection, Jennifer concludes that she would like for her daughter to be a stay-at-home mother and, afterward, a career woman.

Besides her children's programs and music, Jennifer is not an avid media consumer. She sees herself as standing apart from popular culture and its values, unconnected to much of what media portray and promote. However, she does recall day care disaster stories in detail, and she can easily articulate some work–family dilemmas in fictional media. Examples include a single mom torn between child and work in *NYPD Blue* and the dangerous situations to which a woman's job exposed her stepchildren in the film *Stepmom*.

Jennifer's favorite television program is *A Baby Story*, on the Learning Channel. Jennifer says she loves the show and cries at the end of almost every episode, when the infant is delivered. The program reminds her of the birth of her own children. *A Baby Story* fulfills many functions for Jennifer. Its very presence on the air speaks to the cultural importance of having children, validating Jennifer's own choices. Its couple-based focus gives a fairy tale flavor to the narrative, supporting Jennifer's own world-view, in which the desired ending comes about through finding a good man, marrying him, and having children. This televised daily reminder of the centrality of husband and babies to a woman's happiness helps distance Jennifer from a sense of her own alienation.

Jennifer often sees herself as an outsider, somewhat left behind by the women's movement and contemporary culture. Before joining our study, Jennifer never had listened to Laura Schlessinger's radio show, although she had heard of Dr. Laura as a controversial host with a no-nonsense attitude. Exposed to comments about Dr. Laura by other mothers in our study, Jennifer sought out and enjoyed that program. On our fourth ethnographic visit, Jennifer mentioned that she tries to catch it now when she can.

Like several other parents in our study, Jennifer also has media exposure through her religious activities. She attends a weekly mothers' Bible study group, coordinated by the church she attends. Participants use the Bible and a workbook to focus discussion. One week's topic was family conflict. The women shared and commented on conflict situations they'd experienced, primarily with their husbands. In the discussion, it became apparent that Jennifer was striving to understand her husband's enthusiasm for argument through an ideology that high-lighted masculine–feminine difference and a certain level of masculine aggression.

THE MOTHER KEEPS TRACK: GAIL FOGARTY, PART TIME WORKING MOTHER

Gail is an energetic mother of three children ranging in age from three to twelve years old. She was exceedingly generous with her time for our

132 · Media and Middle Class Moms

research. Gail and her husband, Kevin, live on the outskirts of town in a modest ranch house. Their home is a casually furnished mix of cheerful clutter. Gail and her children are always on the go, since each of them has a variety of extracurricular activities. The children are bright, energetic, and sociable. Among the few families we spent time with who are not new arrivals in the Dexter area, they are involved in a local network of family and old friends. These contacts add to their overall busyness, but also to their support, providing services including intermittent day care. The Fogartys' socioeconomic status is somewhat lower than that of other families in our study.

Gail's husband works full time, while she works part time, mostly from home. She has cut back her paid employment hours gradually in accordance with time constraints and day care costs. Gail says she is happy to keep on working. Her income enables her children's many sports activities, and she enjoys the adult contact. Until recently Gail worked in an office, but when one of her young sons became anxious after a bus driver's drop-off mistake, she arranged to work from home. Now Gail has the flexibility to pick her children up after school and to spend time in their classrooms, as well as more time to transport them to their many activities.

Gail treasures the in-home day care facility she uses. The couple who runs it, Gail thinks, have the same moral values she does, and she approves of the way their own children turned out. Her eldest two children, now in school, went there, as her youngest still does, part time. Gail considers it beneficial for children to spend some time away from their parents. She contrasts her own children to others she knows who have full time stay-at-home mothers and who are somewhat immature by her standards.

While Gail does most of the child transportation and housework, Kevin picks up the slack when she has a heavy workload at her job. This work–family balancing has had some adverse effects for him. One year, Gail's substantial job demands, and the family responsibilities that Kevin assumed as a result, cut into the time he had to study for a licensing exam, which he failed. Usually, however, Gail's workload is lighter, and she does most of the work of home and family. She and Kevin occasionally argue about their division of labor, and one of our visits occurred right after a tiff over housework: after dealing with a small family crisis, Gail had come home to a house with dirty dishes, an uncleaned refrigerator, her prepared meal spoiling in the oven, and the family sitting on the couch, watching TV, and eating fast food. Descartes' field notes from that day read, "[Gail] didn't want to complain too much about the incident and mentioned what an involved father [Kevin] was. We talked a bit about generational changes in men in terms of housework and child care and how her husband's generation did a little more than their fathers had done."

Besides his periodically heavy work within the home and with the children, Kevin deals primarily with the family vehicles and outdoor chores. During our five visits with Gail, she also did things for the car and minivans, but Kevin organizes vehicular maintenance, even when Gail is the one who takes the car for servicing. This arrangement recalls the pattern in which the mother keeps track of and manages housework, and the husband occasionally does some of the actual labor.

Gail's media consumption is fairly light, a by-product of her busy schedule. She watches some television news, scans local papers when she can, and reads a family magazine and a religious magazine. Gail's faith is important to her. She prays regularly, and frequently refers the children to Jesus and God as guides for their behavior, asking them if he would approve of certain actions, particularly naughty ones.

Because she spends so much time driving, one of Gail's main media sources is radio, and her favorite program is Laura Schlessinger's talk show. The family minivan is set up to fit Gail's tastes, with multiple media capabilities and dual sound controls. The children can listen to music or watch videos in back while Gail listens to *Dr. Laura* in the front seat. Because of the dual sound controls, she doesn't have to worry about the children hearing adult subject matter on *Dr. Laura*. Gail feels supported by Dr. Laura's overall moral stance and many of her messages, including her anti-abortion position, a cause for which Gail has volunteered her time. Gail does not accept all of Dr. Laura's positions, however. Unlike Schlessinger, for example, Gail sees a limited amount of day care as good for a child's social development.

Gail listens particularly to calls about teenaged children, keeping Dr. Laura's advice for future reference, especially in regard to girls. Gail is somewhat anxious about future situations her daughter may face involving friends, peer pressure, and dating. Her concern highlights a pattern we noted among other informants with both sons and daughters: parents' concerns about their children's behavior and its potential ramifications centered more on girls than boys. Mothers illustrated this theme in discussing the kinds of advice—based on a fairly traditional morality—they valued in Dr. Laura's program. These women tend to come from religious traditions that stress women's purity as an ideal state. Their apprehensions make sense in a culture in which girls bear the brunt of public censure and real consequences if they test the boundaries of moral conventions. Simultaneously, of course, such

134 • Media and Middle Class Moms

misgivings and the actions that result work to maintain and reproduce gendered inequities.

Gail uses media mainly for practical purposes. The children endure long waits more patiently while watching a video in the minivan. Gail finds it easier to do household chores when a video is playing to distract her children. Gail wants her own media to be useful as well. She chooses her media sources (like her child care providers) to fit her own beliefs and values. She trusts her carefully chosen media sources to provide valid, if not infallible, advice. Gail turns to the media for help with what she sees as her most important work: raising her children to be happy, healthy, and moral beings.

PATROLLING BOUNDARIES: JULIE BLANDING, PART TIME WORKING MOTHER

Julie radiates an intense energy that sometimes crosses over into obvious irritation. The Blandings live with their two lively children in one of Dexter's older subdivisions, near the center of town, in a large home furnished with contemporary pieces. Both Julie and her husband have advanced professional training. Julie works two days a week, having cut back from five to four to three to the current two during the course of her child-rearing. Of this she says: "I cut my hours back every year. As they get older, it's harder!" Even her currently reduced schedule leaves Julie visibly frustrated and frazzled, and she only works to maintain her credentials. Describing the days when she goes to her job, Julie peppers the word "crazy" throughout. Her son, Bobby, and daughter, Ruth, pursue a number of extracurricular activities, including sports and church groups. Julie doesn't foresee going back to work full time until her children are in college, saying, "I don't want to leave them! I don't want to miss all the practices and games and come home exhausted with no meals on the table."

When Julie discusses her husband's household participation, her frustration is evident. Asked whether he had made any changes in his work patterns because of family, she replied:

> No, he just keeps going! No, I worry about it, he does not. I'm the one that's always changing . . . No, he's never even considered changing his work schedule. And I'm trying to get him into work earlier, so he can get home earlier, and we can't even do that. Because he's not an early person, he's not an early riser, and he has hours where he could do that.

She continued, "I do the juggling. I do it all. He's oblivious to it. It's like, he gets up, he goes to work." Julie is dissatisfied with her husband's contribution to housework and child care. If she leaves the children with him while she goes to her job, she faces a mess to clean up when she gets home. If he puts the children to bed, they aren't in bed at the proper time because, says Julie, he doesn't watch the clock. Julie does the house cleaning, although her husband sometimes helps her if she asks him to do so. She admits he is a loving father, although this accolade comes with a small sting. "What he likes to do is sit and watch videos with the children," while "I'm running around."

When Julie's children were young, she used her workplace child care facility, where she felt they were safe, and which, she says, helped prepare them for school. When Julie discussed what she disliked about child care, however, a theme of boundary control emerged. After talking about the day care in both positive and neutral ways, she rather suddenly labeled her attitude toward it as "hate." Julie's concerns about how other people might influence her children became even more evident as we spent more time with her and her children.

Descartes spent one afternoon with Julie as she picked up her children from school and ran several errands. Arriving at the school and seeing her daughter, Ruth, standing in line, Julie encouraged her to disobey the teacher's rules and break formation so that they could leave. Once the children were with her, the day was full of admonitions about health and safety. One of the first things Julie asked her son, Bobby, to do when he came home was to throw out bubble gum his teacher had given him. She wondered acerbically if the teacher intended to pay Bobby's dental bills. Julie worries a great deal about her son, saying quite specifically that she does so because he is social and gregarious. She discussed her dismay when at one of his sports events she saw little girls chasing him around.

Stories she tells further illustrate Julie's concerns about her children's environment and her wish to control their physical and moral world. When Bobby (age eight) asked her what "gay" meant, she avoided answering. He persisted for several weeks, however, and she finally told him it meant "happy." Bobby replied that children on the playground had said it meant boys falling in love with other boys. Julie stuck to her guns, however, insisting it meant "happy." When Bobby asked his father about how babies are made, Julie's husband explained the mechanics of pregnancy. When Julie found out, she was furious, and told her husband never to have discussions like that without speaking with her first. Julie seemed to feel that if her husband ever had a right to a say in such matters, he had relinquished it by his limited involvement in the home. Julie wants to maintain what she sees as the children's innocence.

136 • Media and Middle Class Moms

Given how carefully Julie patrols the boundaries of her family's world, it is not surprising that she is equally vigilant about media consumption. She allows only the Disney and Nickelodeon TV channels for the children, although her son now can watch sports reporting as well. When asked about her own media use, Julie expresses disdain at the idea of a regular and unmonitored connection to outside culture, saying she doesn't watch any news, or any other television shows for that matter. Nor does she use the Internet, although she has a computer. She almost never goes out to movies, and rarely rents videos. She reads the village newspaper, and the weather, obituaries, and local section of the *Ann Arbor News*. She scans *Time* magazine, but reports that her primary reading is of children's book series.

The one media source Julie does consume, and fairly regularly, is talk radio. One of her favorite radio hosts is Laura Schlessinger. Julie says Dr. Laura "believes in families." Julie mentions she doesn't always enjoy the program, but that she often gets good advice from it. When asked what that advice is, she says "Just staying home." Julie is aware that Dr. Laura might not approve that she herself works part time, but says it doesn't matter to her because Dr. Laura is not in her shoes.

Julie, a highly trained professional, has curtailed her career substantially because of her beliefs about how children should be raised. In doing so, she has entrusted her family's livelihood to a man whom she considers to be a good provider, while something of a bumbler who needs constant monitoring (fitting the media stereotype of the dad as domestic dunce). Julie gains validation for her choices from Dr. Laura, her primary media source. She sees her frustrations as endurable for an immensely worthwhile purpose. When a disparity arises between her own viewpoints and those of her chosen media source, Julie uses the text (Dr. Laura) selectively, taking from it only what fits her own beliefs and circumstances.

MEN CAN BALANCE, TOO: PENNY WHITCOMB, FULL TIME WORKING MOTHER

Penny is a full time working mother with two young children. She and her husband, Seth, have less formal education, household income, and job prestige than most of our other informants. This is a second marriage for Penny, who has one other child, a daughter, who lives with Penny's ex-husband. Penny and Seth rent rather than own a home, which also makes them a minority in our sample. Penny is a mild-mannered and friendly woman who scheduled an interview during her work hours because it was easier for her to find uninterrupted time there. Descartes met her in her office, where photos of her husband and children were tucked under the glass top of her desk, which was piled high with paperwork.

Penny was a full time stay-at-home mother only once, when she was temporarily unemployed. Seth has been a stay-at-home father twice, both times when he was disabled. Penny feels this experience was good for Seth, allowing him to develop different expectations about men's and women's roles in the home. She says, "I think it's good that a man go through that, it makes him appreciate the mom more. When they walk in the door, and the laundry isn't finished, and the house isn't spotless and she's tired. And 'Well, what did you do all day?' type attitude." When Seth was home full time he did much of the housework and child care. Now that they both work full time, however, Penny does most of the housework. Seth still apparently does more of the child care than many fathers. To illustrate this, Penny mentions that he takes the kids to the doctor.

Penny's family also is unusual in our study in that they live near relatives, including a grandmother and aunt who care for the children after school. Like Gail and her family, the Whitcombs are not migrants to the Dexter area. They do not own a home in one of the new subdivisions, and their jobs do not require a long commute. Like most of our informants, however, Penny feels supported by the fact that the people she knows best, including her family and friends, have similar work–family situations to hers. Others in her social group have experienced divorce and unemployment, and she herself is the child of a dual-income lower middle class couple.

Penny's ideal is to have one parent at home for the children; she believes it is her and her husband's responsibility to raise their children themselves. She also feels it is ideal to have children in the sole care of their parents so parents can instill their own values. She herself needs to keep working full time, she explains, because she and Seth want to buy a home. In the evenings, Penny tries to "make up for the time" she is away from her children, and to make their time together as meaningful and pleasant as possible.

Penny uses media for both practical reasons and for entertainment. Exemplifying the former, she has a Sunday subscription to the *Ann Arbor News*, but she rarely reads the articles. She gets the paper for the enclosed TV guide and grocery coupons. Penny's reading centers on child advice manuals, and her only magazine subscription is to *Parents*. She also reads spiritual texts. When Penny was unemployed, she enjoyed watching Oprah Winfrey's talk show and the *Today Show*. She particularly liked interviews with child psychologists and other experts.

138 • Media and Middle Class Moms

Reflecting their relatively meager incomes, Penny and Seth lacked home Internet access, but they did rent videos and had cable TV.

Much of Penny's media exposure revolves around her children, who watch the Nickelodeon and Disney channels, often with their mother. She can readily cite the children's favorite programs, relating which ones she herself does and doesn't enjoy. She has a similar list for children's movies they have rented. When the children go to bed, Penny and Seth watch TV for entertainment. She enjoys such programs as *Ally McBeal*, with its central female lead. Highlighting the escapist value she finds in the media, Penny is one of the few women in our study who easily named three female characters she would want to be. All were carefree, zany women with few responsibilities. Penny also is one of the few to mention watching a show specifically because she finds a male star, in this case Don Johnson, attractive.

Penny also enjoys *The Sopranos*, which she began watching with her husband. At first she didn't like what she perceived as overt sexism in the husband–wife relationship, which she described as "The Italian old way of the woman stays home and you're not supposed to know nothing, and what I do is my business. And it just drove me nuts and I wouldn't watch it." Then an episode got her hooked: "It wasn't so much demeaning, it was just more on the face." She elaborates:

> It shows in a way the woman saying, "Okay, fine, you're going to use me, I'm going to use you right back. I'm not going anywhere, I've got everything I could possibly want. And then the main family that it focuses on, the Sopranos, she would kind of stand up for herself. So I'd be, "Oh right, you go girl!"

Penny pays attention to media portrayals of gender roles, such as women having access to the same career paths as men, or men participating in domestic work. She is one of the few people we interviewed who elaborated on the latter theme. Penny has direct experience with non-traditional gender roles; her ex-husband has custody of their daughter, and her current husband has spent time as a stay-at-home father.

Penny pays attention to media that promote fathers' participation in the home and in child-rearing, from her religious readings, to a discussion of conventional roles on *Happy Days*, to the news frenzy surrounding the Elián González case, in which a young boy residing in the United States was returned to Cuba. The last example, she thought, demonstrated greater public attention to the importance of fathers. This trend, beneficial in her view, encourages men to "realize they're able to prioritize and balance, just like the woman would balance, work

and home." Here she sees the media as a very positive influence, showing the importance of fathers as well as mothers. This is one way in
which she feels the media support dual-income families like hers.

A WEB OF CONNECTIONS: GWEN ROGERS,
FULL TIME WORKING MOTHER

Descartes met Gwen, the mother of two elementary-school age sons, in
her spacious new home on the far outskirts of Dexter. Her residence
is isolated at present, although signs of new construction abound. Both
Gwen and her husband, Pete, greeted the researcher warmly, after
which Pete worked all morning in their large garden. Both the Rogers
work full time, both primarily from home, although Gwen's position
involves traveling out of state two or three days a week, sometimes
overnight. Gwen is one of the few wives we interviewed who earns
more than her husband.

Like other mothers who travel, Gwen plans ahead for her trips, preparing and freezing meals, and keeping up with the laundry. She says of
her husband, "He helps out when I'm traveling—just with the kids,
fixing dinner and stuff like that." She does most of the housework and
cooking; Pete is responsible for most outside chores, and both drive
their sons to their many activities.

Gwen, who very much enjoys her job, thinks she would not have
made a wonderful stay-at-home mother. She has too much energy, she
says, and child care eventually would have driven her crazy. Gwen does
wish she could have had a longer maternity leave, but it wasn't a company option. Gwen and Pete managed to find, and have been delighted
with, a private day care provider. Gwen values the flexibility and adaptability that she feels non-kin care has given her children. In her work
and family decisions Gwen feels supported by her family and female
friends, most of whom work part time. Most mothers she knows in
Dexter work at least part time, and are professional people like Gwen
and Pete. She meets them primarily through her sons' activities. Her
acquaintance pool is somewhat homogeneous, because, as Gwen herself notes, those activities are expensive enough that only professional
parents can afford them.

Gwen and Pete spend considerable time doing physical and outdoor
activities with their sons, both of whom are avid readers, as are the
parents. Media provide Gwen with a web of connections to both the
outside world and her family. She gains information and pleasure from
media that help her professionally and personally, and uses media at
home to relax and bond with her husband and children. Gwen relates

140 • Media and Middle Class Moms

that they visit the card store together for Pokémon cards and the video store to rent videos. They all play Nintendo games together and watch movies as well. Weekend evenings are a special family time for the Rogers. Gwen makes a nice dinner, then serves popcorn as they watch DVDs. The family reads together for about a half-hour each day as well. Everyone in this family is an avid media user, consuming newspapers, magazines, books, and Internet material, as well as watching TV and DVDs and listening to music.

Their informational media include television news, the cooking magazine *Bon Appétit*, and the *Wall Street Journal*. Gwen also likes diversionary media, such as television dramas and situation comedies. She appreciates intelligent female characters and views as "stupid" media products lacking such portrayals, noting that her husband and sons do tend to like the latter. Of Pete, Gwen says he enjoys programs such as *The Man Show*, a Comedy Central feature that reveled in (barely post-adolescent) masculinity. Gwen reports that the show portrays women as stupid. Of her husband she laughingly remarks, "He's kind of a chauvinist in his own little way, and he gets stuck with me!" Simultaneously, in a bit of a contradiction, Gwen says she likes her favorite movie, *Terms of Endearment*, because it deals with women's feelings: "I could feel the pain that she was going through, because we're more emotional."

Gwen is very much aware of gender roles and stereotyping in the media. In general she feels supported in her work and family choices by the media she consumes regularly, such as the *Ann Arbor News* and *Cosmo*, saying that both frequently run articles that address work and family issues. She also has observed commercials' tendency to portray women as stay-at-home mothers who are normatively responsible for all housework and child care. She dismisses such depictions as old-fashioned but says they don't bother her.

Of her regular shows, Gwen enjoyed the drama *Ally McBeal* and related to the title character, in part because she worked. Her favorite show, however, was the science fiction drama *The X-Files*:

> I like [Scully's, the main female character's,] personality. She's a very hard core woman. Maybe hard core's not the right word. But I mean she represents women well. I mean, don't get me wrong, I'm not a hard person, but some women don't portray themselves like they should and that's why we always get the bad name.

Gwen dislikes media characterizations that demean women, such as Phoebe, a character in the sitcom *Friends*, who, she says, propagates the "dumb blonde" stereotype. Gwen also disapproves of characters that run counter to how she thinks women should be, such as Lucy Liu's character on *Ally McBeal*, whom she sees as "too mean."

Gwen's reflections on media illuminate aspects of her own family life. Her father was a high-ranking professional, while her mother stayed home, then worked part time at pink collar jobs during school hours. Gwen broke that gendered mold by achieving parity in job prestige and income with her husband, whose career she enabled by supporting him while he got his degree. Despite her accomplishments, Gwen agrees with certain gender stereotypes, including the notion that women are more emotional than men. Conventional standards of femininity are important to her, as is shown by her carefully made-up face, manicured and polished nails, and concern over her figure. *Cosmo*, which she reads regularly, is essentially a manual on norms of American femininity.

Gwen is doing a balancing act, not just between work and family, but between ideas of proper gender roles. She is atypical in a social world in which most mothers she knows work only part time. One approach to her responsibilities is to try to "do it all"—succeed at work, raise happy and healthy children, and ensure the housework is done even when she is away from home. She derives support from media she feels show working women in a positive light, such as *The X-Files* and *Ally McBeal*. She identifies with intelligent women pursuing high-profile, exciting careers—women who take it for granted they can succeed in competitive jobs formerly open only to men. Still, and also like Gwen, the women she admired from *The X-Files* and *Ally McBeal* were conventionally feminine. They were attractive in culturally approved ways, as expressed through make-up, slender bodies, and fashionable office wear. While working in a man's world, these women did not seriously challenge male authority. They got along well with men and didn't threaten any status quo. The main female character on *The X-Files* was almost always incorrect, for example, in her theories about any given case. Typically, her more experienced male partner proved to be right as each episode progressed (and he almost always got to drive the car!).

Gwen's media sources, besides connecting her to her family and to the outside world, also helped her reconcile her identities as a feminine woman and a successful careerist. Gwen's favorite TV shows validated and helped normalize, because of their popularity and mass distribution, the desirability of such a blending of roles. Such media portrayals provided Gwen (and others like her) with confidence and ideological support in a physical community whose typical gender roles and ideologies tend to be very different, and not nearly as supportive to mothers like Gwen.

142 • Media and Middle Class Moms

SCOURING THE MEDIA: CORINTH JASPER, SINGLE FULL TIME WORKING MOTHER

Corinth Jasper, a woman in her mid-thirties, has two children. Besides her status as a single parent, which is rare in Dexter, Corinth is anomalous among our informants in other ways. In an overwhelmingly white community, Corinth and her children are racial/ethnic minorities. Each child has a different father, neither of whom Corinth married, and from both of whom she is separated.

Corinth also contrasts with most parents in our study in that she is a renter rather than a homeowner, and her rent is subsidized. Corinth moved to Dexter specifically because she knew of special school programs and funding available there for her children, based on their minority status and her low income. Finances are a serious and ongoing issue for Corinth. She participated in our focus group and asked her second child's father, Toby, to join one of our men's groups, specifically for the monetary incentives we offered. She also belongs to a non-mainstream religion, in contrast to the conventional Christian affiliations of our other informants.

Corinth separated from Toby over the course of our study. She asked him to move out because of his ongoing reluctance to contribute financially and to do work around the house. Corinth said that Toby's career drive does not match her own. He seemed content to continue with menial labor, whereas she wants a middle class lifestyle.

Corinth's life has been and continues to be somewhat haphazard in terms of her domestic partners, residential patterns, work history, and long-term goals. She works very diligently, however, at making a living and providing a nice home for her children. She is concerned about their physical, emotional, and intellectual development. When her first child was very young, Corinth gave up an office position to become a full time nanny for a co-worker. Although she did not really like working with children exclusively and missed adult contact, her nanny position allowed her to bring her own children to work and thus be with them full time, as she also saved on child care costs. Corinth supplemented her income in a number of creative ways, but never so as to enhance her professional credentials. During our research period, her nanny position was drawing to an end, because those children had outgrown the need for a nanny. When we met her, Corinth had worked as a nanny and had been out of the formal labor force for six years. In a tight job market, her recent forays into job seeking had been unsuccessful.

Corinth, who tends to be hard on herself, is quick to discuss flaws she perceives in her own parenting. She criticizes herself for being too tidy when her need to clean cuts into her time with the children. An avid media consumer, she reads articles on parenting and children in *Parents* magazine and *Working Mother*. She gets free subscriptions to both through her son's school program. She posts snippets of advice from *Parents* on her refrigerator to remind herself of them during the day, and she quotes them to her children. Corinth's religion also provides literature for herself and her children. The main reason she converted to that religion was that an adherent visited her while she was pregnant, and offered her supportive birthing and parenting advice. Her new religion also saves Corinth time, because meetings are held at her home, so she doesn't need to get herself and the children to and from church.

Corinth has substantial media exposure. She reads her employer's copies of *Time, Newsweek*, and the *Ann Arbor News* regularly. Her own book collection contains authors from Jane Austen to Rita Mae Brown. Books on wellness, nutrition, and healthful cooking are special favorites because of physical problems Corinth shares with one of her children. Corinth's media tastes are substantial and diverse; she listens to folk, soul, and heavy metal music and watches TV programs that range from PBS to *America's Funniest Home Videos.*

Media enter Corinth's work–family situation in concrete and pervasive ways. First, mass media provide a cost-effective and readily available source of entertainment and education for her and her children. Her cable service is connected to three TV sets throughout the house. Cable can reduce the burden of parental monitoring if children's viewing is limited to specific channels such as Nickelodeon. Corinth rents videocassettes, buys used videos, and gets music CDs and other materials from the local library. Scouring garage sales, she brings home items ranging from children's books to a used television. Second, media give Corinth a chance to accomplish household tasks by distracting her children in a way that is safe and economical. The kids watch TV or a video, put in a music CD, or play a video game when Corinth needs time to complete a chore. Third, media are tied intimately to Corinth's search for employment now that her nanny position is ending. Using the Internet for assistance, she mentions other single mothers in her apartment complex who have done so as well, such as by posting résumés online. Corinth spends considerable time researching career- and degree-related information online. She investigated legal requirements for small businesses, hoping she could turn a botanical hobby into a source of income. When the lack of start-up money posed an obstacle to that endeavor, Corinth researched other forms of

144 • Media and Middle Class Moms

training, including online degree programs. Although she found the cost prohibitive, such a program could bring the classroom to her home and offer the flexibility of staying home with her children while training for a career.

ISOLATION OR CONNECTION

Throughout this book we have argued that the media, and the representations they offer, significantly influence the ways in which people organize themselves and their expectations. We see mass media as important sources of "scripts" or cultural models that contemporary people may draw on as they strive to understand and evaluate who they are, and what they might or should be and do. Although people everywhere probably select media messages to support and reinforce their opinions and life choices, some people are much more dismissive of, distrustful of, or hostile to media than others are. How do our findings in Dexter compare with those of anthropological studies of media use and impact in other places? Kottak's (1990) Brazilian research found suspicion of the media to be most typical of traditional information brokers and moral guardians, including elites, intellectuals, educators, writers, and (especially) the clergy. Kottak's team concluded that, by fuelling information hunger, television had fostered overall media use in Brazil, even promoting literacy. These findings contradict the common American assumption that TV is hazardous to the reading habit, as does the Rogers family, as described in this chapter. In Brazil (a country with a much weaker print history than the United States), TV stimulates overall media use, including reading, by hooking people on information and stimulating curiosity. For Brazilians, heavy viewing was part of an external orientation, a general thirst for information, contacts, models, and support beyond those that are locally and routinely available. Based on their lifestyles and patterns of media use, there is every reason to believe that this finding may be equally true of Dexter's more locally unorthodox women, such as Penny, Gwen, and Corinth.

For some people, such as Penny, Gwen, and Corinth, the media offer a rich web of connections that offer information, entertainment, and social validation. Others, including Jennifer, Gail, and Julie, who can see more mothers and families like themselves locally, limit their own and their children's media exposure, choosing reduced connectivity, greater isolation, and tighter boundaries. The worldly images of difference and diversity that are so pleasing to some can be much less appealing to others, particularly those who feel most comfortable with Dexter's social homogeneity and its opportunities for privacy. The first group may admire Scully and Ally, as the second turns to Disney and Dr. Laura. In the next, and final, chapter we return to this idea of connection, representing one of the key social functions of media, along with the themes of comparison and common ground.

8

COMPARISON, CONNECTION, AND COMMON GROUND

A hassled stay-at-home mother of two compares her own competence unfavorably with a news story about a mother who manages a family of 14. An employed mother sees her own juggling act in the context of a TV nurse's balancing ER work with the care of infant twins. A stay-at-home mother feels in good company with one who calls Dr. Laura Schlessinger to say how happy she is with her work/family choice. A protective mom contrasts her own domestic vigilance with the absenteeism of the parents of two murderous Columbine teenagers. A dad who can "handle a little Springer" contrasts its love/marriage and social class dynamics with his own, and finds it easy to feel superior.

Virtually every American understands a reference to a "Beaver Cleaver family" or "a dad like in *The Cosby Show*." A Vice President comments on the pregnancy of an unmarried professional woman on TV, and the entire country takes notice and debates *Murphy Brown*'s decision. Comparisons of Al Gore to Eddie Haskell don't help his presidential prospects. For older Americans, penny-pinching and the refusal to age beyond 39 are forever associated with Jack Benny.

Media matter—a lot. *Ozzie and Harriet, Leave it to Beaver, The Brady Bunch*: these programs from bygone days speak to us nostalgically of an idealized time when family roles were simpler and less ambiguous. Those TV sitcoms portrayed a set of interlinked conceptions of family, gender, class, and work that is powerful enough to keep shaping Americans' vision of the ideal, even as reality continues to diverge from that model (and, in fact, always has [Coontz 1992]). Today's media remain in dialogue with those earlier tropes, as Americans grapple with the past five decades' reshaping of family roles and gender relations. The major themes emerging from our media content analysis demonstrate this. Child and home care remain depicted primarily as female concerns. The difficulty of combining the roles of worker and parent, particularly for women, is a common focus of fictional and non-fictional media. Child endangerment, due to absent or inattentive working parents, was a third, related, theme, with mothers usually portrayed as more blameworthy than fathers (cf. Douglas and Michaels 2004). The underlying message of these depictions is this: if the mother had been fulfilling her primary role, that of nurturer, everything would have turned out better. Media representations generate a sense of guilt that many of our informants felt, or believed others felt, about their work/family choices.

In real life in Dexter, structural forces, particularly inflexible workplace and school schedules, made it difficult to combine two full time jobs with child care. In the context of inertial cultural values and current structural realities, most parents in our study adopted work–family solutions that worked to reproduce gendered inequalities. Most fathers were employed full time, and most mothers worked for pay part time or not at all. Fathers, working full time and with gender norms on their side, contributed less to child care and much less to housework than their wives did, regardless of employment status.

In their media exposure, the parents in our study processed considerable work and family content, and were well aware of the kinds of messages being transmitted and received. They proved to be attentive and critical consumers of media who could discuss, often eloquently, portrayals of men's and women's roles in families and the workplace. They expressed concern when content seemed to do a disservice to real parents and children. Our informants tended to select media messages that validated and reinforced their own opinions, aspirations, and life choices. Media served several social functions for these parents, of which three deserve particular emphasis: comparison, connection, and common ground.

COMPARISON

Americans readily admit that their educations and their families influence their character, their decisions, and their lives in general. Most Americans are just as apt to deny that the mass media influence them. Such denial is suspect, considering that mass media typically enter our lives long before we enter the school system, or that the TV outlasts the father in many American homes. This tendency to recognize that media

148 • Media and Middle Class Moms

impact others, "but not me," is common. Americans tend to evaluate media influence negatively, seeing those who are influenced as weak, gullible, and childlike. For social scientists, however, media impact has been confirmed again and again—and for Americans of all social classes.

Our study in Dexter showed how parents used varied media images of work and family to get a sense of what others were thinking and doing, and to identify, or contrast themselves, with media representations. Media personalities and messages often were cited in ways that highlighted the function of social comparison. Our informants compared themselves with people and situations from the media as well as with people in their own lives. Media suggest, proclaim, or demonstrate (no matter how accurately) how other people, including unorthodox people, live, behave, and cope with life circumstances. Responses to media accounts varied from "I can do that" to "That's so not me."

Some informants were explicit that they used media to keep in touch with what other people were thinking and doing, even if they disagreed with or disapproved of that information. Sometimes a media message provoked a contrast: "I know I'm not going to think that way, but I want to hear what they have to say." Parents tended to approve particularly—saying they could "relate to"—media accounts that depicted choices they had made. They felt that "if it's there [presented in the media] I'm not alone and not so unusual," for example, in forsaking office work for telecommuting from home.

Our informants took note of how media figures handled situations similar to their own. If they thought those situations were handled well, they could try to cope similarly with like circumstances. They found useful examples and role models in the media. As one mother put it, "Gosh, that's how I'd like to be." For many of our informants (and Americans more generally), certain social comparisons *only* take place via the media. Dexter parents lacked firsthand knowledge of the parenting skills of the mothers and fathers of mass murderers. Nor did most people in our study have direct knowledge of the demands facing ER personnel. Particularly in the absence of real life models, the media provide material for comparisons that allow people to think through and evaluate their own circumstances and decisions. The extreme nature of some situations depicted in the media starkly illuminates contrasts, making them easier to see.

In our study, we found that social comparison (whether with real life others, such as family and friends, or via the media) allowed people to evaluate their own decisions and effectiveness in work and family roles. Our informants compared and contrasted their own situations, favorably and unfavorably, with those of their parents, siblings, co-workers,

Comparison, Connection, and Common Ground • **149**

friends, neighbors, and with what they saw on television or heard about on the radio. The media, they felt, often provided validation for their own personal choices, whether through negative or positive contrasts. Mothers who saw media figures complain about the competing demands of work and family could empathize with those mothers while feeling good about their own decision to stay home. Knowing that others felt similar pressures, but still managed to juggle work and family responsibilities and raise well-adjusted children, could help a parent feel better about the way she or he coped. And unlike neighbors and family, the media (with the exception of Dr. Laura) usually don't talk back. People can compare and contrast at will, picking and choosing the depictions, messages, and meanings to support, or not, their own choices.

Upward social comparison, as discussed in Chapter 1, isn't always positive; it can provoke feelings of inadequacy. "If she can do all that, what's wrong with me?" However, we found that parents used potentially threatening messages selectively; sometimes they simply rejected them. Our informants were especially suspicious of what they saw as idealized images in parenting magazines and child care and pregnancy manuals. Such media, they felt, promoted busywork, an unnecessary form of overparenting. One mother discarded one magazine because it "made me feel like I was doing everything bad—too many duties, like elaborate Halloween costumes." Busy with the many demands of parenting, this mother never had the time for the myriad activities and crafts suggested by *Parenting*.

Some felt awash in a sea of child care information, idealized and inflated expectations for mothers, and "expert" opinions and advice. Asserting the value of parental authority, autonomy, and judgment (mother knows best!), some extolled the "inner voice": "You don't have to call four people before you say to yourself, 'The kid's got a cold.'"

An important component of self-validating social comparison can be summed up as: bad things happen to people unlike me. Downward social comparisons allowed our informants to feel better about their own lives in contrast to all the sick, stupid, unfortunate, and misguided people seen on TV (think Jerry Springer, Anna Nicole Smith, and the latchkey kid who grows up to be Jeffrey Dahmer). Our informants paid special attention to media accounts that they felt illustrated the dangerous results of improper choices. They saw the media as playing to parental guilt and other emotions (cf. Douglas and Michaels 2004), but also as confirming the results of lackluster and failed parenting. Often cited were disastrous outcomes when parents weren't with their children at critical times. Media accounts stoked fears about day care,

150 • Media and Middle Class Moms

kidnapping, abusive—even murderous—nannies, and deadly results when children were left alone. As one mother put it, "I see so many kids being left home alone and then a fire starting."

Had she ever really seen this—outside the media? When asked why she chose to stay home, another woman said it had a lot to do with the negative things she had observed in the children of working parents, both in "real life" and on TV. She distilled the Columbine killings into an issue of parental neglect: the killers' parents had chosen to work outside the home, to abandon family responsibilities, and to remain ignorant while their sons made bombs in the garage. Her knowledge of the circumstances surrounding Columbine could have come only from the media.

To be sure, and just as importantly, social comparison also is a feature of everyday life: People make social comparisons when they attend public functions and events, including church, religious meetings, school functions, and after school activities. One stay-at-home mother believed she could identify the children of working parents by their behavior at school, which she perceived as less controlled and more disruptive than that of children like her own. An employed mother saw children of stay-at-home mothers as less mature socially than those from dual-income families.

No matter what their work–family decision, parents usually felt supported by their family and friends. Occasional negative statements and incidents tended to reflect stereotypes of one camp—stay-at-home mothers or employed mothers—about the other. Our informants commonly described their own work/family choices favorably via vignettes that contrasted their situations with presumably less desirable circumstances and outcomes involving other families and children.

Social comparison can turn into a class-based competition, as when people compare their homes or vehicles with those of other parents. Wealthier stay-at-home parents may overlook their own comfortable homes and privileged means as they criticize the assumed consumption mania of the dual-earner couple. Social comparison proceeds in the classroom, as parents who are able to take the time to assist there compare their own and other children, as they also compare themselves with other parents who do, or do not, help out at school. Transportation choices (e.g., school bus or private vehicle) and clues about parental schedules and priorities (e.g., the tendency to be on time or late) are on display as children arrive at and leave school, or partake in after school care or activities. People compare as well with their co-workers, like the pink collar worker who notes and resents the more flexible work hours of professionals and bosses.

The consumption stimulation industry, particularly as represented by advertising on TV and in glossy magazines, assumes that people will compare those ads with, and find wanting, their own lives, and that they will desire products that draw them closer to the media imagery. As well, for generations, explicitly and implicitly, the media have promoted images of particular kinds of (sanitary) families and the products associated with their lifestyles. It makes sense for the media, as agents of commerce and consumption, to promote upward mobility, illustrated by the disproportionately large number of professionals shown on TV (Signorielli and Kahlenberg 2001). And don't forget the ads for (and sales of) SUVs and minivans, which became the quintessential family vehicles in turn-of-the-century America. These well-equipped vehicles were an important part of the landscape of family life in Dexter, enabling the endless child transportation and commuting that characterized life there.

People compare children, in themselves, and as a reflection of parental competence. Parents must be able to afford, in time and money, education and extracurricular activities for their offspring. Dexter offers an excellent public education system, and good schooling, with the goal of a college degree, has become mandatory for middle class Americans of the twenty-first century. With an eye to enhancing the chance of college admissions, parents involve their children in a host of activities. These further encourage social comparison through conspicuous displays of parental commitment and/or investment. Raising the middle class child has become increasingly pricey. Far from being the economic helpmeets of earlier centuries, children now truly are dependents. They represent an ever-increasing investment. *Consumer Reports* magazine (2005) noted that parents with a $70,200-plus income, like many of those in our study, will spend about $353,000 raising their child to age 18. Four years at a public university would add another $130,000 by the year 2021. Today, keeping up with the Joneses means keeping up not only with a breadwinner, but matching the Joneses' kids, activity by activity. This social comparison extends beyond homes, cars, and possessions. As suggested by Garey's (1999) concept of maternal visibility, parenting itself has become a product to be performed, displayed, and socially evaluated, with children's successes and failures the key performance indicators.

CONNECTION

When people seek certain messages and cannot easily find them in their home communities, they are likely to look somewhere else. Today's

152 • Media and Middle Class Moms

media and technology, including cable, satellite, the Internet, VCRs, DVDs, television, movies, radio, print, and other sources, offer a dazzling array of immediately accessible alternatives to what is available locally. The media offer a rich web of connections that can provide information, entertainment, social validation, and designs for living.

Through research in several Brazilian communities, a team led by one of us (Kottak 1990) found that exposure to television fueled an information hunger that fostered overall media use, including print, thus contradicting the common American assumption that TV is hazardous to the reading habit. In Brazil, greater interest in media was part of an external orientation, a general wish for information, contacts, models, and support beyond those that were locally and routinely available. Based on their lifestyles and patterns of media use, there is every reason to believe that this finding may be equally true of certain parents in Dexter, Michigan (and probably throughout the United States as well).

This linking role of media probably is less important for people who feel most comfortable in and with the local setting. For some of our informants, media offered a welcome gateway to a wider world, while others were comfortable with, and even sought to enhance, their seclusion, limiting both media exposure and the outside social contacts of themselves and their children. Some mothers had chosen to stay home specifically because they saw the child care options available outside as unsatisfactory and felt that their role was to be with their children throughout the day. (Demonstrating an external orientation, by contrast, most working mothers viewed outside child care as beneficial to their children's development.) It's likely as well that women who see more mothers and families like themselves locally may limit their media exposure. Wary about external threats, discordant messages, and alien models, they opt for reduced connectivity and a more confined social world with tighter boundaries. They choose the local and the familiar to the national, the global, and the alien. The messages about diversity, difference, and escape that are so pleasing to some people can pose a threat to women who, for more than a generation, have been told their "traditional" choices are not modern ones.

Connection to a wider world, real or imagined, is a way to move beyond local standards and expectations, even if the escape is only temporary and vicarious. David Ignatius described the escapist value of nineteenth century English novels, expressed particularly through their heroines—woman who are "passionate seekers," pursuing "free thought and personal freedom," rejecting the "easy comforts and arranged marriages of their class" in their quest for something more. Despite (and/or because of) their independent or rebellious temperaments, characters such as Elizabeth Bennet in Jane Austen's *Pride and Prejudice* almost always find a happy ending. Sympathetic readers find the heroine's success "deeply satisfying" when there are limited opportunities in real life (the local community) to see such behavior and choices (all quotes from Ignatius 2007:A21). We heard similar comments from some mothers, mostly employed, about TV heroines, such as Agent Scully from *The X-Files* or the title character of *Ally McBeal*.

The flip side of connectivity is a wish to separate—to draw and maintain boundaries, to isolate and protect from dangers real and imagined. For most of the parents in our study, the very choice of moving to Dexter indicates a desire to create a haven for their families, to keep them separate from the perils of contemporary life. Many chose to live in homes on large lots in sparsely populated neighborhoods. Neighbors, living not too close by, tended to be people like themselves who had made similar life choices, as were the mothers who helped out in the schools and handled after-school activities. Most of the parents in our study were very comfortable with the middle class homogeneity that was a hallmark of their community. Only one commented negatively upon the lack of racial and class diversity.

Many of the mothers in this study, especially those who stayed at home full time, said they avoided TV news in order to shield themselves and their children from all the bad things happening in the world. Many women were strict media monitors. Men tended to be more tolerant of discordant media messages than women were, and worried less about the influence of the media on their children. As suggested by Parsons and Bales (1955), these fathers saw their role specifically as one involved with introducing the outside world to their children. Tensions related to the differential media tolerance of husbands and wives surfaced occasionally in many informants' homes.

Paradoxically, the bleakness of the real world also can be seen as a reason to seek out escapist media. Many of the women in our study avoided news media, but eagerly consumed fare that presents a safer vision of the world, where things are as they "should" be—where following the normative life script of marriage and motherhood culminates in safe, happy, and healthy families (*A Wedding Story, A Baby Story*) or where sanitized adventuring is rewarded with fame and fortune (*Survivor, Amazing Race*). Writing in summer 2007, Ignatius proclaimed: "If ever there were a summer for escapist literature, this is it. The news of the real world is so bleak that it's a blessing to retreat for a while into the imagined worlds of fiction" where goodness more clearly prevails (2007:A21). Take that, Lord Voldemort!

COMMON GROUND

A third social function of the media is to provide common ground, shared cultural knowledge and expectations. As noted earlier, one ironic commonality in our study was for people to underestimate their media use and to deny the influence of media on their lives. Yet our research revealed considerable shared knowledge of media, which in fact were an ongoing and regular presence in our informants' lives, offering an array of work and family content that people were aware of and reflected upon. Initial disclaimers notwithstanding, most of our informants turned out to be habitual and even enthusiastic media consumers. Media entertained and informed them, and, as became especially evident in our focus groups, let them participate in a shared culture (common ground).

Media images of work and family provide fodder for discussions with family and friends, and across the nation. Recently the media have tried to make us care about how such figures as Lindsay Lohan, Paris Hilton, and Britney Spears have managed to screw up their privileged lives. And, given the ubiquity of the coverage, we indeed must care, perhaps again as a point of social comparison. Do their mistakes tell us something about poor choices or poor parenting? Does their unhappiness make the rest of us more content with more modest means?

Several years ago, one of us (Kottak 2004:496–497) adopted a teaching technique that took advantage of his students' familiarity with television: he demonstrated changes in American kinship and marriage patterns by contrasting the TV programs of the 1950s and 1960s with more recent ones. (Students know about the history of sitcom families from syndicated reruns, especially on the cable/satellite channel Nickelodeon.) As Kottak began to diagram family structure using old sitcom material, some students immediately recognized (from reruns) the nuclear families of the 1950s and 1960s, especially the Beaver Cleaver family. When he started diagramming *The Brady Bunch*, even more students joined in, shouting out names: "Jan," "Bobby," "Greg," "Cindy," "Marcia," "Peter," "Mike," "Carol," "Alice." As the Brady cast recitation neared completion, most students were shouting out in unison, as though at a religious revival, names made as familiar as their parents' through exposure to TV reruns.

Were reruns not so easily available, this continuing familiarity with old sitcoms would not exist. But why, one wonders, within the wide world of syndicated reruns, do certain shows, such as *The Brady Bunch*, enjoy such enduring popularity. Two cultural reasons come to mind. First, such programs (and add to them *Leave it to Beaver, The Waltons,* and *Little House on the Prairie*—all mentioned by our informants in Dexter) offered idealized images of family life even when they first aired. The family affairs portrayed in the old sitcoms appear yet more romanticized in the face of today's work, marriage, and family realities. A graduate student, now in his fifties, once told Kottak he had always wanted his family to be like the one on *The Brady Bunch*. An African American informant in a different study told Descartes that when she was growing up she wanted her family to be white like the families on 1960s TV, because they all seemed so happy. Although contemporary Americans never will experience the myriad realities of the past, idealized images of what can only be perceived as a mythic golden age of the American family linger there in the museum of syndication. Such programs exert a powerful draw—one that appeals to parents as well as children. A second cultural reason for this enduring popularity is that parents encourage their children to consume certain media. Disney and PBS were prominent in the fare our informants offered their children, but also the old television shows, the "family" shows—how can contemporary children possibly be harmed by exposure to Beaver and Wally Cleaver or Greg and Marcia Brady? American parents can relive moments of their own past as they direct their sons and daughters toward such relished relics. In so doing, they inculcate a new generation in an older generation's values.

The media provide social cement as families watch favorite programs together or plan events around *Harry Potter*. Media offer common ground for family members and for much larger groups. Simply by invoking certain media sources, one is cued in to the very values that define a person: the man who tells us he visits James Dobson's website and listens to Dr. Laura is telling us what his moral code is. He believes in a strong, breadwinner father and a nurturant stay-at-home mother, and he has worked to make that work and family configuration a reality in his life. The woman who tells us she listens to NPR, watches *ER*, and reads *Working Mother* is giving us a different set of clues as to her values. She combines paid employment and family in her own life, and doesn't see that as a bad thing. She might wish for a more flexible schedule, as she is still likely bound by norms dictating that she is the primary caregiver for her children, but she doesn't want to stay at home full time.

MEDIA AND MIDDLE CLASS (WHITE) MOMS IN DEXTER

The parents participating in our research by and large have a narrow profile. They are white, middle class and upper middle class

156 • Media and Middle Class Moms

professionals. They can afford to live in the largely white, largely middle class community of their choice. They are able to organize their work and family lives as they best see fit, frequently by having one parent (the mother) stay at home to keep close tabs on their children's development and daily experiences. In our analyses we make no secure claims for generalizability. It is true, however, that the "white flight" trend has been present for decades, and that the new suburbia continue to spread. Throughout the nation, previously cultivated fields now sprout suburban-looking developments of large, comfortable, costly homes. Affluent parents seeking safe, prosperous environments for their children find ways to access them. Many of the parents in our study had done just that: living in Dexter they inhabit a town that harkens back, visually and demographically, to the homogeneous depictions of *Ozzie and Harriet* and *Leave it to Beaver*. Dexter's class and racial/ethnic variation, which is minimal, largely is confined to the rental units in the village center. For many Dexter residents, prosperity enables the kind of work/family choices portrayed in those old shows and promoted today by media sources such as Dr. Laura.

Dexter's homogeneity in race, class, and ethnicity is part of what makes our research population distinct. The parents who participated had the means to create a way of life for their families that suited them. Many in America do not. Our informants had a considerable amount of control over their surroundings and their children's activities. The cost of this was male commuting out to far-flung jobs and female homekeeping that precluded employment at their level, even had it been wanted. These were choices that most men and women in our study easily accepted and justified. Their preferred lifestyles fit in with traditional middle class gender norms, the practices of their friends and families, and many, if not most, media representations (note the dearth of magazines called *Fathering* or *Working Father*).

For the most part, these parents easily saw themselves reflected in popular media and did not seek out heterogeneity there any more than they did in their own lives. As mainstream media now depict both working mothers and stay-at-home mothers, there was sufficient material there for parents with either preference to pick and choose selectively. Very few parents spoke of consuming alternative or "niche" media, with the exception of Christian media. Most of their media consumption featured white middle class people much like themselves. Two exceptions were *The Cosby Show* and *The Bernie Mac Show*, mentioned as favorites by several informants. These two comedies featured African American families—economically secure ones—with lifestyles that middle class white Americans probably can identify

Comparison, Connection, and Common Ground · **157**

with fairly easily. Few parents in our study consumed any other African American-centered media; even fewer mentioned seeking out media that featured poor people, gay men, lesbians, Latinos, Asians, Muslims, or Jewish people (with the exception of the comedy *Seinfeld*). When they did use media that portrayed others' realities, often those media did so in ways that elicited and illustrated unfavorable and frightening impressions: the local news flashes a photo of an African American criminal suspect, *Jerry Springer* stages another chaotic confrontation between people who obviously have little material or social capital, and so on. The media our informants used on a regular basis consistently reinforced the valuation of homogeneity represented by their lives in Dexter. For the most part, these parents consumed mainstream media—sources that reflected themselves most positively. Their media use reinforced the presumed normalcy of their own lifestyles and experiences, their gender-based decisions, and their status with respect to race and class. For our informants, the media offered little reason to question the assumed naturalness of their lifestyle choices.

Based on our research in Dexter, Michigan, we have concluded, and have argued throughout this book, that the media, and the representations they offer, contribute substantially to the ways in which people organize themselves and their expectations. The mass media provided "scripts" or cultural models that Dexterites used to understand and evaluate their identities, situations, decisions, and life possibilities. We have reflected at length on how the parents in our study experienced their work and family lives and how media informed and connected to those experiences. We have used their words and our own experiences with them to paint a picture of their circumstances and decisions against the broader backdrop of changes in work, family, and media in America. We wonder, however, whether media—and particular representations in them—were so meaningful because they were especially well suited to Dexter—its specific demographics, character, and location. To what extent do our results, such as those about the media's social functions of comparison, connection, and common ground, apply to Americans more generally? Our research calls out for similar studies to be conducted in different and more diverse communities within twenty-first century America.

APPENDIX A: DEMOGRAPHIC DATA

Table 1
The Research Community in 1990 and 2000

	Village 1990	Village 2000	Township 1990	Township 2000
Total population	1,497	2,338	4,407	5,248
Sex				
Male	49.23%	48.63%	51.24%	50.57%
Female	50.77%	51.37%	48.76%	49.43%
Race[a]				
White	98.73%	96.58%	98.32%	97.52%
Black	0.07%	0.43%	0.29%	0.38%
Asian	0.13%	1.03%	0.45%	0.61%
American Indian, Eskimo, or Aleut	0.80%	0.30%	0.62%	0.29%
Hispanic or Latino of any race	0.73%	0.98%	1.07%	1.03%
Total households	633	1,013	1,527	1,863
Family[b] households	64.61%	63.28%	81.47%	79.92%
Married couple families	49.45%	46.59%	73.74%	71.82%

Source: U.S. Census (1990a, 1990b, 2000b, 2000c)

[a] Column totals may not add to 100 percent due to rounding and exclusion of the category of "other."
[b] "Family" is defined by the Bureau of the Census as two or more people related by birth, marriage, or adoption.

160 • Appendix A

Table 2
The Research Community, 2000 Employment Statistics

Presence and age of children by employment status of parents	Village	Township
Under 6 years	224	412
Living with two parents	151 (67.41%)	364 (88.35%)
Both parents in labor force	66.23%	64.29%
Father only in labor force	29.80%	34.34%
Mother only in labor force	3.97%	1.37%
Living with one parent	73 (32.59%)	48 (11.65%)
Living with father	22	20
In labor force	100.00%	100.00%
Not in labor force	0.00%	0.00%
Living with mother	51	28
In labor force	86.27%	100.00%
Not in labor force	13.73%	0.00%
6 to 17 years	338	1020
Living with two parents	193 (57.10%)	1013 (99.31%)
Both parents in labor force	82.38%	84.30%
Father only in labor force	12.44%	13.33%
Mother only in labor force	5.18%	2.37%
Living with one parent	145 (42.90%)	7 (00.69%)
Living with father	7	0
In labor force	100.00%	0.00%
Not in labor force	0.00%	0.00%
Living with mother	138	7
In labor force	84.78%	100%
Not in labor force	15.22%	0%

Source: U.S. Census (2000e)

Table 3
Gender and Paid Labor Status

Sex by work status in 1999, usual hours worked per week in 1999	Village	Township
Male:	879	1,964
Usually worked 35 or more hrs/week	75.77%	75.71%
Usually worked 15 to 34 hrs/week	10.92%	6.87%
Usually worked 1 to 14 hrs/week	1.25%	2.39%
Did not work in prior year	12.06%	15.02%
Female:	975	1,946
Usually worked 35 or more hrs/week	52.41%	47.23%
Usually worked 15 to 34 hrs/week	21.23%	20.66%
Usually worked 1 to 14 hrs/week	3.90%	5.50%
Did not work in prior year	22.46%	26.62%

Source: U.S. Census (2000g)

APPENDIX B: INDIVIDUAL INTERVIEW GUIDE

Interview #_____   Date _____

Interview Questions—Work, Family, Media
Tell me about your work and family situation.

> The people in your household: [ages, relationship to respondent, work/school/care schedules]

> The kind of work you do [(if applicable) nature of work, job title, hours per day, days per week, temporary/full time/part time, length of time at this position, benefits, hours and time off flexibility, company policies, etc.]

> Why did you take this particular position? Did your work schedule change with the birth of your children and then with their entrance into school? If currently not working for pay, what was the last time you worked for pay?

> Same for spouse.

What is a typical weekday routine for you and your family? Weekend?

How are household chores divided up in your family?

Media
What forms of media do you watch, listen to or read?

Television. Radio. Newspapers. Magazines. Books. Movies and videos. Internet. How many hours per day (or week) for each? Which are your favorites in each? Which characters or personalities do you identify with the most in each? Why?

Is anything in the media you use related to family issues, or more specifically, to work–family issues? In what ways?

What types of images or messages do you get from the media you use about work and family? How do those images or messages make you feel? Are they helpful? Do they support or undermine the choices your family has made?

What sort of media did you watch, read, or listen to when you were a child? Teen? Expecting your children?

Have you ever listened to Dr. Laura or Dr. Joy Browne or a similar person? What do you think of their messages about work and family? (This can be extended to other specific shows/personages/media forms dealing with work and family: *The Cosby Show, Home Improvement, Roseanne, Jesse, Leave it to Beaver, The Brady Bunch, Family Ties, Growing Pains, ER*, Dr. Spock, *Baby Boom, Parenting Magazine*, etc.)

Do you recall a specific time when you got advice, reinforcement, or new ideas about work and family issues from the media? What was it? Do you recall a specific time when you disagreed with a work–family issue presented in the media or felt that a message was undermining your own choices? What was it?

Demographic Information
This sheet is for classification purposes only, so that we can compare results from different kinds of people in the study. Again, all information is completely confidential.

Your race/ethnicity _____

Your religion _____

Education _____ (highest degree completed)

164 • Appendix B

Please describe your marital history. Is this your first marriage? What year were you married?

_____

Length of time in Dexter: _____ years

Does your family rent or own your home? _____

Household income (please circle one)

None	$30,000–$39,999	$70,000–$79,999
Under $10,000	$40,000–$49,999	$80,000–$89,999
$10,000–$19,999	$50,000–$59,999	$90,000–$99,999
$20,000–$29,999	$60,000–$69,999	$100,000 and over

Your income (please circle one)

None	$30,000–$39,999	$70,000–$79,999
Under $10,000	$40,000–$49,999	$80,000–$89,999
$10,000–$19,999	$50,000–$59,999	$90,000–$99,999
$20,000–$29,999	$60,000–$69,999	$100,000 and over

Your spouse's income (please circle one)

None	$30,000–$39,999	$70,000–$79,999
Under $10,000	$40,000–$49,999	$80,000–$89,999
$10,000–$19,999	$50,000–$59,999	$90,000–$99,999
$20,000–$29,999	$60,000–$69,999	$100,000 and over

APPENDIX C: INTERVIEW DATA ENTRY FORM

INTERVIEW #

Household

Relationship to Informant	Age	Weekday Schedule (Work, School, Care, Activities)	Weekend Schedule
Self			

Paid Work

First Name	Job Title (if not working for pay, when last time?)	Hours per Day	Days per Week	Flexibility? Hours and Time Off	Length of Time at Job	Job and/or Schedule Change at Child's Birth?	Job and/or Schedule Change at Child's School Entrance?	Job and/or Schedule Change Plans for Future?
Informant								

Comparative Work–Family Patterns

	Work–Family Patterns
Parents	
Parents-in-Law	
Siblings	
Friends	
Neighbors	

HOUSEHOLD WORK

First Name	Child Care	Cooking	Cleaning	Laundry	Other Chores	Outside Chores
Informant						

Media Consumed by Household

First Name	Television	Radio	Newspapers	Magazines/ books	Movies/ videos	Internet
Informant						

Informant Media Questions

	Television	Radio	Papers	Magazines/ books	Movies/ videos	Internet
Regular Media						
Frequency						
Favorite Media						
Characters/Personalities Identify With?						
Work/Family Content/Messages?						
Specific Time when got Advice/ Reinforcement?						
Specific Time when disagreed or felt undermined?						
What do you think of Dr. Laura/ Dr. Joy Browne messages on work and family?						

APPENDIX D: FOCUS GROUP SCRIPT AND INTERVIEW GUIDE

Focus Group Interview Guide—Work, Family, Media

When they come in, give them the consent forms to look over and sign, the envelope with the cash, and maybe a sheet explaining the ethnography part, with a sign-up spot. Get consent forms before the group starts.

Opening Script

Hi everyone, my name is Lara and I'm the moderator for this focus group. As you know, I work for the University of Michigan. For the past two years we've been working on a project in Dexter that studies how parents decide to balance work and family, and what kind of messages they hear from the media about the best way to do that.

Some people balance work and family by having one parent stay home to care for the children, and some families have two full time working parents, and some have one part time, one full time. Some families are single-parent families. We all know that everyone is different. That's why we've invited a group of people here, so we can hear about a range of different experiences and views.

The way to do that in a focus group is to discuss your thoughts and experiences with each other. I'll give you questions to discuss, but the key thing is to discuss, not to listen to me! So most of what you'll be doing tonight is talking to each other and I'll pretty much stay out of it except to ask more questions.

170 • Appendix D

Inviting a whole group of people to talk means that we need to think about how to have a good discussion. One thing that helps is if you all respond to each other by sharing and comparing your different experiences and ideas. That's pretty easy when you all agree, but what about if you disagree? We certainly want to hear about that, but the main thing is to be polite about how you express your disagreement. Essentially we want a safe space, and a good experience here for everyone.

You already know that we plan to tape-record this so we don't have to take notes, and what that means is that it helps a lot if you only talk one at a time. And you've seen the confidentiality statement that we will only discuss results in confidential ways that use aliases, not names, etc. But the other confidentiality issue is each other, and this is a small community. So please, although we don't foresee talking about anything too sensitive, it's best if you keep things private that you feel are private, and that you respect each other's confidentiality outside of this room.

Can I answer any questions about any of that? Okay, great!

[Turn tape recorder on now]

The Focus Group

First we'd like to go around the room and just hear a little bit about you. Can you say your name and a few words about yourself? How many kids you have, their ages, what kind of work you and your husband do, including whether one of you stays home to care for your children?

Great! Thank you.

My first question is about how you made the work–family choice you did. Can you talk about that?

How do you feel about the work–family choice you made?

Great! Now let me ask about media, since that's a particular focus of our study.

Lets just start with which are your favorites programs in the media? Which characters or personalities do you like the most? Why?

Focus Group Script and Interview Guide • 171

Okay, great, now, in your favorite programs, what types of images or messages are there about work and family?

What about in other programs on television? Here we could think of fiction shows or non-fiction news-type programs.

(IF THIS HASN'T COME UP) How do these images or messages that we've been talking about make you feel? Are they helpful or undermining?

Great! Let's think about other forms of media now. What kinds of messages are out there in the radio that you listen to?

How about in the magazines that you read?

What about newspapers?

Have you ever gotten work and family input from any other type of media? Websites? Books, fiction or non-fiction? Anything else?

(IF THIS HASN'T COME UP ON ITS OWN) Supermom?

(IF THIS HASN'T COME UP ON ITS OWN) Have you ever listened to Dr. Laura or Dr. Joy Browne or a similar radio personality? What do you think of their messages about work and family? Can play Dr. Laura/Dr. Browne excerpts to get feedback.

[Turn off tape recorder.]

Concluding Script: Thank you so much for your help! I really, really appreciate it. Also, let me describe another phase of the project that we've been working on, and that we want to ask you for your help with. It was described on this sheet (discuss sheet explaining ethnography, and collect any signed ones afterward).

APPENDIX E: RESEARCH PARTICIPANTS' DEMOGRAPHIC INFORMATION

Table 1
The Male Interview Participants

Work status	Wife's work status	Number of children
Full time, plus.	Stays home, crafts for sale.	2
Full time.	Stays home.	2
Full time, plus.	Part time, some from home.	3
Full time, plus.	Part time, during school hours.	4
Full time.	Half time, during school hours.	3
Full time, about half time from home.	Full time, about half from home.	3
Half time, plus, mostly from home.	Full time.	2
Full time, telecommutes from home.	Divorced.	2

Participants' Demographic Information • 173

Table 2
The Female Interview Participants

Work status	Husband's work status	Number of children
Stays home.	Full time, plus.	2
Stays home.	Full time, plus.	2
Stays home.	Full time, plus.	2
Stays home.	Full time, plus.	3
Stays home.	Full time.	3
Stays home.	Full time.	5
Stays home. Owns a home business but very few hours.	Full time.	1
Part time, from home.	Full time.	5
Part time, much from home.	Full time.	3
Part time, some from home.	Full time, plus, but temporarily unemployed.	2
Part time, some from home.	Full time.	2
Part time to full time, mostly from home.	Full time, plus.	2
Part time to full time, mostly from home.	Full time.	2
Part time.	Full time, plus.	3
Part time.	Full time, plus.	2
Part time.	Full time.	2
Part time.	Full time.	2
Part time.	Full time.	3
Part time.	Full time.	3
Part time.	Full time.	2
Part time.	Full time.	2
Part time.	Full time.	2
Full time in school year, part time in summer, all from home.	Full time, plus, some from home.	6
Full time, some from home, some travel.	Full time, some from home.	2
Full time, some from home, some travel.	Full time.	2
Full time.	Full time.	2
Full time.	Full time.	6
Full time, plus.	Divorced.	2

174 • Appendix E

Table 3
The Male Focus Group Participants

	Work status	Wife or partner's work status	Number of children
Group 1	Stays home.	Works full time.	2
	Works part time, retired.	Retired.	2
	Works full time, from home.	Stays home.	2
	Works full time.	Stays home.	2
	Works full time.	Stays home.	1
	Works full time.	Student.	2
	Works full time.	Divorced.	2; he has >50% custody
Group 2	Not working.	Disabled.	1
	Works full time.	Stays home.	1
	Works full time.	Works part time.	4
	Works full time.	Works full time.	2; 1 does not live with him
	Works full time.	Works full time.	2
	Works full time.	Works full time.	3
	Works full time.	Works full time.	2

Participants' Demographic Information • 175

Table 4
The Female Focus Group Participants

	Work status	Husband or partner's work status	Number of children
Group 1	Stays home.	Works full time.	2
	Stays home.	Works full time.	2
	Stays home.	Works full time.	2
	Works part time.	Works full time.	2
	Works full time.	Works full time.	2
Group 2	Stays home.	Works full time, from home.	2
	Stays home.	Works full time.	2
	Stays home.	Works full time.	2
	Stays home.	Works full time.	1
	Stays home.	Works full time.	1
Group 3	Stays home.	Works full time.	1
	Stays home.	Works full time.	2
	Stays home.	Works full time.	1
	Stays home.	Works full time.	1
Group 4	Retired, works part time.	Retired, works part time.	2
	Works part time.	Works full time.	2
	Works part time.	Works full time.	2
	Works full time.	Works full time.	2
	Works full time.	Works full time.	3
Group 5	Works full time, mostly at home, but a lot of travel.	Works full time, some from home.	3
	Works nearly full time, telecommutes one day a week.	Works full time.	2
	Works full time.	Works full time.	1
	Works full time.	Works full time.	2
	Works full time.	Works full time	3
	Works full time.	Works full time.	1; 1 stepchild
	Works full time, plus.	Works full time.	2
Group 6	Works full time.	Works full time.	2; 1 stepchild
	Works full time.	Works full time.	1
	Works full time.	Works full time.	2
	Works full time.	Works full time.	1
	Works full time.	Works full time.	2
	Works full time.	Works full time.	1

176 • Appendix E

Table 5
The Ethnographic Observation Participants

Wife's work status	Husband's work status	Number of children
Stays home.	Full time.	1
Stays home.	Full time.	1
Stays home.	Full time.	2
Stays home.	Full time.	3
Stays home.	Full time, plus.	2
Part time, much of it from home.	Full time.	3
Part time, some from home.	Full time.	3
Part time.	Full time.	2
Part time.	Full time.	3
Part time.	Full time.	2
Part time.	Full time, plus.	2
Full time.	Not applicable.	2

REFERENCES

Abu-Lughod, Lila (1997) The Interpretation(s) of Culture After Television. *Representations* 59:109–134.

Agar, Michael H. (1985) *Speaking of Ethnography*. Beverly Hills, CA: Sage.

Alexander, Alison (1993) Exploring Media in Everyday Life. *Communication Monographs* 60:55–61.

Andrews, Arlene B., Irene Luckey, Errol Bolden, Judith Whiting-Fickling, and Katherine A. Lind (2004) Public Perceptions about Father Involvement: Results of a Statewide Household Survey. *Journal of Family Issues* 25:603–633.

Arendell, Teresa (2000) *Soccer Moms and the New Care Work. Center for Working Families Working Paper* No. 16. Berkeley, CA: University of California Press.

Axinn, William, and Arland Thornton (2000) The Transformation in the Meaning of Marriage. In Linda Waite, Christine Bachrach, Michelle Hindin, Elizabeth Thomson, and Arland Thornton (Eds.), *Ties That Bind: Perspectives on Marriage and Cohabitation* (pp. 147–165). New York: Aldine de Gruyter.

Bandura, Albert (1977) *Social Learning Theory*. Englewood Cliffs, NJ: Prentice Hall.

Becker, Penny Edgell, and Phyllis Moen (1999) Scaling Back: Dual-Career Couples Work-Family Strategies. *Journal of Marriage and the Family* 61(4):995–1007.

Blodgett, Harriet (1990) Not Such a Long Way, Baby: Women and Televised Myth. In Katherine Usher Henderson and Joseph Anthony Mazzeo (Eds.), *Meanings of the Medium: Perspectives on the Art of Television* (pp. 57–77). New York: Praeger Publishers.

Buunk, Abraham P., and Frederick X. Gibbons (2007) Social Comparison: The End of a Theory and the Emergence of a Field. *Organizational Behavior and Human Decision Processes* 102(2007):3–21.

178 · References

Caplan, Pat (1993) Learning Gender: Fieldwork in a Tanzanian Coastal Village, 1965–85. In Diane Bell, Pat Caplan, and Wazir J. Karim (Eds.), *Gendered Fields: Women, Men, and Ethnography* (pp. 168–181). New York: Routledge.

Casper, Lynne M., and Suzanne M. Bianchi (2002) *Continuity and Change in the American Family.* Thousand Oaks, CA: Sage Publications.

Chambers, Deborah (2001) *Representing the Family.* Thousand Oaks, CA: Sage Publications.

Chatzky, Jean Sherman (2000) Working at Home: Can It Work for You? *USA Weekend,* August 25–31.

Chira, Susan (1998) *A Mother's Place: Taking the Debate About Working Mothers Beyond Guilt and Blame.* New York: HarperCollins Publishers.

Coltrane, Scott (1989) Household Labor and The Routine Production of Gender. *Social Problems* 36(5):473–490.

Coltrane, Scott (1996) *Family Man: Fatherhood, Housework, and Gender Equality.* New York: Oxford University Press.

Coltrane, Scott (2000) *Gender and Families.* Walnut Creek, CA: Altamira.

Conant, Jennet (1994) Family First: Tipper Gore Gave Up a Career to Support Her Husband, Al, and Their Four Children, but She Has No Regrets. *Redbook* 182(5):80.

Consumer Reports (2005) Bringing Up Baby on a Budget. *Consumer Reports,* June. http://www.consumerreports.org/cro/babies-kids/the-cost-of-raising-a-baby-605/overview/index.htm.

Coontz, Stephanie (1992) *The Way We Never Were: American Families and the Nostalgia Trap.* New York: Basic Books.

Cornfield, Daniel B., and Bill Fletcher (2001) The U.S. Labor Movement: Toward a Sociology of Labor Revitalization. In Ivar Berg and Arne L. Kalleberg (Eds.) *Sourcebook of Labor Markets: Evolving Structures and Processes* (pp. 61–82). New York: Kluwer Academic/Plenum Publishers.

Crary, David (2007) Marital Priorities Change. *Hartford Courant.* July 1, 2007, A2.

Darrah, Charles, James Freeman, and Jan English-Lueck (2007) *Busier than Ever!: Why American Families Can't Slow Down.* Stanford: Stanford University Press.

DeNavas-Walt, Carmen, Bernadette D. Proctor, and Cherry Hill Lee (2006) *Income, Poverty, and Health Insurance Coverage in the United States: 2005.* U.S. Census Bureau. Current Population Reports, Consumer Income. http://www.census.gov/prod/2006pubs/p60-231.pdf

Descartes, Lara (2007) Rewards and Challenges of Using Ethnography in Family Research. *Family and Consumer Science Research Journal* 36(1):22–39.

Descartes, Lara, and Conrad P. Kottak (2008) "Patrolling the Boundaries of Childhood in Middle Class 'Suburbia'." In Elizabeth Rudd and Lara Descartes (Eds.), *The Changing Landscape of Work and Family in the American Middle Class: Reports from the Field* (pp. 141–155). Lanham, MD: Rowman & Littlefield.

References • 179

Descartes, Lara, Conrad P. Kottak, and Autumn Kelly (2007) Chauffeuring and Commuting: A Story of Work, Family, Class, and Community. *Community, Work, and Family* 10(2):161–178.

Deutsch, Francine (1999) *Halving it All: How Equally Shared Parenting Works.* Cambridge, MA: Harvard University Press.

DeVault, Marjorie (1991) *Feeding the Family: The Social Organization of Caring as Gendered Work.* Chicago, IL: University of Chicago Press.

di Leonardo, Micaela (1987) The Female World of Cards and Holidays: Women, Families, and the Work of Kinship. *Signs: Journal of Women in Culture and Society* 12(3):440–453.

Douglas, Susan J., and Meredith W. Michaels (2004) *The Mommy Myth: The Idealization of Motherhood and How it has Undermined Women.* New York: Free Press.

Douglas, William and Beth Olson (1995) Beyond Family Structure: The Family in Domestic Comedy. *Journal of Broadcasting and Electronic Media* 39(2):236–261.

Dube, Arindrajit (2006) *Where Have all the Wages Gone? Jobs and Wages in 2006.* UC Berkeley Labor Center Policy Brief. Berkeley, CA: UC Berkeley Labor Center.

Elasmar, Michael, Kazumi Hasegawa, and Mary Brain (1999) The Portrayal of Women in U.S. Prime Time Television. *Journal of Broadcasting and Electronic Media* 43(1):20–35.

Festinger, Leon (1954) A Theory of Social Comparison Processes. *Human Relations* 1:117–140.

Fields, Jason M., and Lynne M. Casper (2001) America's Families and Living Arrangements: Population Characteristics, 2000. U.S. Census Bureau. *Current Population Reports*, P20–537, June 2001. http://www.census.gov/prod/2001pubs/p20-537.pdf.

Fischbach, Dirk (2000) Editorial. *Dexter Leader.* January 20.

Fiske, John (1989) *Understanding Popular Culture.* London: Routledge.

Fouad, Nadya and Howard E. A. Tinsley (1997) Wor–Family Balance. *Journal of Vocational Behavior* 50(2):141–144.

Francese, Peter (1995) America at Mid-Decade. *American Demographics* 17(2):23–31.

Fuchs Epstein, Cynthia, Carroll Seron, Bonnie Oglensky, and Robert Sauté (1999) *The Part-Time Paradox: Time Norms, Professional Lives, Family and Gender.* New York: Routledge.

Garey, Anita Ilta (1999) *Weaving Work and Motherhood.* Philadelphia: Temple University.

Gerbner, George, and Larry Gross (1976) Living With Television: The Violence Profile. *Journal of Communication* 26:173–199.

Gerson, Kathleen (1991) Coping with Commitment: Dilemmas and Conflicts of Family Life. In Alan Wolfe (Ed.), *America at Century's End* (pp. 36–58). Berkeley, CA: University of California Press. http://www.escholarship.org/editions/view?docId=ft158004pr&chunk.id=nsd0e745&toc.id=d0e11176&brand=eschol

180 • References

Gibbons, Frederick X., and Meg Gerrard (1997) Health Images and their Effect on Health Behavior. In Bram P. Buunk and Frederick X. Gibbons (Eds.), *Health, Coping and Well-being: Perspectives from Social Comparison Theory* (pp. 63–94). Mahwah, NJ: L. Erlbaum Associates.

Gifford, Susan K. (2001) You Can Have a 50/50 Marriage! *Redbook* 196(3):116.

Gillespie, Marie (1995) *Television, Ethnicity, and Cultural Change*. London: Routledge.

Ginsburg, Faye (1994) Culture/Media: A (Mild) Polemic. *Anthropology Today* 10(2):5–15.

Goad, Kimberly (2001) How I Work at Home and Make $50,000+. *Redbook* 196(3):86.

Gornick, Janet C., Alexandra Heron, and Ross Eisenbrey (2007) The Work–Family Balance: An Analysis of European, Japanese, and U.S. Work-Time Policies. *Economic Policy Institute Briefing Paper* #189. May 24, 2007 Washington, D.C.

Grote, Nancy K., Kristen E. Naylor, and Margaret S. Clark (2002) Perceiving the Division of Family Work to be Unfair: Do Social Comparisons, Enjoyment, and Competence Matter? *Journal of Family Psychology* 16(4):510–522.

Hakmiller, Karl L. (1966) Threat as a Determinant of Downward Comparison. *Journal of Experimental Social Psychology* (Suppl. 1):32–39.

Hamilton, Brady E., and Stephanie J. Ventura (2006) Fertility and Abortion Rates in the United States, 1960–2002. *International Journal of Andrology* 29:34–45.

Hansen, Karen (2005) *Not-So-Nuclear Families: Class, Gender, and Networks of Care*. Piscataway, NJ: Rutgers University Press.

Hartmann, Heidi, Ariane Hegewisch, and Vicky Lovell (2007) *An Economy that Puts Families First: Expanding the Social Contract to Include Family Care*. EPI Briefing Paper. Washington D.C.: Economic Policy Institute.

Hays, Sharon (1996) *The Cultural Contradictions of Motherhood*. New Haven, CT: Yale University Press.

Heintz, Katharine E. (1992) Children's Favorite Television Families: A Descriptive Analysis of Role Interactions. *Journal of Broadcasting and Electronic Media* 36(4):443–451.

Himmelstein, Hal (1984) *Television Myth and the American Mind*. New York: Praeger Publishers.

Hochschild, Arlie (1997) *The Time Bind: When Work Becomes Home and Home Becomes Work*. New York: Henry Holt and Company.

Hochschild, Arlie (1989) *The Second Shift*. New York: Avon Books.

Hodges, Michael H. (2000) The Family Juggling Act: As School Gets Under Way, Many Students Are Stretched Thin and Family Time Takes a Hit. *Detroit News*, September 4.

Holcomb, Betty (1998) Work at Home: How to Make the Dream Happen. *Redbook* 192(2):124.

Hoover, Stewart M. (2001) Visual Religion in Media Culture. In David Morgan and Sally M. Promey (Eds.), *The Visual Culture of American Religions* (pp. 146–159). Berkeley, CA: University of California Press.

Hoover, Stewart M., Lynn Schofield Clark, and Diane F. Alters (2004) *Media, Home, and Family*. New York: Routledge.

Houseman, Susan N. (2001) Why Employers Use Flexible Staffing Arrangements: Evidence from an Establishment Survey. *Industrial and Labor Relations Review* 55(1):149–170.

Hoyt, Carolyn (2000) When Wives Earn More: He Works. She Works. But Her Paycheck's Bigger. How Much Does it Stress Their Relationship? Four Couples Confess. *McCall's*, January.

Hubbert, Wendy, and David Hubbert (2000) The Dirty Work. *Redbook* 194(5):104.

Ignatius, David (2007) Summer's Escape Artists. *Washington Post*. Thursday July 26, A21.

Itzkoff, Dave (2007) A Brave New World for TV? Virtually. *New York Times*, June 24, 2007. Accessed June 24, 2007 from http://www.nytimes.com/2007/06/24/arts/television/24itzk.html?th&emc=th

Jacobs, Jerry A. and Kathleen Gerson (2004) *The Time Divide: Work, Family, and Gender Inequality*. Cambridge, MA: Harvard University Press.

Kalleberg, Arne L., Barbara F. Reskin, and Ken Hudson (2000) Bad Jobs in America: Standard and Nonstandard Employment Relations and Job Quality in the United States. *American Sociological Review* 65(2):256–278.

Kalleberg, Arne L., Jeremy Reynolds, and Peter V. Marsden (2003) Externalizing Employment: Flexible Staffing Arrangements in US Organizations. *Social Science Research* 32(4):525–552.

Keller, Kathryn (1992) Nurture and Work in the Middle Class—Imagery from Women's Magazines. *International Journal of Politics, Culture, and Society* 5(4):577–600.

Kendall, Diana (2005) *Framing Class: Media Representations of Wealth and Poverty in America*. New York: Rowman and Littlefield.

Kitzinger, Jenny (1995) The Face of AIDS. In Ivana Marcova and Robert Farr (Eds.), *Representations of Health and Illness*. Amsterdam: Harwood Academic Publishers.

Kottak, Conrad P. (1982) Anthropological Analysis of Mass Enculturation. In Conrad P. Kottak (Ed.), *Researching American Culture: A Guide for Student Anthropologists* (pp. 40–74). Ann Arbor, MI: University of Michigan Press.

Kottak, Conrad P. (1990) *Prime-Time Society: An Anthropological Analysis of Television and Culture*. Belmont, CA: Wadsworth Publishing Company.

Kottak, Conrad P. (2004) *Mirror for Humanity: A Concise Introduction to Cultural Anthropology*. Boston: McGraw-Hill.

Kottak, Conrad P. (2008) *Cultural Anthropology*. 12th ed. Boston: McGraw-Hill.

Kottak, Conrad P., and Kathryn A. Kozaitis (2008) *On Being Different: Diversity and Multiculturalism in the North American Mainstream*. 3rd ed. Boston: McGraw-Hill.

182 • References

Kubey, Robert and Mihály Csikszentmihályi (1990) *Television and the Quality of Life: How Viewing Shapes Everyday Experience*. Hillside, NJ: Lawrence Erlbaum.

Ladies' Home Journal (2000) My Balanced Life: *Career Switch*. January.

Landry, Bart (2000) *Black Working Wives: Pioneers of the American Family Revolution*. Berkeley, CA: University of California Press.

Lareau, Annette (2003) *Unequal Childhoods: Class, Race, and Family Life*. Berkeley, CA: University of California Press.

Larmoyeux, Mary, and Ethan Pope (2001) *There's No Place Like Home: Steps to Becoming a Stay-at-Home Mom*. Nashville, TN: Broadman and Holman Publishers.

Lee, Raymond L. M., and Susan E. Ackerman (1994) Farewell to Ethnography? Global Embourgeoisement and the Disprivileging of the Narrative. *Critique of Anthropology* 14:339–354.

Lester, Bijou Yang (1996) Part-time Employment of Married Women in the U.S.A. *American Journal of Economics and Sociology* 55:61–72.

Levine, James A. (1999) The Other Working Parent. *New York Times*, March 4.

Lipsitz, George (1990) *Time Passages: Collective Memory and American Popular Culture*. Minneapolis, MN: University of Minneapolis Press.

Makarushka, Irena S. (1995) Family Pictures. In William Doty (Ed.), *Picturing Cultural Values in Postmodern America* (pp. 140–157). Tuscaloosa, AL: University of Alabama Press.

Margolis, Maxine L. (1984) *Mothers And Such: Views of American Women and Why They Changed*. Berkeley, CA: University of California Press.

Marin, Rick (2000) Dads in Charge: At-Home Fathers Step Out to Find They Are Not Alone. *Ann Arbor News*, February 1. Reprinted from *New York Times*.

Marlino, Deborah, and Fiona Wilson (2003) *Teen Girls on Business: Are They Being Empowered?* Full Report. Simmons School of Management and The Committee of 200. Boston and Chicago.

McMahon, Martha (1995) *Engendering Motherhood: Identity and Self-Transformation in Women's Lives*. New York: The Guilford Press.

Milgrom, Melissa (2000) The Balancing Act: Real-Life Survival Tactics for Working Mothers That Are Guaranteed to Inspire. *Real You*, Spring.

Miller, Leslie (2000) The Babysitter Club: Massachusetts Lieutenant Governor Under Fire for Using State Resources to Help Care for Child. *Ann Arbor News*, January 14.

Minton, Torri (2002) No Time for Errands? Rent a Wife. *San Francisco Chronicle*, February 10.

Moores, Shaun (1993) *Interpreting Audiences: The Ethnography of Media Consumption*. London: Sage Publications.

Moran-Ellis, Jo, Victoria D. Alexander, Ann Cronin, Mary Dickinson, Jane Fielding, Judith Sleney, and Hilary Thomas (2006) Triangulation and Integration: Processes, Claims and Implications. *Qualitative Research* 6:45–59.

Morley, David (1986) *Family Television: Cultural Power and Domestic Leisure.* New York: Routledge.

Murphy, Patrick D. (1999) Media Cultural Studies' Uncomfortable Embrace of Ethnography. *Journal of Communication Inquiry* 23(3):205–221.

Mussweiler, Thomas, Shira Gabriel, and Galen V. Bodenhausen (2000) Shifting Social Identities as a Strategy for Deflecting Threatening Social Comparisons. *Journal of Personality and Social Psychology* 79(3):398–409.

Newitz, Annalee (1998) *ER*, Professionals, and the Work–Family Disaster. *American Studies* 39(2):93–105.

Newman, Katherine S. (1993) *Declining Fortunes: The Withering of the American Dream.* New York: Basic Books.

Nielsen Media Research (2000) Report on Television. New York: Nielsen Media Research.

Nielsen Media Research (2001) *Television Audience 2001.* New York: Nielsen Media Research.

Nippert-Eng, Christena E. (1996) *Home and Work: Negotiating Boundaries Through Everyday Life.* Chicago: University of Chicago Press.

O'Crowley, Peggy (2002) Career Mothers: Trend of Mothers Going Back to Work After Having Baby Has Reversed. *Ann Arbor News*, April 30.

Papper, Robert A., Michael E. Holmes, and Mark N. Popovich (2004) Middletown Media Studies. *International Digital Media and Arts Association Journal.* 1(1):4–56.

Parsons, Talcott, and Robert F. Bales (1955) *Family, Socialization, and Interaction Process.* New York: Free Press.

Paul, Pamela (2001) The New Nesters. *Redbook* 196(2):104.

Pew Research Center (2007a) As Marriage and Parenthood Drift Apart, Public Is Concerned about Social Impact. Downloaded July 1, 2007 from http://pewresearch.org/pubs/526/marriage-parenthood

Pew Research Center (2007b) Fewer Mothers Prefer Full-Time Work. Downloaded July 13, 2007 from http://pewresearch.org/pubs/536/working-women.

Potuchek, Jean L. (1997) *Who Supports the Family? Gender and Breadwinning in Dual-Earner Marriages.* Stanford, CA: Stanford University Press.

Randolph, Laura B. (1998) Superwomen: How They Manage to (Almost) Do It All. *Ebony* 53(6):60.

Reskin, Barbara F., and Irene Padavic (1994) *Women and Men at Work.* Thousand Oaks, CA: Pine Forge.

Ribbens, Jane (1994) *Mothers and Their Children: A Feminist Sociology of Childrearing.* London: Sage Publications.

Roach, Mary (2000) He Came. He Saw. He Cleaned. *Redbook* 194(5):134.

Roberts, Sam (2007) 51% of Women Are Now living without a Spouse. *New York Times*, January 16. http://select.nytimes.com/search/restricted/article?res=F50B11F83B540C758DDDA80894DF404482.

184 · References

Roberts, Cokie, and Steve Roberts (2000) Parents Need Help Fighting for Time. *Detroit News*, September 27.

Rose, Stephen J., and Heidi I. Hartmann (2004) *Still a Man's Labor Market: The Long-Term Earnings Gap*. Report C355, Institute for Women's Policy Research. Washington, D.C.

Rubin, Courtney (2000) The New Domestic Gods: 2 Million U.S. Dads Now Stay Home with the Kids. *USA Weekend*, August 25–27.

Rudd, Elizabeth (2004) Family Leave: A Policy Concept Made in America. In Marcia Pitt-Catsouphes and Ellen Kossek (Eds.), *Work-Family Encyclopedia*. Chestnut Hill, MA: Sloan Work and Family Research Network at Boston College.

Rudd, Elizabeth, and Lara Descartes (Eds.) (2008) *The Changing Landscape of Work and Family in the American Middle Class: Reports from the Field*. Lanham, MD: Rowman and Littlefield.

Sado, Stephanie, and Angela Bayer (2001) Executive Summary: The Changing American Family. Population Resource Center. http://www.prcdc.org/summaries/family/family.html. Accessed June 18, 2007.

Savacool, Julia A. (2000) Becoming "Mommy" Again. *Child*, March.

Schlessinger, Laura (2000) *Parenthood by Proxy: Don't Have Them If You Won't Raise Them*. New York: HarperCollins.

Schor, Juliet B. (1998) *The Overspent American: Upscaling, Downshifting, and the New Consumer*. New York: Basic Books.

Seiter, Ellen (1999) *Television and New Media Audiences*. Oxford, UK: Oxford University Press.

Seymour, Lesley Jane (1999) This Photo Is a Lie. *Redbook* 192(3):8.

Shellenbarger, Sue (1999) Sizing Up Employers—What Job Candidates Really Want to Know: Will I Have a Life? *Ann Arbor News*, January 4.

Shelton, Beth Anne (1990) The Distribution of Household Tasks: Does Wife's Employment Status Make A Difference? *Journal of Family Issues* 11(2):115–135.

Shrum, L. J., Robert S. Wyer, and Thomas C. O'Guinn (1998) The Effects of Television Consumption on Social Perceptions: The Use of Priming Procedures to Investigate Psychological Processes. *Journal of Consumer Research* 24 (4):447–458.

Signorielli, Nancy (1999) Recognition and Respect: A Content Analysis of Prime-Time Television Characters Across Three Decades. *Sex Roles: A Journal of Research* 40(7–8):527–544.

Signorielli, Nancy, and Susan Kahlenberg (2001) Television's World of Work in the Nineties. *Journal of Broadcast and Electronic Media* 45(1):4–22.

Silberstein, Lisa R. (1992) *Dual-Career Marriage: A System in Transition*. Hillsdale, NJ: Lawrence Erlbaum.

Skill, Thomas, and James D. Robinson (1994) Four Decades of Families on Television: A Demographic Profile, 1950–1989. *Journal of Broadcasting and Electronic Media* 38(4):449–465.

Skill, Thomas, and Sam Wallace (1990) Family Interactions on Prime-Time

References • **185**

Television: A Descriptive Analysis of Assertive Power Interactions. *Journal of Broadcasting and Electronic Media* 34(3):243–262.

Smith, Joan (2000) Why You *Don't* Need a Balanced Life. *Redbook* 194(5):96.

Stacey, Judith (1990) *Brave New Families: Stories of Domestic Upheaval in Late Twentieth Century America*. New York: Basic Books.

Stacey, Judith (1996) *In the Name of the Family: Rethinking Family Values in the Postmodern Age*. Boston: Beacon Press.

Stier, Haya, and Noah Lewin-Epstein (2000) Women's Part-Time Employment and Gender Inequality in the Family. *Journal of Family Issues* 21(3):390–410.

Strobel, Frederick R. (1993) *Upward Dreams, Downward Mobility: The Economic Decline of the American Middle Class*. Lanham, MD: Rowman and Littlefield Publishers.

Taflinger, Richard F. (1996) Sitcom: What it Is, How it Works, A History of Comedy on Television: 1970–1992. www.wsu.edu:8080/~taflinge/comhist2.html

Tawa, Renee (1999) Identity Issues Haunt House-Husbandhood. *Ann Arbor News*, December 7. Reprinted from *Los Angeles Times*.

Tiedge, James T., Arthur Silverblatt, Michael J. Havice and Richard Rosenfeld (1991) Discrepancy Between Perceived First-Person and Perceived Third-Person Mass Media Effects. *Journalism Quarterly* 68:141–154.

Tittle, Carol Kehr (1981) *Careers and Family: Sex Roles and Adolescent Life Plans*. Beverly Hills, CA: Sage Publications.

Townsend, Nicholas W. (2002) *The Package Deal: Marriage, Work and Fatherhood in Men's Lives*. Philadelphia: Temple University Press.

U.S. Census Bureau (n.d.) Households, Persons Per Household, and Family Households, 1990. Retrieved December 27, 2007 from http://quickfacts.census.gov/qfd/meta/long_58580.htm

U.S. Census Bureau (1990a) General population and housing characteristics: Dexter village, Michigan. Retrieved February, 20 2006 from http://factfinder.census.gov/servlet/QTTable?_bm=y&-context=qt&-qr_name=DEC_1990_STF1_DP1&-ds_name=DEC_1990_STF1_&-CONTEXT=qt&-tree_id=100&-all_geo_types=N&-redoLog=true&-geo_id=label&-geo_id=16000US260695&-search_results=16000US260695&-format=&-_lang=en

U.S. Census Bureau (1990b) General population and housing characteristics: Dexter township, Michigan. Retrieved February, 20 2006 from http://factfinder.census.gov/servlet/QTTable?_bm=y&-context=qt&-qr_name=DEC_1990_STF1_DP1&-ds_name=DEC_1990_STF1_&-CONTEXT=qt&-tree_id=100&-keyword=dexter%20township,%20MI&-all_geo_types=N&-redoLog=true&-geo_id=06000US26161025&-search_results=16000US260695&-format=&-_lang=en

U.S. Census Bureau (2000a) Travel time to work for workers 16 years and over: Dexter township and village, Michigan. Retrieved January 16, 2007 from http://factfinder.census.gov/servlet/DTTable?_bm=y&-context=dt&-

186 • References

ds_name=DEC_2000_SF3_U&-mt_name=DEC_2000_SF3_U_P031&-CONTEXT=dt&-tree_id=403&-all_geo_types=N&-geo_id=06000US2616122180&-geo_id=16000US2622160&-search_results=16000US2622160&-format=&-_lang=en

U.S. Census Bureau (2000b) Profile of general demographic characteristics. Dexter village, Michigan. Retrieved February 20, 2006 from http://factfinder.census.gov/servlet/QTTable?_bm=y&-context=qt&-qr_name=DEC_2000_SF1_U_DP1&-ds_name=DEC_2000_SF1_U&-CONTEXT=qt&-tree_id=100&-redoLog=false&-all_geo_types=N&-geo_id=16000US2622160&-search_results=16000US260695&-_sse=on&-format=&-_lang=en

U.S. Census Bureau (2000c) Profile of general demographic characteristics. Dexter township, Michigan. Retrieved February 20, 2006 from http://factfinder.census.gov/servlet/QTTable?_bm=y&-context=qt&-qr_name=DEC_2000_SF1_U_DP1&-ds_name=DEC_2000_SF1_U&-CONTEXT=qt&-tree_id=100&-redoLog=false&-all_geo_types=N&-geo_id=06000US2616122180&-search_results=16000US260695&-_sse=on&-format=&-_lang=en

U.S. Census Bureau (2000d) Profile of general demographic characteristics. United States. Retrieved February 13, 2007 from http://factfinder.census-.gov/servlet/QTTable?_bm=y&-context=qt&-qr_name=DEC_2000_SF1_U_DP1&-ds_name=DEC_2000_SF1_U&-CONTEXT=qt&-tree_id=100&-all_geo_types=N&-redoLog=false&-_caller=geoselect&-geo_id=01000US&-search_results=16000US260695&-format=&-_lang=en

U.S. Census Bureau (2000e) Age of own children under 18 years in families by living arrangements by employment status of parents. Dexter township and village, Michigan. Retrieved February 13, 2007 from http://factfinder.census.gov/servlet/DTTable?_bm=y&-state=dt&-context=dt&-ds_name=DEC_2000_SF3_U&-mt_name=DEC_2000_SF3_U_P046&-CONTEXT=dt&-tree_id=403&-keyword=dexter%20township&-redoLog=false&-all_geo_types=N&-geo_id=06000US2616122180&-geo_id=16000US2622160&-search_results=04000US26&-format=&-_lang=en

U.S. Census Bureau (2000f) Age of own children under 18 years in families by living arrangements by employment status of parents. United States. Retrieved February 13, 2007 from http://factfinder.census.gov/servlet/DTTable?_bm=y&-state=dt&-context=dt&-ds_name=DEC_2000_SF3_U&-mt_name=DEC_2000_SF3_U_P046&-CONTEXT=dt&-tree_id=403&-keyword=dexter%20township&-redoLog=false&-all_geo_types=N&-_caller=geoselect&-geo_id=01000US&-search_results=04000US26&-format=&-_lang=en

U.S. Census Bureau (2000g) Sex by work status in 1999 by usual hours worked per week in 1999 by weeks worked in 1999 for the population 16 years and over. Dexter township and village, Michigan. Retrieved February 20,

2006 from http://factfinder.census.gov/servlet/DTTable?_bm=y&-state=dt&-context=dt&-ds_name=DEC_2000_SF3_U&-mt_name=DEC_2000_SF3_U_P047&-CONTEXT=dt&-tree_id=403&-keyword=dexter%20township&-all_geo_types=N&-geo_id=06000US2616122180&-geo_id=16000US2622160&-search_results=04000US26&-format=&-_lang=en

U.S. Census Bureau (2000h) Sex by work status in 1999 by usual hours worked per week in 1999 by weeks worked in 1999 for the population 16 years and over. United States. Retrieved February, 20 2006 from http://factfinder.census.gov/servlet/DTTable?_bm=y&-geo_id=01000US&-ds_name=DEC_2000_SF3_U&-_lang=en&-redoLog=false&-mt_name=DEC_2000_SF3_U_P047&-format=&-CONTEXT=dt

U.S. Census Bureau (2000i) Profile of Selected Economic Characteristics. United States. Retrieved January 20, 2007 from http://factfinder.census-.gov/servlet/QTTable?_bm=y&-context=qt&-qr_name=DEC_2000_SF3_U_DP3&-ds_name=DEC_2000_SF3_U&-tree_id=403&-redoLog=true&-all_geo_types=N&-_caller=geoselect&-geo_id=01000US&-search_results=06000US2616122180&-format=&-_lang=en

U.S. Census Bureau (2000j) Profile of Selected Economic Characteristics. Dexter township and village, Michigan. Retrieved January 20, 2007 from http://factfinder.census.gov/servlet/QTTable?_bm=y&-context=qt&-qr_name=DEC_2000_SF3_U_DP3&-ds_name=DEC_2000_SF3_U&-tree_id=403&-redoLog=true&-all_geo_types=N&-_caller=geoselect&-geo_id=06000US2616122180&-geo_id=16000US2622160&-search_results=16000US2622160&-format=&-_lang=en

U.S. Census (2006) 2006 American Community Survey Data Profile Highlights: Washtenaw County. Accessed December 27, 2007 from http://factfinder.census.gov/servlet/ACSSAFFFacts?_event=&geo_id=05000US26161&_geoContext=01000US%7C04000US26%7C05000US26161&_street=&_county=washtenaw&_cityTown=washtenaw&_state=04000US26&_zip=&_lang=en&_sse=on&ActiveGeoDiv=geoSelect&_useEV=&pctxt=fph&pgsl=050&_submenuId=factsheet_1&ds_name=DEC_2000_SAFF&_ci_nbr=002&qr_name=DEC_2000_SAFF_R1050&reg=DEC_2000_SAFF_R1050%3A002&_keyword=&_industry=

U.S. Department of Labor (2004) Time Use Survey. Accessed January 17, 2008 from http://www.bls.gov/tus/home.htm

Upton, Rebecca (in press). *The Next One Changes Everything.* Ann Arbor, MI: University of Michigan Press.

USA Weekend (2000) "Webcams" at Day Care Let Mom and Dad Check in Any Time. January 21–23.

Van Buren, Abigail (2000) Daily Column. *Ann Arbor News*, January 11.

Vande Berg, Leah R. and Diane Streckfuss (1992) Prime-Time Television's

188 · References

Portrayal of Women and the World of Work: A Demographic Profile. *Journal of Broadcasting and Electronic Media* 36(2):183–194.

Walzer, Susan (1998) *Thinking About the Baby: Gender and Transitions into Parenthood.* Philadelphia, PA: Temple University Press.

Warren, Elizabeth, and Amelia Warren Tyagi (2003) *The Two-Income Trap: Why Middle-Class Mothers and Fathers are Going Broke.* New York: Basic Books.

Watson, Joanne (2001) *Team Work: How to Help Your Husband Make More Money, So You Can Be a Stay-at-Home Mom.* Glendale, CA: Family Books.

Weston, Liz Pulliam (2006) Is Your Degree Worth $1 Million, or Worthless. *MSN Money.* http://articles.moneycentral.msn.com/CollegeAndFamily/SavingForCollege/IsYourDegreeWorth1million.aspx?page=all

Williams, Joan (2000) *Unbending Gender: Why Family and Work Conflict and What to Do About It.* Oxford: Oxford University Press.

Wisensale, Steven K. (2001) *Family Leave Policy: The Political Economy of Work and Family in America.* Armonk, NY: M. E. Sharpe.

Wolf, Jeanne (2000) Jamie Lee Lets Go. *Redbook* 195(5):126.

Yellowpages.com (n.d.) Churches and Religious Organizations, Dexter, MI. Accessed on January 17, 2007 from http://www.switchboard.com/bin/cgidir.dll?PR=120&MEM=1&ST=1&C=Churches&C2=church&CID=36&T=Dexter&S=MI&HA=1&LNK=54:4&SO=2

zap2it.com (2007) http://www.zap2it.com/tv/ratings/ Retrieved June 24, 2007.

INDEX

This index, following the text, uses 'working' mothers as a convenient shorthand meaning mothers who work for pay as well as inside the home. It is not intended to imply that stay-at-home mothers do not work.

1950s model of family life, 14, 40, 41–3, 51, 55–7, 154
1980s, as golden decade of the 'TV family', 42

A

about, discourses about the media, 9, 71–3
Abu-Lughod, L., 5–6
Ackerman, S., 33
advertisements: consumption stimulation industry, 151; idealized home life portrayals, 72; not showing working mothers, 113, 140; women portrayed in, 110, 113, 140; work and family portrayed as opposing forces, 51–2
African American families, 52, 156–7
after-school activities, 88–9
Agar, M., 5
Alexander, A., 5
Alters, D., 6, 18, 66, 67
Andrews, A., 37
Arendell, T., 37
Arthur, 60, 69, 112, 123, 130
autonomy in the workplace, 87
Axinn, W., 13

B

Bandura, A., 8
Bayer, A., 12
Becker, P., 14
beliefs, selecting media to reinforce, 8–9, 134, 136
Bianchi, S., 11
Blodgett, H., 45
Bolden, E., 37
books: about staying at home, 54; child care/ parenting manuals, 66, 123–4, 149; consumption by Dexter residents, 60; gender differences in choosing, 66; reading with children, 61
boundaries, 153; 'Julie' case study, 135–6
Brady Bunch, The, 83, 111, 154–5
Brain, M., 45
Browne, Dr. Joy, 121, 163
Buunk, A., 17

C

Caplan, P., 35
case studies, 127–45
Casper, L., 11, 12, 13
celebrities: celebrity magazines'

190 · Index

portrayal of motherhood, 51; social comparison, 154; and the 'supermom' image, 116
Center for the Ethnography of Everyday Life (CEEL), 4, 27
Chambers, D., 44
child care, 94–9; *see also* day care
child care manuals, 66, 123–4, 149
children, endangered by work/ family choices, 48–51, 147, 149–50
children's media: as babysitter, 58, 70, 143; concerns over 'too much', 70, 136; monitoring use of, 63–5, 136; parents' consumption of, 61
Chira, S., 16, 45, 49
Christian media, 61–2, 74–5, 131
Clark, L., 6
Clark, M., 15, 18, 66, 67
Coltrane, S., 15, 45, 91, 92
commercials: *see* advertisements
common ground (social function of media), 3–5, 8, 9, 66–7, 154–5
commuting, 22, 156
competitive consumption, 98–9, 151
Conant, J., 51
connection to wider world (social function of media), 3–4, 8, 144–5, 151–3
consumption of media: admitting own use, 73–5; children's use, 64–5, 70, 136; demonization of media, 8, 10; denial of media influence, 68–71, 147–8, 154; in Dexter, 58–77; influence on work/family choices, 78–106, 155–7; justifications of media consumption, 69–70; stigmatization of excessive media use, 7–8, 76–7
Coontz, S., 44, 146
'Corinth' case study, 142–4
Cornfield, D., 10
Cosby Show, The, 42, 60, 114, 156
Crary, D., 15
Csikszentmihályi, M., 8

D

Daddio, 55, 109
Darrah, C., 6
day care, 49, 96–9, 114
daytime TV, 69–70

Dear Abby, 50, 74
demonization of media, 8, 10
DeNavas-Walt, C., 11
denial of media influence, 68–71, 147–8, 154
Descartes. L., 4, 6, 12, 25, 26; as ethnographic researcher, 33–8
Dexter: demographic tables, 159–61; description of town, 20–6
di Leonardo, M., 14
diversity, 4, 153, 156–7
divorce, 13
Dobson, James, 13, 62, 74
'domestic dunces', men as (stereotype), 45, 54–6, 109–10, 136
Douglas, S., 7, 41–2, 44, 46
downward social comparison, 17, 102–3, 149–50
Dr. Laura (Schlessinger): as common ground, 117–21; endangered children/ anti-daycare, 3, 49–50; integrated data, 30–1; parents' use of her messages, 9, 72, 74–5, 98, 107–8, 133, 136
dual earner households, 11, 14, 25–6, 80–3
Dube, A., 11
dysfunctional families, on TV, 43

E

earnings, average, 86
Elasmar, M., 45
employed mothers: *see* working mothers
endangered children, 48–51, 147, 149–50
English-Lueck, J., 6
entertainment, media as, 68, 69, 138
equipment, placement of, 62–3
ER, 40, 42, 46–7, 49, 125–6
escapism, 75–6, 153
ethnography: generally, 5–7; ethnographic observation (research method), 28–9, 32, 33–8
Everybody Loves Raymond, 7, 43, 47–8, 111
exposure to media, concerns over effects: admitting own use, 73–5; children's use, 64–5, 70, 136; demonization of media, 8, 10; denial of media influence, 68–71, 147–8, 154;

Index · **191**

justifications of media consumption, 69–70; stigmatization of excessive media use, 7–8, 76–7

extended families, 44–5

extracurricular activities, mother's presence at, 88–9

F

faith-centered activities, media exposure via, 61–2, 74–5, 131

families: 1950s model, 14, 40, 41–3, 51, 55–7, 154; extended families, 44–5; family composition, 12–13, 25; family size, 12; portrayal in TV shows, 43–6

Father Knows Best, 1–2, 39, 41

fathers: and flexible working/ caring responsibilities, 87; as media 'exposers' for children, 63–4, 153; portrayed as incompetent, 45, 54–6, 109–10, 136; single fathers, 45; stay-at-home fathers, 55, 89–91, 136–9; superman/ superdad image - lack of, 53; on TV, 45; working fathers as unmarked category, 51

femininity, 141

Festinger, L., 17, 126

fictional and non-fictional media, blurry divide, 46

Fields, J., 12, 13

Fischbach, D., 50

Fiske, J., 9, 108, 122

Fletcher, B., 10

flexible working arrangements, 85–9, 91

focus groups (as research method), 27–8, 32, 162–8

Fouad, N., 52

Francese, P., 12

Freeman, J., 6

G

'Gail' case study, 131–4

Garey, A., 6, 15–16, 81, 89, 151

gender: gender norms, 147; influences on media consumption, 59, 63–6; portrayal of gender differences in media, 109–10

Gerard, M., 17

Gerbner, G., 17

Gerson, K., 11, 37, 52, 53, 85, 98–9, 101, 108

Gibbons, F., 17

Gillespie, M., 6

Ginsburg, F., 5–6

Gross, L., 17

Grote, N., 15

guilt, 115–16, 147

'Gwen' case study, 139–41

H

Hakmiller, K., 17

Hamilton, B., 12

Hansen, K., 6

Hasegawa, K., 45

Havice, M., 68, 70

Hays, S., 6, 8, 16, 46, 49, 96

Heintz, K., 45

'helpless man' stereotype, 45, 54–6, 109–10, 136

Himmelstein, H., 44

Hochschild, A., 6, 14, 16, 37, 87, 91, 92

Holmes, M., 7

home working, 53–4, 61, 79–80

homogeneity, 26, 153, 156

Hoover, S., 6, 8–9, 18, 66, 67, 71

household income, 11, 25–6

Houseman, S., 10

housework, 14–15, 18, 54–6, 91–6, 132–5

Hudson, K., 10

I

I Love Lucy, 41

Ignatius, D., 152–3

in, about, of typology of media in people's lives, 8–9

income, household, 11, 25–6

influence of media: admitting own use, 73–5; denial of media influence, 68–71, 147–8, 154; justifications of media consumption, 69–70; over families' work/family choices, 107–27

information, media as source of, 74, 113–14

intended meanings, 9, 108–9

192 · Index

internet: as common ground, 67; consumption by Dexter residents, 60, 61; entwined with TV, 7
interviews (research method), 26–7
isolation, 'Jennifer' case study, 129–31
Itzkoff, D., 7

J

Jacobs, J., 11, 37, 52, 53, 98–9, 108
'Jennifer' case study, 129–31
Jerry Springer Show, The, 17, 124, 149, 157
Jesse, 48
'Julie' case study, 134–6

K

Kahlenberg, S., 45, 151
Kalleberg, A., 10
Kelly, A., 12, 25
Kendall, D., 4
Kitzinger, J., 8, 27
Kottak, C., 4, 6, 11, 12, 25, 26, 40, 70, 128, 144, 152, 154
Kozaitis, K., 12
Kubey, R., 8

L

Landry, B., 11, 52
Lareau, A., 12
Larmoyeux, M., 54
Dr. Laura (Schlessinger): as common ground, 117–21; endangered children/anti-daycare, 3, 49–50; integrated data, 30–1; parents' use of her messages, 9, 72, 74–5, 98, 107–8, 133, 136
Law and Order, 42, 48–9, 68, 121
Leave it to Beaver, 1–2, 5, 7, 39, 41, 42, 154, 156
Lee, C., 11, 33
Lester, B., 10
Lewin-Epstein, N., 14
lifestyle pressures, coming from media, 70–1
Lind, K., 37
Lipsitz, G., 44
Luckey, I., 37

M

magazines: gender differences in choosing, 66; for ideas and tips, 74, 113–14; parenting magazines, 111, 123, 149; portrayals of men and domestic work, 55–6; portrayals of stay-at-home mothers, 111–12, 113; portrayals of work and family as opposing forces, 51–3; working mothers, 114
Makarushka, I., 45
Mama (I Remember Mama), 41
Margolis, M., 11
Marlino, D., 13
marriage, 12–13
Marsden, P., 10
maternal visibility, 16, 151
maternity leave, 87
McMahon, M., 14
media content analysis: media in Dexter, 39–57; as research method, 29–30
media discourses, 7–10
media equipment, placement of, 62–3
media monitors, women as, 63–4, 153
media pressures, 70–1
men: as breadwinners, 84, 90; and domestic work, 55–7; 'helpless man' stereotype, 45, 54–6, 109–10, 136; involvement in child care, 94–5; as media exposers, 63–4, 153; superman/superdad image - lack of, 53
methods of research: discussion of, 26–31; focus group guides, 162–8; interview guides, 162–8; research participants, 31–3, 172–6
Michaels, M., 7, 41–2, 46
middle class families: changes since 1950s, 2; definition, 2, 4, 31; as different to usual ethnographic subjects, 34; summary of research results, 155–7
Moen, P., 14
Moran-Ellis, J., 30
motherhood, cultural model of, 50–1
movies, as common ground, 66, 67
multi-tasking (media consumption while doing other things), 60–1; *see also* traveling
Murphy, P., 5
Mussweiler, T., 17

Index · 193

N

Naylor, K., 15
Newman, K., 16
news media: consumption by Dexter residents, 60; gender differences in choosing, 65, 66, 153; men and domestic work portrayals, 55–6; social comparison, 124–5; women's avoidance of, 153; work and family portrayed as opposing forces, 49, 52–4
'niche' media, 156; *see also* Christian media
Nippert-Eng, C., 15, 37
nuclear families, 12–13, 16, 44

O

of, discourses of the media, 9–10, 71–3
O'Guinn, T., 17
Olson, B., 44
Ozzie and Harriet, The Adventures of, 1–2, 41, 156

P

Padavic, I., 10, 11
Papper, R., 7
parenting magazines, 123–4, 143, 149
part-time working, 14, 82–3, 118; 'Gail' case study, 131–4; 'Julie' case study, 134–6
paternity leave, 87
'Penny' case study, 136–9
personal space, 36–8
personalization of media messages, 9
physical environment as factor in contextualizing media use, 62–3
Pope, E., 54
Popovich, M., 7
'postmodern' families, 13
Potuchek, J., 14
power: empowerment of employment for women, 82; between researcher and ethnographic subjects, 33–6
privacy, 36–8
'privilege gap', 34
Proctor, B., 11

R

radio, 60, 63, 67; *see also* Dr. Laura (Schlessinger)
research methods: discussion of, 26–31; focus group guides, 162–8; interview guides, 162–8; research participants, 31–3, 172–6
Reskin, B., 10, 11
Reynolds, J., 10
Ribbens, J., 15
ripple effect, 62
Roberts, S., 12
Robinson, J., 44
role models: flawed, 109–10; positive, 113, 123, 148
Rosenfeld, R., 68, 70
Rudd, E., 6

S

Sado, S., 12
Schlessinger, Dr. Laura: as common ground, 117–21; endangered children/anti-daycare, 3, 49–50; integrated data, 30–1; parents' use of her messages, 9, 72, 74–5, 98, 107–8, 133, 136
Schor, J., 98–9
scrutiny, of research by participants, 33, 36
Seiter, E., 6, 8, 59
Shellenbarger, S., 51–2
Shelton, B., 14
Shrum, L., 17
Signorielli, N., 45, 151
Silberstein, L., 14, 15
Silverblatt, A., 68, 70
Simpson, The, 43
single parents: 'Corinth' case study, 142–4; prevalence of, 12–13; single fathers, 45; on TV, 44–5, 48
Skill, T., 44
social cement: *see* common ground
social comparison (social function of media), 3–4, 17–18, 102–3, 121–7, 147–51
social networks, 103–5
social reality in Dexter, 78–106
Sopranos, The, 44, 138

194 · Index

Stacey, J., 13
Star Trek, 40
stay-at-home fathers, 55, 89–91; 'Penny' case study, 136–9
stay-at-home mothers: as idealized category, 51; influence of childhood patterns, 100–1; 'Jennifer' case study, 129–31; making work/family choices, 83–5, 89–91, 98, 104; media portrayals, 111–12, 113
stereotypes: 'helpless man' stereotype, 45, 54–6, 109–10, 136; as media tools, 72; superwoman/ supermom image, 52, 53, 54, 78–9, 115–16
Stier, H., 14
Streckfuss, D., 45
Strobel, F., 10, 11
superman/ superdad image - lack of, 53
superwoman/ supermom image, 52, 53, 54, 78–9, 115–16

T

Taflinger, R., 45
telecommuting (working from home), 52–4, 61, 79–80
texts, media as, 9, 108–9
Thornton, A., 13
Tiedge, J, 68, 70
time: commodification of, 37–8; time pressures, 11, 16, 37–8, 52–3, 112
Tinsley, H., 52
Tittle, C., 13
Townsend, N., 6, 84
traveling, media consumption whilst, 63, 75, 133–4
treats, media consumption as, 67
TV shows: changes since 1950s, 41–6; consumption by Dexter residents, 60; daytime TV, 69–70; media content analysis, 39–57; *see also* titles of individual shows
Tyagi, A., 12

U

Upton, R., 105

V

Van Buren, A., 50
Vande Berg, L., 45
vehicles, media in, 63, 75, 133–4
Ventura, S., 12
violence, 8

W

Wallace, S., 44
Waltons, The, 4, 44, 111, 154
Warren, E., 12
Weston, L., 12
'white flight' trend, 156
Whiting-Fickling, J., 37
Williams, J., 14
Wilson, F., 13
women: in the labor market, 11, 13–15; as media monitors, 63–4, 153; media portrayals, 7, 40–2, 110; portrayals of home as women's primary role, 40–1
work/family balance: changing patterns, 10–15; competing demands, 51–3; deciding who stays at home, 89–91; dual earner households, 11, 14, 25–6, 80–3; influence of childhood patterns, 100–1; institutional barriers to choices, 85–9; media influences over choices, 107–27; portrayed as opposing forces, 46–53, 126, 147; social reality in Dexter, 78–106; social support for choices, 103–5; *see also* stay-at-home mothers; working mothers
work/family studies, place of this work within, 6–7
working class families, 44
working fathers, as unmarked category, 51
working mothers: generally, 13–15; 'Corinth' case study, 142–4; 'Gwen' case study, 139–41; media specifically aimed at, 114; 'Penny' case study, 136–9; portrayed as disadvantaging their children, 48–51
workplaces, TV portrayals, 42–3, 45–6
Wright Mills, C., 11–12
Wyer, R., 17

Reading Materials Evolved.

Introducing the

SOCIAL ISSUES COLLECTION

A Routledge/University Readers Custom Library for Teaching

Customizing course material for innovative and excellent teaching in sociology has never been easier or more effective!

Choose from a collection of more than 300 readings from Routledge, Taylor & Francis, and other publishers to make a custom anthology that suits the needs of your social problems/ social inequality, and social issues courses.

All readings have been aptly chosen by academic editors and our authors and organized by topic and author.

Online tool makes it easy for busy instructors:

1. *Simply select your favorite Routledge and Taylor & Francis readings, and add any other required course material, including your own.*

2. *Choose the order of the readings, pick a binding, and customize a cover.*

3. *One click will post your materials for students to buy. They can purchase print or digital packs, and we ship direct to their door within two weeks of ordering!*

More information at www.socialissuescollection.com

Contact information: Call your Routledge sales rep, or
Becky Smith at University Readers, 800-200-3908 ext. 18, bsmith@universityreaders.com
Steve Rutter at Routledge, 207-434-2102, Steve.Rutter@taylorandfrancis.com.